First World War
and Army of Occupation
War Diary
France, Belgium and Germany

12 DIVISION
Headquarters, Branches and Services
General Staff
1 August 1918 - 27 June 1919

WO95/1827

The Naval & Military Press Ltd
www.nmarchive.com
Published in association with The National Archives

Published by

The Naval & Military Press Ltd

Unit 10 Ridgewood Industrial Park,

Uckfield, East Sussex,

TN22 5QE England

Tel: +44 (0) 1825 749494

www.naval-military-press.com

www.nmarchive.com

This diary has been reprinted in facsimile from the original. Any imperfections are inevitably reproduced and the quality may fall short of modern type and cartographic standards.

© **Crown Copyright**
Images reproduced by permission of The National Archives, London, England, 2015.

Contents

Document type	Place/Title	Date From	Date To
Heading	Gen. Staff Aug 1918-Jun 1919		
Heading	General Staff. 12th Division, August, 1918. June 1919		
War Diary	Vignacourt	01/08/1918	03/08/1918
War Diary	Beaucourt	04/08/1918	09/08/1918
War Diary	Ribemont	10/08/1918	24/08/1918
War Diary	Ribemont And Morlancourt	25/08/1918	25/08/1918
War Diary	Morlancourt And Meaulte	26/08/1918	26/08/1918
War Diary	Meaulte	27/08/1918	29/08/1918
War Diary	Hidden Wood	30/08/1918	31/08/1918
Miscellaneous	12th Division Order No. 270. Appendix I.	01/08/1918	01/08/1918
Miscellaneous	Move Table Attached To 12th Division Order No. 270.		
Miscellaneous	12th Division Order No. 271. Appdx. II	06/08/1918	06/08/1918
Miscellaneous	Addition To 12th Division Order No. 271.	07/08/1918	07/08/1918
Miscellaneous	Artillery Arrangements With Reference To 12th Division Order No. 271.	06/08/1918	06/08/1918
Miscellaneous	12th Division Order No. 272. Appdx III	06/08/1918	06/08/1918
Miscellaneous	Table To Accompany 12th Division Order No. 272, Dated 6th August, 1918.	06/08/1918	06/08/1918
Miscellaneous	Addendum And Corrigendum No. 1 To 12th Division Order No. 272.	06/08/1918	06/08/1918
Miscellaneous	Arrangements For Signalling To Aeroplanes With Reference To 12th Division Order No. 271.	06/08/1918	06/08/1918
Miscellaneous	12th Division Order No. 273. Appdx. IV	06/08/1918	06/08/1918
Miscellaneous	Arrangements With Regard To Gas And Smoke.	07/08/1918	07/08/1918
Miscellaneous	Correction No. 1 To 12th Division G.X. 3331 Of 6th Aug.- Artillery Arrangements With Reference To 12th Division Order No. 271. Appdx. V	07/08/1918	07/08/1918
Miscellaneous	Addition To 12th Division Order No. 271. Appdx. VI.	07/08/1918	07/08/1918
Miscellaneous	Addendum And Corrigendum No. 1 To 12th Division Order No. 272. Appdx. VII	06/08/1918	06/08/1918
Miscellaneous	12th Division Order No. 274. Appdx. VIII	12/08/1918	12/08/1918
Miscellaneous	Messages And Signals.	12/08/1918	12/08/1918
Miscellaneous	36th Inf. Bde.	12/08/1918	12/08/1918
Miscellaneous	12th Division Warning Order No. 275. Appdx. IX	13/08/1918	13/08/1918
Miscellaneous	12th Division Order No. 276.	13/08/1918	13/08/1918
Miscellaneous	12th Division Warning Order No. 277.	15/08/1918	15/08/1918
Miscellaneous	Amendment To 12th Division Warning Order No. 277.	18/08/1918	18/08/1918
Miscellaneous	D.R.L.S.		
Miscellaneous	12th Division Order No. 278	19/08/1918	19/08/1918
Miscellaneous	C Form. Messages And Signals.	21/08/1918	21/08/1918
Miscellaneous	Addendum To 12th Division Order No. 278.	19/08/1918	19/08/1918
Miscellaneous	A Form Messages And Signals.	19/08/1918	19/08/1918
Miscellaneous	12th Division Order No. 279. Appdx. XI	21/08/1918	21/08/1918
Miscellaneous	12th Division No. G.X. 3657. Appdx. X.	19/08/1918	19/08/1918
Miscellaneous	Notes On The Attack-No. 2.	19/08/1918	19/08/1918
Miscellaneous Map	12th Division Instructions For Attack No. 3.	20/08/1918	20/08/1918
Miscellaneous Map	12th Division Instructions For Attack No. 4.	21/08/1918	21/08/1918
Miscellaneous	35th Inf. Bde.	21/08/1918	21/08/1918

Map	12th. B.N. M.G.C.		
Map	To Accompany 12th Div. No. G.X:		
Map			
Miscellaneous	Message Form.		
Miscellaneous	Instructions For Attack No. 1	19/08/1918	19/08/1918
Map			
Miscellaneous	Legend Map. A.		
Miscellaneous	A Form Messages And Signals.	23/08/1918	23/08/1918
Miscellaneous	A Form. Messages And Signals.		
Miscellaneous	A Form. Messages And Signals.	25/08/1918	25/08/1918
Miscellaneous	Appdx. XIII		
Miscellaneous	35th Inf. Bde. Appdx. XIV	20/08/1918	20/08/1918
Miscellaneous	III Corps.	16/08/1918	16/08/1918
Miscellaneous	C Form. Messages And Signals.	24/08/1918	24/08/1918
Miscellaneous	A Form Messages And Signals.	24/08/1918	24/08/1918
Miscellaneous	C Form. Messages And Signals.	24/08/1918	24/08/1918
Miscellaneous	35th Inf. Bde.	23/08/1918	23/08/1918
Miscellaneous	35th Inf. Bde. III Corps.	24/08/1918	24/08/1918
Miscellaneous	Messages And Signals.	12/08/1918	12/08/1918
Miscellaneous	36th Inf. Bde.	12/08/1918	12/08/1918
Miscellaneous	Buvu Wura A.D.M.S. Rovua		
Miscellaneous	35th Inf: Bde: 36th Inf. Bde.		
Miscellaneous	A Form Messages And Signals.		
Miscellaneous	C Form. Messages And Signals.	02/08/1918	02/08/1918
Miscellaneous	A Form Messages And Signals.	01/08/1918	01/08/1918
Miscellaneous	12th. Division. A.D. Signals.	30/07/1918	30/07/1918
Miscellaneous		02/08/1918	02/08/1918
Miscellaneous	W In 12 Div		
Miscellaneous	C Form. Messages And Signals.	01/08/1918	01/08/1918
Miscellaneous	Warning Order.	31/07/1918	31/07/1918
Miscellaneous	A Form Messages And Signals.	24/08/1918	24/08/1918
Miscellaneous	35th Inf. Bde.	23/08/1918	23/08/1918
Miscellaneous		23/08/1918	23/08/1918
Miscellaneous	C Form. Messages And Signals.	23/08/1918	23/08/1918
Miscellaneous	C Form. Messages And Signals.		
Miscellaneous	C Form. Messages And Signals.	23/08/1918	23/08/1918
Miscellaneous	A Form Messages And Signals.	19/08/1918	19/08/1918
Miscellaneous	12th Division No. G.X. 3598.	17/08/1918	17/08/1918
Miscellaneous	C' Form. Messages And Signals.☐20/08/1918☐20/08/1918☐ Miscellaneous☐C" Form. Messages And Signals.	18/08/1918	18/08/1918
Miscellaneous	C.R.E. 35th Inf. Bde.	18/08/1918	18/08/1918
Miscellaneous			
Miscellaneous		12/08/1918	12/08/1918
Miscellaneous	A Form Messages And Signals.		
Miscellaneous	Arrangements With Regard To Gas And Smoke.	07/08/1918	07/08/1918
Miscellaneous	Correction No. 1 To 12th Division G.X. 3331 Of 6th Aug.- Artillery Arrangements With Reference To 12th Division Order No. 271.	07/08/1918	07/08/1918
Miscellaneous	Table 'B'.	07/08/1918	07/08/1918
Map			
Miscellaneous	Arrangements With Regard To Gas And Smoke.	07/08/1918	07/08/1918
Miscellaneous	35th Inf. Bde.	19/08/1918	19/08/1918
Map			
Miscellaneous	247 R.I.R.		
Map			

Type	Description	Start	End
Miscellaneous Map	Map 'B'		
Miscellaneous	12th Division August 1918		
Miscellaneous	Bde Instructions		
Map Miscellaneous	57 S.E.		
Map Miscellaneous	57 S.W.		
Map Miscellaneous	62 N.W.		
Map Miscellaneous	57 C.S.E.		
Map Miscellaneous	62 C. N.E.		
Heading	General Staff. 12th Division. September, 1918.		
War Diary	Hidden Wood	01/09/1918	04/09/1918
War Diary	Combles.	05/09/1918	06/09/1918
War Diary	Vaux Wood	07/09/1918	16/09/1918
War Diary	Epinette Wood	17/09/1918	30/09/1918
Miscellaneous	12th Division Order No. 280.	04/09/1918	04/09/1918
Miscellaneous	C Form Messages And Signals.	04/09/1918	04/09/1918
Miscellaneous	C Form. Messages And Signals.		
Miscellaneous	A Form Messages And Signals.	05/09/1918	05/09/1918
Miscellaneous	A Form Messages And Signals.		
Miscellaneous	C Form. Messages And Signals.	05/09/1918	05/09/1918
Miscellaneous	C Form. Messages And Signals.		
Miscellaneous	C Form. Messages And Signals.	05/09/1918	05/09/1918
Miscellaneous	C Form. Messages And Signals.		
Miscellaneous	C Form. Messages And Signals.	05/09/1918	05/09/1918
Miscellaneous	C Form Messages And Signals.	06/09/1918	06/09/1918
Miscellaneous	C Form. Messages And Signals.		
Miscellaneous	12th Division Instructions For Defence No. 2.	11/09/1918	11/09/1918
Miscellaneous	C Form. Messages And Signals.	12/09/1918	12/09/1918
Miscellaneous	12th Division Order No. 282.	14/09/1918	14/09/1918
Miscellaneous	12th Division Order No. 283.	16/09/1918	16/09/1918
Miscellaneous	12th Division No. G.O. 132.	15/09/1918	15/09/1918
Miscellaneous	Addendum To 12th Division Order No. 283-Divisional O.P. Arrangements.	17/09/1918	17/09/1918
Miscellaneous			
Miscellaneous	Addition To 12th Division Order No. 283.		
Miscellaneous	Addition No. 2 To 12th Division Order No. 283.		
Miscellaneous	A Form Messages And Signals.	16/09/1918	16/09/1918
Miscellaneous	A Form Messages And Signals.	18/09/1918	18/09/1918
Miscellaneous	A Form Messages And Signals.	19/09/1918	19/09/1918
Miscellaneous	A Form Messages And Signals.		
Miscellaneous	A Form Messages And Signals.	20/09/1918	20/09/1918
Miscellaneous	A Form Messages And Signals.		
Miscellaneous	Warning Order.	21/09/1918	21/09/1918
Miscellaneous	12th Divnl. Artillery.	22/09/1918	22/09/1918
Miscellaneous	12th Division Order No. 284.	22/09/1918	22/09/1918
Miscellaneous	A Form Messages And Signals.	23/09/1918	23/09/1918
Map	Divn Boundary		
Miscellaneous	A Form Messages And Signals.	26/09/1918	26/09/1918
Map	Map 'A'		
Map			
Map	Dispositions At 9 A.M. 19-9-18.		

Map			
Miscellaneous			
Miscellaneous	VIII Corps.	19/02/1919	19/02/1919
Miscellaneous	List Of Officers Recommended For The Staff College In Accordance With Para. 721 K.R.	01/03/1919	01/03/1919
Heading	General Staff. 12th Division, October 1918.		
War Diary	Bois De L'Epinette	01/10/1918	01/10/1918
War Diary	Villers Chatel.	02/10/1918	06/10/1918
War Diary	Chateau De La Haie.	07/10/1918	11/10/1918
War Diary	Lievin	12/10/1918	15/10/1918
War Diary	Henin Lietard	16/10/1918	18/10/1918
War Diary	Raimbeaucourt	19/10/1918	21/10/1918
War Diary	Orchies	22/10/1918	22/10/1918
War Diary	Sameon	23/10/1918	29/10/1918
War Diary	Flines	30/10/1918	31/10/1918
Miscellaneous	Report On Operations Of October, 1918	28/11/1918	28/11/1918
Miscellaneous	The Work Of The 12th Divisional R.E. And 5th Northamptonshire Regt. (Pioneers) During The Operations 7/10/18 To 11/11/18 East Of Vimy Sector. Appendix 'A'	24/11/1918	24/11/1918
Miscellaneous	Appendix "B". Prisoners of War		
Miscellaneous	Appendix "D". Lessons Learnt During The Operations.	28/11/1918	28/11/1918
Miscellaneous	12th Division Order No. 287 App 1.	03/10/1918	03/10/1918
Miscellaneous	Movement Table Issued With 12th Division Order No. 287		
Miscellaneous	Addendum No. 1 To 12th Division Order No. 287	04/10/1918	04/10/1918
Miscellaneous	12th Division Order No. 288 App No 2	04/10/1918	04/10/1918
Miscellaneous	A Form. Messages And Signals. App No 3	08/10/1918	08/10/1918
Miscellaneous	12th Division Order No. 289. App No 4	09/10/1918	09/10/1918
Miscellaneous	A Form. Messages And Signals. App No 5	10/10/1918	10/10/1918
Miscellaneous	A Form. Messages And Signals.	10/10/1918	10/10/1918
Miscellaneous	March And Relief Table-Issued With 12th Division Order No. 292.		
Miscellaneous	VIII Corps. App No. 4.	26/10/1918	26/10/1918
Miscellaneous	12th Division Order, No. 290. App No 6	11/10/1918	11/10/1918
Miscellaneous	12th Division Order No. 292. App No 7.	27/10/1918	27/10/1918
Heading	Maps Operations 12th Division 6th To 29th October 1918		
Map			
Map	France. Sheet 44 S.W.		
Map			
Map	France. Sheet 44 S.W.		
Map			
Heading	12th Division Operations 6th-29th Oct 1918		
Heading	General Staff. 12th Division November 1918.		
War Diary	Flines	01/11/1918	09/11/1918
War Diary	Flines Sameon.	10/11/1918	19/11/1918
War Diary	Sameon	20/11/1918	25/11/1918
War Diary	Masny	26/11/1918	30/11/1918
Miscellaneous	12th Division Order No. 293. App. No. I	04/11/1918	04/11/1918
Miscellaneous	12th Division Order No. 294. App No 2	09/11/1918	09/11/1918
Miscellaneous	March Table issued with 12th Division Operation Order 29? - 9th November 1918	09/11/1918	09/11/1918
Miscellaneous	12th Division Order No. 295. App No 3	10/11/1918	10/11/1918
Miscellaneous	App No 4		
Miscellaneous	App No 5		

Miscellaneous	12th Division Order No. 296. App. No 6	23/11/1918	23/11/1918
Miscellaneous	March Table Issued With 12th Division Order No. 296.		
Miscellaneous	Addendum And Corrigendum No. 1. 12th Division Order No. 296	24/11/1918	24/11/1918
Miscellaneous	12th Division Order No. 297. App. No. 7.	27/11/1918	27/11/1918
Miscellaneous	35th Inf. Bde.	07/11/1918	07/11/1918
Miscellaneous	12th Division (G),	08/11/1918	08/11/1918
Miscellaneous	12th Div.		
Miscellaneous	Headquarters, 12th Division "G"	18/11/1918	18/11/1918
Miscellaneous	12th Division.	20/11/1918	20/11/1918
Miscellaneous	12th Division "G".	08/11/1918	08/11/1918
Miscellaneous	Headquarters, 12th. Division. "G"	08/11/1918	08/11/1918
Miscellaneous	Lessons Learnt During The Operations Of 12th Division During October, 1918.	10/11/1918	10/11/1918
Miscellaneous	C.R.A. C.R.E. 35th Inf. Bde.	27/11/1918	27/11/1918
Miscellaneous			
Map			
Miscellaneous			
Heading	General Staff, 12th Division, December 1918. 1918 Dec-1919 June		
War Diary	Masny	01/12/1918	31/12/1918
Miscellaneous	11th Division.	12/12/1918	12/12/1918
Miscellaneous	12th Division G.	18/12/1918	18/12/1918
Miscellaneous	12th Division.	22/12/1918	22/12/1918
Miscellaneous	12th Divisional Artillery.	31/12/1918	31/12/1918
Miscellaneous	List Of Officers Recommended For The Staff College In Accordance With Para. 721 K.R.	01/01/1919	01/01/1919
Miscellaneous	VIII Corps.	06/01/1919	06/01/1919
Miscellaneous	11th Division.	04/01/1919	04/01/1919
Heading	War Diary 12th Divn G S December 1918		
Heading	War Diary 12th Divn G S January 1919		
War Diary	Masny	01/01/1919	31/01/1919
Heading	War Diary 12th Divn H.Q. G February 1919		
War Diary	Masny	01/02/1919	03/02/1919
War Diary	Erre	04/02/1919	04/02/1919
War Diary	Somain	04/02/1919	04/02/1919
War Diary	Auberchicourt	04/02/1919	04/02/1919
War Diary	Masny	05/02/1919	28/02/1919
Heading	War Diary General Staff 12th Division. March 1919 (Vol)		
War Diary	Masny	01/03/1919	27/03/1919
War Diary	Somain	28/03/1919	31/03/1919
Heading	War Diary Of April 1919		
War Diary	Somain	01/04/1919	30/04/1919
Heading	War Diary Of May 1919 (Vol)		
War Diary	Somain	01/05/1919	31/05/1919
Miscellaneous	Administrative Instructions In Conjunction With Forecast No. 7. Appendix 'a'	03/05/1919	03/05/1919
Miscellaneous	Administrative Instructions No. 2. Appendix "B"	09/05/1919	09/05/1919
Miscellaneous	Appendix "A" Issued In Conjunction With Administrative Instructions No. 2.		
Miscellaneous	12th Division Brigade Group. Appendix 'C'	28/05/1919	28/05/1919
Miscellaneous	Appendix 'A'. To accompany 12th Div Admin Inst No 3		
War Diary	Somain	01/06/1919	22/06/1919
War Diary	Dunkirk	23/06/1919	27/06/1919

Miscellaneous	Appendix "A" to Administrative Instructions No 4		
Miscellaneous	Administrative Instructions No. 4.		
Miscellaneous	Appendix "A" To Administrative Instructions No. 4.		
Miscellaneous	Appendix "B".		
Heading	Appendix To War Diary Of General Staff 12th Division August And September, 1918.		
Miscellaneous	Historical Section Of War Cabinet, 2 Whitehall Gardens, London, S.W.	18/03/1919	18/03/1919
Miscellaneous	Report On Operations By 12th Division. Phase I. August 2nd To August 21st 1918.		
Miscellaneous	12th Division. Narrative Of Operations 4th To 8th September 1918.		
Miscellaneous	Narrative Of Operations From 18th To 30th September, 1918		
Miscellaneous Map	12th Division.		
Miscellaneous	Map "Z" 12th Division Operation		

12TH DIVISION

GEN. STAFF
AUG 1918 - JUN 1919

GENERAL STAFF,

12th DIVISION,

AUGUST, 1918.

June 1919

NARRATIVE OF OPERATIONS

and

MAP SHOWING ADVANCE OF DIVISION

from 8th Aug. to 30th Sept. 1918

IN SEPARATE COVER

Army Form C. 2118.

WAR DIARY
12th DIVISION. AUGUST. 1918.
INTELLIGENCE SUMMARY.
(Erase heading not required.)

Place	Date	Hour	Summary of Events and Information	Remarks and references to Appendices
VIGNACOURT	1st.		Reconnaissances of line carried out by 35 and 37 Infantry Brigades. Operation Order No 270 issued today. Fine day.	App No 1
VIGNACOURT	2nd		Reconnaissances carried out by 36th Infantry Brigade and advance parties proceeded to the trenches. Weather broke and rain fell heavily. Movements in accordance with Operation Order No 270 carried out.	
VIGNACOURT	3rd.		Movements in accordance with Operation Order No 270 continued. Weather still very wet. Relief of 173rd Infantry Brigade complete by 35th Infantry Brigade by 3.50 a.m. Lieut-Col J.D. Belgrave, R.A., D.S.O. joined for duty as Acting G.S.O.1. 58th Division reported that enemy was withdrawing from his trenches W. of the ANCRE.	
BEAUCOURT.	4th		Relief of 175th Brigade by 37th Infantry Brigade complete by 2.45 a.m. G.O.C. took over command at 10 a.m. Weather showery. G.O.C. and G.S.O.1. attended Conference at Corps Headquarters at 5 p.m. A quiet day in the line - patrols confirmed that enemy had withdrawn across RIVER ANCRE.	
BEAUCOURT	5th		Weather still very showery and trenches in a bad condition. Commander-in-Chief called at Divisional Headquarters in the afternoon. Conference at Divisional Headquarters at 9.30. p.m. attended by B.G.G.C 35th Infantry Brigade; 36th Infantry Brigade; C.R.A.; G.S.O.1.; G.S.O.2; and A.A.Q.M.G. Proposed scheme of operations explained by G.O.C.: 36th Infantry Brigade to be withdrawn on night 6th/7th to Corps Reserve, 37th Infantry Brigade to be relieved by 47th Division on night 7th/8th. 35th Infantry Brigade to attack on morning of the 8th, and 37th Infantry Brigade on morning of 9th or 10th, depending on results of operations on 8th. A quiet time in the line.	
BEAUCOURT	6th		G.S.O.2 sent about 1 a.m. to III Corps to explain situation regarding relief of 37th Infantry Brigade to B.G., G.S. and also to ask that 30 guns under C.R.A., 25th Division not accounted for in Corps R.A. Scheme might be at disposal of G.O.C. for assisting 35th Infantry Brigade. O.O. 271 issued.	App 11
			About 4 a.m. Germans attacked 18th Division on our right and succeeded in capturing their trenches on a front of about 2,000 yards to a depth of about 1,000 yards. Situation on our front quiet except for some gas shelling of batteries in vicinity of both Brigade Headquarters. G.S.O.2. visited 37th Brigade and explained scheme of operations to Brigadier General Commanding/	

Army Form C. 2118.

WAR DIARY

12th DIVISION or AUGUST, 1918.

INTELLIGENCE SUMMARY.

(Erase heading not required.)

Instructions regarding War Diaries and Intelligence Summaries are contained in F. S. Regs., Part II. and the Staff Manual respectively. Title pages will be prepared in manuscript.

Place	Date	Hour	Summary of Events and Information	Remarks and references to Appendices
	6th	(Continued). :-	37th Infantry Brigade, who proceeded to carry out the necessary reconnaissance. G.O.C. held a conference at 2.30 p.m. at which the following were present:- G.S.O.1; G.S.O.2; O.C.; 12th Bn M.G.C.; B.G.C. 35th Infantry Brigade and C.R.A. Artillery and M.G. arrangements for operation by 35th Infantry Brigade were discussed and settled. At about 4.30 p.m. G.O.C. 12th Division came to Headquarters and saw B.G.C. 36th Infantry Brigade, warning having been received earlier that 36th Infantry Brigade would probably be put into 18th Division, as their Divisional Reserve subsequently to take part in the operations of the 18th Division under their orders. Operation Order 272 was issued with regard to moves and reliefs in connection with the above. At 8.40 p.m. confirmation was received or telephone message at about 6.30 p.m. that 36th Infantry Brigade was to move and come under orders of 18th Division. Orders had previously been issued for this move. (Operation Order 273). G.O.C. visited B.G.C. 37th Infantry Brigade in the evening. Weather still very wet, with fine intervals. quiet day. Signalling to aeroplanes, maps and lights issued.	App 111 App 1V
BEAUCOURT	7th		G.X. 5380 issued with reference to extension Southwards of 35th Infantry Brigade's objective. Addendum and Corrigendum No.1 to 12th Division Order No 272 issued. Arrangements made for attack by 12th Division to take place two hours after that of 58th and 18th Divisions (on right) to give time for wire to be cut. Zero hour for 58th and 18th Divisions 4.20 a.m. for the 12th Division 6.20 a.m. At 10 p.m. heavy enemy Mustard Gas shelling of area North and East of MARETT WOOD. Correction No.1 to 12th Division G.X.5331 of 6th August - Artillery arrangements - issued.	App V. App VI App VIII
BEAUCOURT	8th		Gas shelling continued until 12.30 a.m. - Troops in assembly positions by 5.20 a.m. - attack launched on 3 Battalion front at 6.20 a.m. Centre (7th Norfolks) and left battalion (9th Essex) reached and consolidated their objectives. - Left Coy of right battalion (1/1st Cambs.) reached its objective, but the right Coy met with strong resistance owing to troops on our right not being able to get forward. - Under Heavy and Field Artillery support, and in co-operation with 18th Division on right, 2 Coys. of 1/1st Cambs. attacked again at 12.15 p.m. and were completely successful in gaining their objectives - 316 prisoners, 14 M.gs., 8 L.t.m.s and 2 M.T.M.S being captured. At 4 p.m. orders were received that 37th Infantry Brigade	

Army Form C.2118.

WAR DIARY
12TH DIVISION or AUGUST, 1918.
INTELLIGENCE SUMMARY.

(Erase heading not required.)

Instructions regarding War Diaries and Intelligence Summaries are contained in F. S. Regs., Part II. and the Staff Manual respectively. Title pages will be prepared in manuscript.

Place	Date	Hour	Summary of Events and Information	Remarks and references to Appendices
	8th (continued):-		((less one battalion with 35th Brigade) to be placed under orders of 18th Division - 37th Infantry Brigade moved to ROMA-BALLARET LINE (J.25.17.10) arriving there at 9 p.m. At 8.45 p.m. orders were received by telephone to continue attack in conjunction with flank Division - 8 Tanks allotted - Zero hour probably 4.30 a.m., 9th - Orders sent to 37th Infantry Brigade to assemble in K.2.a. and 13.d. ready to attack at dawn. On evening of 8th line ran E.26.b.3.9. - due South - MORLANCOURT (exclusive) K.8.c.8.0.	
BEAUCOURT	9th		At 1.45 a.m. Zero hour postponed by telephone order from III Corps till the evening. It was only possible to stop the leading Battalion of 37th Infantry Brigade after they had already penetrated the enemy defences. Attack finally ordered to take place at 5.30 p.m. 6th R.W.Kent Regt on left very successful - Centre and Right Battalions and troops on right of the Division met with strong opposition. Line E.21.d.5.7 - E.28.a.4.4 - E.4.a.3.0. - In touch on right at K.10.b.3.7. 350 prisoners, M.gs and T.Ms and two 77mm guns taken. At 10 p.m. Divisional Headquarters moved to RIBEMONT (D.27.a.1.3.)	
RIBEMONT.	10th		9th Essex Regt placed under orders of 37th Inf. Bde - Orders issued for attack to be resumed at 6 p.m. Supported by tanks, attack was successful - main line of Amiens DEFENCES captured. 58th Division attacked simultaneously - as soon as they had passed through 36th Brigade, latter reverted to 12th Division- 9th R. Sussex Regt was attached to 37th Infantry Brigade and moved in close support to its right in attack on the 10th. After this attack 7th R. Sussex relieved 9th Essex. Line on evening of 10th - E.22.a.5.2. - E.28.c.8.8. - K.5. central - K.5.d.4.8. This line was consolidated during the night - wired and strong points made under orders of C.R.E. by Field Coys., Pioneers and American Engineers.	
RIBEMONT.	11th		Quiet Day.	
RIBEMONT	12th		In the evening, 36th Infantry Brigade took over right and centre Sub-sectors from 37th Infantry Brigade. There were then two Brigades in the line - 36th on right on two Battalion Front - 37th Brigade on left on one battalion front.	

CASUALTIES. Officers Killed. 11; 26 wounded; Nil Missing.
O.R. " " 88; 685 " " 158 "

Army Form C.2118.

WAR DIARY

12TH DIVISION — AUGUST, 1918.

INTELLIGENCE SUMMARY.

(Erase heading not required.)

Instructions regarding War Diaries and Intelligence Summaries are contained in F.S. Regs., Part II. and the Staff Manual respectively. Title pages will be prepared in manuscript.

Place	Date	Hour	Summary of Events and Information	Remarks and references to Appendices
RIBEMONT.	13th		At 4.55 a.m. two Coys of right Battalion, 36th Infantry Brigade, and two platoons left Battalion under heavy concentration of guns attacked trench running through 105 Contour in E.29. Trench taken but lost as result of a counter-attack at 6.30 a.m. - some prisoners, M.Gs and T.Ms taken - our casualties 1 Officer and 66 other ranks.	App VIII
RIBEMONT.	13th to 21st		Fine weather, which had prevailed during the preceeding operations continued. Line held was consolidated during this pause in the operations - our patrols active, and enemy line accurately located.	App. IX.
RIBEMONT.	22nd		Division ordered to continue attack - 35th Brigade on the right - 36th Brigade on the left - One battalion of the 36th Brigade had the special task of clearing MEAULTE. At Zero (4.45 a.m.), D. Special Coy. R.E. fired 50 drums of Burning Oil into the head of the valley in E.29.a. Considerable opposition but attack went well. Total prisoners reported at 1.40 p.m. - 8 officers and 374 Other Ranks. Hostile Artillery and M.G. fire was very heavy through-out the engagement and became more intense so that our line remained on the general line CARLAILOT FARM (E.18.a.) - STRAGGLY TREE (E.20.a.). Cavalry who had been sent on in advance were help up by Machine Guns - 37th Brigade were detailed to be ready to act as Advanced Guard to the Division and to exploit success if gained. At 6 p.m. Corps Commander and Mr Winston Churchill visited Divisional Headquarters.	App X App XI
RIBEMONT	23rd		37th Brigade (on a two battalion front) passed through 35th Brigade at 10 p.m., with orders to attack in conjunction with 36th Brigade on left, at 1 a.m. 24th instant.	App XII
RIBEMONT.	24th		Heavy Machine Gun fire was met from a German Strong Point in F.20.a. and at 6 a.m. the 6th R.W. Kent Regt was forced to retire to the Road in E.19.c. about the PEAR TREE - 35th Brigade on left reached and held the general line from F.14.c.5.5. to Railway Junction F.7.b.8.7. Order sent out to Brigades to postpone further exploitation until following day. Artillery engaged F.20.a. and F.14.c. (centre of opposition) during day.	
RIBEMONT and Morlancourt	25th		At 2.30 a.m. 36th and 37th Brigades attacked in direction of FRICOURT and MAMETZ - little opposition - 35th Brigade ordered to form an advance Guard - At 8 a.m. XXII Corps mounted troops pushed forward followed by 35th Brigade Group who got in touch on their left with 18th Division at F.5.b.9.5. and on their right with 58th Division in LAPREE WOOD. Night passed quietly. Weather still fine - heavy ground mist in the morning. DIVISIONAL Headquarters moved from RIBEMONT to MORLANCOURT (K.9.b.2.3.) at 12 noon	

Army Form C. 2118.

WAR DIARY

12TH DIVISION.   of   AUGUST. 1918.

INTELLIGENCE SUMMARY.

(Erase heading not required.)

Instructions regarding War Diaries and Intelligence Summaries are contained in F. S. Regs., Part II. and the Staff Manual respectively. Title pages will be prepared in manuscript.

Place	Date	Hour	Summary of Events and Information	Remarks and references to Appendices
MORLANCOURT and MEAULTE.	26th		Divisional Headquarters moved to MEAULTE (E.23.b.2.3.) at 7 p.m. 36th Infantry Brigade continued advance by pushing out strong patrols - at nightfall the line ran approximately through COKE AVENUE A.14 and 9 - A.9.a.35.85. - A.3.c.3.0 - A.3.c.25.00 - A.3.c.0.0.60 - A.2.d.8.9. and thence along CARNOY - MONTAUBAN ROAD to A.3.a.4.9.	
MEAULTE	27th		37th Infantry Brigade passed through 36th Brigade and formed Advance Guard. Opposition was encountered but advance went well. At 9 p.m. line held was A.16.b.8.9.(in touch with 58th Division.) - N.W. corner of FAVIERE WOOD - thence to junction with 18th Division) S.E. corner of BERNAFAY WOOD.	
MEAULTE	28th		35th and 36th Infantry Brigades attacked through 37th Infantry Brigade and stubborn resistance put up by M.G. Line held - S.E. corner of TRONES WOOD (in touch with 18th Division) MALTZ HORN FARM and RIDGE - A.6.c.7.5 - A.6.d.0.0 - A.12.a.4.5. - A.12.c.1.0. Line consolidated - 30 M.Gs and 150 prisoners captured.	Appx XIII
MEAULTE	29th		At 7 a.m. 37th Infantry Brigade passed through 35th and 36th Infantry Brigades - Cavalry were sent on ahead closely followed by Infantry - 37th Infantry Brigade reached a general line - East of SAVERNEKE WOOD and west of LE FOREST in touch with 18th Division on left - 6th Buffs on right were unable to gain touch with 58th Division and were ordered to form a defensive flank - Patrols were sent out and touch established with the Australians at Hill 110 in B.23.c and d. Captures 2 Officers, 66 Other Ranks. Divisional Headquarters moved to HIDDEN WOOD (F.10.b.) at 1.30 p.m.	Appx XIV
HIDDEN WOOD	30th		At 6 a.m. 142nd Infantry Brigade, 47th Division, passed through 57th Infantry Brigade, when Command passed. Division resting. 35th Infantry Brigade: MALTZ HORN FARM Area. 36th Infantry Brigade: CARNOY Area. 37th Infantry Brigade: FAVIERES WOOD Area. OFFICER CASUALTIES:- Killed 14; Wounded 43; Missing. Nil. O.R. " " :- Killed 211; Wounded 1000; Missing. 103. Weather still fine - Division reorganising. Drafts joined units.	

(A7093). Wt. W12839/M1293. 75.v.o.o. 1/17. D. D. & L., Ltd. Forms/C.2118.14.

Army Form C. 2118.

WAR DIARY
12TH DIVISION or AUGUST, 1918.
INTELLIGENCE SUMMARY.
(Erase heading not required.)

Instructions regarding War Diaries and Intelligence Summaries are contained in F. S. Regs., Part II. and the Staff Manual respectively. Title pages will be prepared in manuscript.

Place	Date	Hour	Summary of Events and Information	Remarks and references to Appendices
HIDDEN WOOD	31st		Day spent reorganizing and resting.	
			Total Casualties for the month of August :-	
			Officers Killed 53 ; Wounded 134 ; Missing 3 ; O.R. ,, 533 ; ,, 3193 ; ,, 399 ;	

Appendix I

SECRET.
Copy No.

12th DIVISION ORDER No. 270.

1st AUGUST, 1918.

Ref: Map Sheets.
LENS and AMIENS 1:100,000.
and 62.D. 1:20,000.

1. The 12th Division (less Artillery) will relieve the 58th Division (less Artillery) in the Centre Sector, III Corps, commencing on August 2nd. in accordance with the attached move and relief table.

2. (a) Details of the various reliefs will be arranged by the Commanders concerned.

   (b) "Q" is arranging for the relief of all Units not specially mentioned in this Order.

   (c) Completion of all moves or reliefs will be reported to the 58th Division and repeated to this Office.

3. (a) All programmes of work in hand and projected, aeroplane photos, Defence Schemes, trench stores, S.O.S.Signal message carrying rockets and A.P.S.A.A. will be taken over on relief.

   (b) Separate instructions will be issued regarding the relief of working parties.

4. (a) Divisional Headquarters will close at VIGNACOURT at 10 a.m. on 4th August, and open at BEAUCOURT CHATEAU at the same time, at which hour the G.O.C. will assume command of the Sector.

   (b) The following troops, covering the Sector, will come under the command of the G.O.C. at 10 a.m. 4th August.

   > 25th Divisional Artillery.
   > 5th Army Brigade, R.H.A.
   > 86th Army Brigade, R.F.A. (in mobile reserve).
   > 1 Coy 50th Battn., M.G.Corps. (~~less 2 Companies~~).

5. ACKNOWLEDGE.

A.Ryan
Major,
General Staff,
12th Division.

Issued at 8.30 p.m.

/Distribution ......

Copies to :-

1. "Q".
2. C.R.A.
3. C.R.E.
4. 35th Inf. Bde.
5. 36th Inf. Bde.
6. 37th Inf. Bde.
7. 5th Northamptonshire Regt. (Pioneers).
8. 12th Battn. M.G.C.
9. 12th Divl. Signal Coy., R.E.
10. A.D.M.S.
11. D.A.D.V.S.
12. A.P.M.
13. Camp Commandant.
14. 12th Divl. Train.
15. S.S.O.
16. 12th Div. Reception Camp.
17. Divl. Gas Officer.
18. D.A.D.O.S.
19. 214th Divl. Employment Coy.
20. O.C., S.A.A.Section, D.A.C.
21. A.D.C.
22. III Corps.
23. 18th Division.
24. 47th Division.
25. 58th Division.
26 - 33. G.S. and Records.
34. Town Major - BAIZIEUX.
35. Area Commdt.- BEAUCOURT.
36. Town Major - BEHENCOURT.
37. Area Commdt.- VIGNACOURT.
38. Do. - PERNOIS & BERTEAUCOURT.
39. Do. - CANAITRES.

MOVE TABLE ATTACHED TO 12th DIVISION "ORDER" No. 270.

Date.	Serial No.	Unit or Formation.	FROM.	TO.	Relieving.	REMARKS.
Aug. 2nd.	I.	35th Inf. Bde. Group. (less Transport). (a) 5th Northamptonshire Regt. (b) 35th Infantry Brigade. (c) 58th Fd. Ambulance. (d) 'C' Coy. 12th Bn. M.G.C.	FLESSELLES CANAPLES etc. Area.	Reserve Bde. 58th Divn.	1/4th Suffolk Regt. 174th Inf.Bde. (less forward Bn.) 2/3rd Field Amb. Reserve Coy., 18th Bn. M.G.C.	Move by bus. Embussing point for serial I (a) FLESSELLES – VILLERS BOCAGE road, facing E., tail just E. of FLESSELLES. Troops to be in position to embus at 12 noon. Embussing point for serials I (b), (c) and (d) CANAPLES – HAVERNAS road, facing S.E., head just N.W. of HAVERNAS. Troops to be in position to embus at 12 noon. Debussing point for all serials X roads on BAIZIEUX – BEHENCOURT & FRANVILLERS – CONTAY roads.
	II.	Transport of 35th Inf. Brigade Group as in Serial I.	CANAPLES – BERTEAUCOURT	Transport lines of Units of 58th Divn. being relieved.	As in Serial I.	To move by road under orders of B.G.C. 35th Infantry Brigade, and clear HAVERNAS by 11 a.m. Route NAOURS – TALMAS, thence as convenient. 5th Northamptonshire Regt. may move direct via VILLERS BOCAGE, clearing FLESSELLES by 11 a.m.

Date.	Serial No.	Unit or Formation.	FROM.	TO.	Relieving.	Remarks.
Aug. 2nd.	III.	37th Inf. Bde. Group. (Less Transport).		Reserve Bde. Area 58th Division.		Move by bus. Embussing point for Serial III (a) VILLERS BOCAGE - MOLLIENS AU BOIS Rd., facing E., tall just E. of VILLERS BOCAGE. Troops to be in position to embus at 9.30 p.m.
	(a)	'D' Coy., 12th Bn.M.G.C.	VILLERS BOCAGE		Serial I (d)	Embussing point for Serial III (b) (c) & (d) BERTEAUCOURT - HALLOY LES PERNOIS road, facing E., head just N. of HALLOY LES PERNOIS. Troops to be in position to embus at 9.0.p.m.
	(b)	'A' Coy. Do.	HALLOY LES PERNOIS.		do.	Embussing point for Serial III (e) VIGNACOURT - FLESSELLE'S road, facing N., just E. of VIGNACOURT. Troops to be ready to embus at
	(c)	37th Inf. Bde.	BERTEAUCOURT Area.		Serial I (b)	8 p.m. This Serial will then accompany main convoy and follow Serials III (b) (c) & (D)
	(d)	36th Fld.Ambulance.	do.		2/2nd.Fd.Ambl.	Debussing point for all serials as for Serial I.
	(e)	70th Fld.Coy. R.E.	VIGNACOURT.		504th Fd.Coy. R.E.	57th Infantry Brigade will have 1 Battalion forward with 2 Coys. in RAIZEUX and 2 Coys. in LAVIEVILLE Line.
	IV.	Transport of 57th Inf. Bde. Group, as in Serial III.	PERNOIS - VIG-NACOURT Area.	Transport Lines of Units of 58th Divn. being relieved.	As in Serial III.	To move under orders of B.G.C. 37th Inf. Bde. via VIGNACOURT - FLESSELLES. Not to pass road junction one third of a mile E. of T of VIGNACOURT before 4 p.m. 70th Field Coy.,R.E.,transport will join remainder of Brigade Group Transport on VIGNACOURT - FLESSELLES Road, just E. of VIGNACOURT, and follow in rear of same.

Date, Serial No.	Unit or formation	Relieving	To	Remarks
Night 2/3rd Aug.	Serial V. 55th Inf. Bde.		Right Sub-sector, 58th Division.	Report to H.Q., 58th Div. at 9.10 a.m.
Do.	Serial VI. 'C' Coy., 12th Battn. M.G.C.		Left Group, 58th Bn. M.G.C.	Report to Left Sub-sector.
Aug 3rd	Serial VII. 36th Inf. Bde. Group.		VILLERS BOCAGE Reserve Bde. Area – 58th Division.	Move by bus. Embussing point for Serial VII (a) VILLERS BOCAGE – MOLLIENS AU BOIS Road, facing E., tail just E. of VILLERS BOCAGE. Troops to be in position to embus at 7.30 p.m. Embussing point for Serials VII (b) (c) (d)(e) VIGNACOURT – FLESSELLES Road, facing E., tail just E. of VIGNACOURT. Troops to be in position to embus at 7 p.m. Debussing point for all Serials as for Serial
(a)	H.Q. & 'A' Coy.; 'B' Coy.; 12th Battn. M.G.C.	HAVERNAS.	H.Q., 36th Inf. Bde. to EBART'S FARM. S.I.O.S.I.	
(b)	59th Fld. Coy., R.E.		503rd Fld.Coy. R.E.	
(c)	57th Fld. Coy., R.E.	BERNAVILLECOURT	511th Fld.Coy. R.E.	
(d)	36th Inf. Bde.	VIGNACOURT.	Serial III(c)	
(e)	7th Fld. Ambulance.	do.	2/1st Fld.Ambn.	

(4)

Date.	Serial No.	Unit or Formation.	FROM	TO	REMARKS
Aug. 3rd.	VIII.	Transport of 36th Inf. Bde. Group - as in Serial VII.	BERTRANCOURT - HAVERNAS - VIGNACOURT Area.	Relieving:- As in Serial VII.	Transport of Units of 36th Bde. being relieved. As convenient - to be East of MONTIGNY by 7 p.m. to march under orders of B.G.C. 36th Inf. Bde. Group.
	IX.	Serial III.(c) 37th Inf. Bde.	Reserve Bde. Area.	Left Sub-sector. H.Q. D.21.a.5.1.	(b) & (c)
6	X.	Serial III.(a) & (b)	Reserve Coy. Area.	Right Sub-sector. Centre and Right Groups 8th Battn. M.G.Corps.	

N O T E S :-

(i) Units of Brigade Groups detailed in Column 3 are to be in the same order as they will be in the Convoy the first group being at the head of the column and the last at the tail.

(ii) Routes for lorries will be as follows :-
   Eastwards. - CONTAY - HERISSART - VILLERS BOCAGE.
   Westwards. - CONTAY - HERISSART - PUCHEVILLERS - MOLLIENS AU BOIS - 13 miles S.W. of BAIZIEUX.

(iii) On return journey Eastwards, lorries of the back Brigades of each Division in the following order:- 17th - 1754.

(iv) All Units and Formations of the Division will come under the command of the 59th Division on the completion of above moves.

(v) Attention is directed to Fourth Army Routine Order No. 2039 regarding orders to be observed on the march.

(vi) There will be no movement E. of a N. & S. line through BRESLE now; 1½ miles S.W. of BAIZIEUX on the CONTAY - FRANVILLERS Rd. S. of the X Rds. 1½ miles S.W. of BAIZIEUX before 9.15 p.m.

Appdx. II

SECRET.
Copy No. 13

12th DIVISION ORDER No. 271.

Reference Map Sheet
62 d N.E. 1/20,000.

6th August, 1918.

1. On Z day at an hour to be notified later 35th Infantry Brigade will attack from their present front and will capture and consolidate the approximate line shown on the attached map.
Patrols will be pushed out forward of this line to ascertain the position of the enemy and give warning of counter-attack.

2. The attack is in conjunction with operations of 18th and 58th Divisions on our right to secure the lines shown on the map.

3. The object of the 35th Infantry Brigade attack is to secure suitable jumping off ground for an attack on the spur N. and N.E. of MORLANCOURT which will probably take place either 24 or 48 hours later.

4. O.C. 12th Machine Gun Battalion will place one Section at the disposal of the G.O.C. 35th Infantry Brigade.

5. Artillery and machine gun barrage arrangements will be notified later.

6. Two Sections Field Company R.E. will be placed at the disposal of G.O.C. 35th Infantry Brigade by C.R.E. for this attack.

7. G.O.C. 35th Infantry Brigade will select a Battle Headquarters from the neighbourhood of which he can see his objective and will report location to this office. Battalion Headquarters J.5.d.7.5. is suggested.

8. Instructions regarding intercommunication, signalling to aeroplanes, medical and administrative arrangements will be issued separately.

9. Watches will be synchronized at 35th Infantry Brigade Headquarters at 7 p.m. on Y day By a staff officer from Divisional Headquarters.

10. ACKNOWLEDGE.

B. Belgrave
Lieut.Colonel,
General Staff,
12th Division.

Issued at 7.45 a.m.

P.T.O

Copies to :-

	No.	
	1	G.O.C.
∅	2	C.R.A. 25th Division.
	3	C.R.E.
∅	4	35th Infantry Brigade.
∅	5	36th Infantry Brigade.
∅	6	37th Infantry Brigade.
	7	5th Northamptonshire Regt.(Pioneers)
∅	8	12th Bn. Machine Gun Corps.
	9	O.C. 12th Div. Signal Coy.
	10	A.D.M.S.
	11	A.P.M.
	12	"A" & "Q".
	13)	War Diary.
	14)	
	15	18th Division.
	16	47th Division.
	17	58th Division.
	18)	
∅	19)	IIIrd Corps.
	20	5th Brigade R.A.F.
	21	10th Tank Battalion.

) for information.

Maps sent only to those marked ∅

SECRET.

12th Division No. G.X. 3380.
7th AUGUST, 1918.

ADDITION TO 12th DIVISION ORDER No. 271.

1.   The objective of the 35th Infantry Brigade has been extended Southwards to include the trench from junction of CULGOA and CLONCURRY at K.13.b.2.8 - K.7.d.9.0 - K.8.a.0.0 - K.8a.2.7.
        Artillery fire will lift off this trench at Zero plus 129 minutes.

2.   Two Companies, 5th Northamptonshire Regt. (Pioneers) will dig a communication trench from our present front line to the new front line about K.2.central during night 8th/9th inst. under orders issued by G.O.C., 35th Infantry Brigade.

3.   North of the grid line through K.13. and 14. the Division on our right is holding BURKE LINE as far North as K.7.c.6.3 thence to CULGOA TRENCH.

        The Northern objective of that Division is CLONCURRY TRENCH as far South as K.13.d.5.8, thence along trench running East through K14 c and d

4.   On the completion of the relief to-night by the 132nd (American) Regt. the 37th Infantry Brigade will place 1 Battalion at the disposal of the 35th Infantry Brigade. Details to be arranged mutually between Brigadiers concerned.

                                        C.R.Ryan
                                        Major for
                                        Lieut.Colonel,
                                        General Staff,
                                        12th Division.

Copies to all recipients of 12th Division Order No. 271.

SECRET.

12th Division No. G.X. 3380.
7th AUGUST, 1918.

ADDITION TO 12th DIVISION ORDER No. 271.

1. The objective of the 35th Infantry Brigade has been extended Southwards to include the trench from junction of CULGOA and CLONCURRY at K.13.b.2.8 - K.7.d.9.0 - K.8.a.0.0 - K.8a.2.7.
Artillery fire will lift off this trench at Zero plus 129 minutes.

2. Two Companies, 5th Northamptonshire Regt. (Pioneers) will dig a communication trench from our present front line to the new front line about K.2.central during night 8th/9th inst. under orders issued by G.O.C., 35th Infantry Brigade.

3. North of the grid line through K.13. and 14. the Division on our right is holding BURKE LINE as far North as K.7.c.6.3 thence to CULGOA TRENCH.

The Northern objective of that Division is CLONCURRY TRENCH as far South as K.13.d.5.8, thence along trench running East through K14 c and d

4. On the completion of the relief to-night by the 132nd (American) Regt. the 37th Infantry Brigade will place 1 Battalion at the disposal of the 35th Infantry Brigade. Details to be arranged mutually between Brigadiers concerned.

CRRyan
Major for
Lieut.Colonel,
General Staff,
12th Division.

Copies to all recipients of 12th Division Order No. 271.

SECRET.

12th Division No. G.X.3331

6th AUGUST, 1918.

ARTILLERY ARRANGEMENTS WITH REFERENCE TO
12th DIVISION ORDER Nº. 271.

1. 18 prs. open at Zero with intense fire on line K.8.a.0.7. - K.2.c.0.8. - K.2.central., thence along Railway in K.2.b.2.0. to E.27.c.2.6.

    After 4 minutes, barrage will creep back 800 yards at normal rate, then backwards and forwards through these 800 yards until Zero plus 30.

2. From Zero plus 30 to Zero plus 120 wire cutting on trench K.8.a.0.7. to K.2.c.0.8. and slow rate of fire on selected trenches.

3. At Zero plus 120 intense bombardment of trench K.8.a.0.7. to K.2.c.0.8. selected trenches, and of railway bends in E.26.d., K.2.b. and K.2.d.

    At Zero plus 123 mins. lift off trench K.8.a.0.7. to K.2.c.0.8. and on more Easterly of two railway bends in K.2.b.

    " " plus 129 mins. lift off trenches West of Westerly Railway bend in K.2.d. and b.& on to Easterly Railway.

    " " plus 132 mins. lift off Western railway and trenches West of the N. and S. line through K.2.b.6.5.

    " " plus 150 mins. lift on to protective barrage on N. and S. grid line through E.27.central and K.3.central.

    " " plus 180 mins. slow down to bursts of fire, until ordered to stop.

4. The S.O.S. barrage will be put down on a North and South line on the Grid between E.26. and E.27. and K.2. and K.3. with special attention to valleys in K.3.a. and c. and E.27.a.

    MACHINE GUN ARRANGEMENTS.

1. O.C., 12th Machine Gun Battalion has detailed two Sections to be attached to 35th Infantry Brigade for consolidation. Of these two Sections, 2 guns have been ordered to Rendezvous with each attack Battalion, to move with their rear waves.

2. In addition 32 guns will be in position to fire on railways and trenches on Spur in K.2.b. and d., K.3.a., E.26.d. and E.27.c. during the attack.

3. S.O.S. Machine Gun barrage will be on valleys in E.27. a. and K.3.c., North and South of the Spur.

A. Belgrave

Lieut-Colonel,
General Staff,
12th Division.

Distribution over/

Copies to :-

    C.O.C.
    C.R.A., 25th Division.
    C.R.E.
    35th Infantry Brigade.
    36th Infantry Brigade.
    37th Infantry Brigade.
    12th Battn. Machine Gun Corps.
    O.C., 12th Div. Signal Coy., R.E.
    18th Division.
    47th Division.
    58th Division.
    III Corps. (2 copies)
    5th Brigade R.A.F.
    10th Tank Battalion.

Appx III

SECRET.
Copy No. 29

12th DIVISION ORDER No. 272.

Ref: 62.d. 1/40,000.
     62.d. N.E. 1/20,000.

6th AUGUST 1918.

1. On the nights 6th/7th and 7th/8th inst. the 36th Inf. Bde. will be withdrawn to BOIS DE MAI, with Headquarters at ALLONVILLE, where it will be in III Corps Reserve.

2. (a) On the night 7th/8th inst. the 37th Infantry Brigade will be relieved in the Left Sub-Sector, as far South as Bridge and Post at E.20.d.2.1 (inclusive) by the 66th American Brigade, which will be under the command of the G.O.C. 47th Division.

   (b) The 35th Infantry Brigade will take over responsibility for the line as far North as Post and Bridge at E.20.d.2.1 (exclusive) where touch will be maintained with the 66th American Infantry Brigade.

   (c) The Divisional Northern boundary will then be E.20.d.2.1 (exclusive) - E. and W. grid line between squares E.19. and E.25. - FRANVILLERS - ROUNDWOOD - BEHENCOURT (all inclusive).

   (d) On relief, the 37th Infantry Brigade will move to billets in the vicinity of ROUND WOOD and FRANVILLERS (Hdqrs. BEHENCOURT), where it will be in Divisional Reserve.

3. At 12 midnight on night 7th/8th instant the G.O.C. 12th Division is handing over command of the sector N. of the boundary in para. 2 (c) above to G.O.C. 47th Division.

4. (a) Relief of Machine Gun Companies, including the Coy. of the 50th Bn. M.G. Corps now under the orders of the G.O.C. 12th Division, Field Companies R.E. and Field Ambulances will be arranged direct between their respective commanders and those of the 47th Division.

   (b) On relief, the Coy. 50th Bn. M.G. Corps will come under the orders of O.C. 50th Bn. M.G. Corps and will be accommodated in the vicinity of QUERRIEU.

   (c) Further orders will be issued regarding the 5th Northamptonshire Regt. (Pioneers).

5. Moves will take place in accordance with the attached table. Completion of each Serial to be reported to Divisional Headquarters.

6. Instructions regarding billetting of all units relieved are being issued by 12th Division "Q".

7. A C K N O W L E D G E.

C.A.Ryan
Major for
Lieut.Colonel,
General Staff,
12th Division.

Issued at 2.30pm

/Copies to...

Copies to :-

1. G.O.C.
2. C.R.A., 25th Division.
3. C.R.E.
4. 35th Inf. Bde.
5. 36th Inf. Bde.
6. 37th Inf. Bde.
7. 5th Northamptonshire Regt. (Pioneers).
8. 12th Bn. M.G.Corps.
9. 12th Div. Signal Coy. R.E.
10. A.D.M.S.
11. A.P.M.
12. 'A' & 'Q'.
13. D.A.D.V.S.
14. Camp Commandant.
15. 12th Div. Train.
16. S.S.O.
17. 12th Div. Recpn. Camp.
18. Div. Gas Officer.
19. D.A.D.O.S.
20. 214th Divl. Empl. Coy.
21. O.C., S.A.A.Sect.,D.A.C.
22.) III Corps.
23.)
24. 18th Division.
25. 47th Division.
26. 58th Division.
27. 33rd American Division.
28.) War Diary.
29.)
30. 66th American Infantry Brigade.
31-34. G.S. and Records.

Table to accompany 12th Division Order No. 272, dated 6th August, 1918.

Serial.	Date.	Unit or Formation.	From.	To.	Relieved by.	Remarks.
A.	6/7 August.	36th Inf. Bde. less 1 Bn. and Brigade Hdqrs.	ROUNDWOOD.	BOIS de MAI.	2 Bns. 132nd (American) Regt.	To move about 10 p.m. after relief by 2 Bns. 132nd (American) Regt. who came under command of B.G.C. 36th Inf.Bde.
B.	do.	1 Coy. 50th Bn. M.G.Corps.	LAVIEVILLE SYSTEM and BAIZIEUX.	Vicinity of QUERRIEU to rejoin their Bn.	1 Coy. 124th (American) M.G. Bn.	
C.	7/8 August.	1 Bn. 36th Inf. Bde., Bde.Hdqrs. 36th Inf. Bde.	do. EKARTS FARM.	BOIS de MAE ALLONVILLE.	1 Bn. 132nd American Regt. Hqrs. 66th American Bde.	
D.	do.	37th Inf. Bde.	Left Sub-Sector, 12th Division.	2 Bns. FRAN-VILLERS, 1 Bn. ROUND-WOOD. Bde. Hdqrs. BEHENCOURT.	132nd (American) Regt. less 1 Bn.	
E.	do.	Left Coy. 12th Bn. M.G.Corps.	do.	BEHENCOURT.	1 Coy. 124th (American) M.G. Bn.	

S E C R E T.

Addendum and Corrigendum No. 1 to 12th Division Order No. 272.
----

1. Para. 1 and serials A. and C. of the move table are cancelled. The 36th Infantry Brigade will move in accordance with orders issued separately to all concerned.

2. With reference to para. 4 (c), the 5th Northamptonshire Regt. (Pioneers) on night of 7th/8th instant will move to the area of the Support Battalion, 35th Infantry Brigade, in accordance with instructions to be issued by 35th Infantry Brigade.
    They will be under the orders of B.G.C. 35th Infantry Brigade tactically from midnight 7th/8th instant, but will not be used except for defensive purposes.

3. In Move Table, Serial E, column 5, for BEHENCOURT read IBARTS FARM.

C.R.Ryan

Major for Lieut.Colonel,
General Staff,
12th Division.

6th August, 1918.

Copies to all recipients of 12th Division Order No. 272.

SECRET

12th Division No. G.X. 3344

6th AUGUST, 1918.

<u>ARRANGEMENTS FOR SIGNALLING TO AEROPLANES WITH
REFERENCE TO 12th DIVISION ORDER N°.271.</u>

1. Red Flares, tin discs, and groups of 3 rifles will all be used to denote "I am here" to aeroplanes. These are the only signals which will be used by Infantry to communicate with aeroplanes.

2. A Contact Aeroplane will fly along the front at Zero plus 240 minutes. At this time Infantry will burn red flares, show their groups of 3 rifles, or their tin discs, turning the latter about to catch the reflection of the sun.
   Tin discs will be issued at the rate of 2 or 3 per Section.

3. All Headquarters will be reminded to display their ground signal sheets and strips.

4. Warning of hostile counter-attack will be given by aeroplanes in the following manner. The aeroplane will fly in the direction of the enemy, dropping a white parachute flare as near to the counter-attacking troops as possible.

- MAPS. -

62.D. N.E. and 62.D. S.E. 1:20,000 Map, of which the message map which will be issued is a facsimile, will be used for all references.

- LIGHT SIGNALS -

The following light signals will be employed :-

(a) No.32.Grenade, GREEN over GREEN over GREEN.
    meaning S. O. S.

(b) No.32.Grenade, WHITE over WHITE over WHITE
    meaning "we have reached objective".

[signature]

Lieut-Colonel,
General Staff,
12th Division.

Copies to :-

G.O.C.
C.R.A., 25th Division.
C.R.E.
35th Infantry Brigade.
36th Infantry Brigade.
37th Infantry Brigade.
12th Bn.Machine Gun Corps.

O.C.,12th Div.Signal Coy.
18th Division.
47th Division.
58th Division.
III CORPS (2 copies)
5th Brigade, R.A.F.
10th Tank Battalion.

Appdx. IV

SECRET.

Copy No. 13

12th DIVISION ORDER No. 273.

Ref: 62.d. 1/40,000.   6th August, 1918.

1. The 36th Infantry Brigade will relieve the 53rd Infantry Brigade, 18th Division, to-night 6th/7th instant, and will come under the orders of G.O.C. 18th Division on the completion of the move.

2. The dispositions of the Brigade will be:- 3 Battalions in trench system in vicinity of FRANVILLERS: Brigade Headquarters to FRECHENCOURT.

3. (a) No move to take place before 9.15 p.m.

   (b) All other details to be arranged direct between Brigades.

4. Completion of the move to be reported to 18th Division and repeated to this office.

5.   A C K N O W L E D G E.

C.Ryan Major for

Lieut. Colonel,
General Staff,
12th Division.

Issued at 7.15 p.m

Copies to :-

   1. "Q".
   2. C.R.A., 25th Division.
   3. C.R.E.
   4. 35th Infantry Brigade.
x 5. 36th Inf. Bde.
   6. 37th Inf. Bde.
   7. 5th Northamptonshire Regt.
   8. 12th Bn. M.G.C.
   9. 12th Div. Train.
  10. III Corps.
x 11. 18th Division.
  12. 47th Division.
  13)
  14) War Diary.
  15 - 18. G.S. and Records.
  19. G.O.C.

x By Special D.R.

SECRET.

12th Division No. C.X. 3362.

7th AUGUST, 1918.

ARRANGEMENTS WITH REGARD TO GAS AND SMOKE.

GAS.

1. If the wind is favourable, Gas will be fired between Zero and Zero plus 30 minutes from Sunken Road K.1.d.1.3 to K.1.d.2.7, with targets in MORLANCOURT and trenches which have been selected in consultation with G.O.C. 35th Infantry Brigade.

2. Os.C. Special Companies have guaranteed that there will be no Gas on or West of the line K.8.c.0.5 - K.8.a.0.0 - K.2.d.0.0 - K.2.central - K.26.central at or after Zero plus 2 hours.

   Patrols will be able to enter MORLANCOURT without respirators at Zero plus 2 hours, but must be warned not to enter cellars or deep dug-outs without putting their respirators on.

3. The wind limits for the operation are W.N.W. through W. to W.S.W., and of a velocity exceeding 4 miles per hour.

4. If at any time up to Zero minus 2 hours it becomes certain that the wind will be unfavourable, the gas operation will be cancelled by a message from Divisional Headquarters.

   The following code will be used :-

   Operation will not take place ... ... VESLE.

   On receipt of this message, Brigade will inform the officer of Special Company, who will be at their Headquarters. This officer will then be responsible for stopping the gas operation. This does not affect the responsibility of the officers in charge of each group of emplacements for deciding whether or not the wind at Zero is safe for discharge.

SMOKE.

Stokes Mortars will fire smoke from Zero plus 120 minutes, under arrangements which have been made direct between O.C. Stokes Mortars and G.O.C. 35th Infantry Brigade, with a view to neutralizing the machine guns in K.2.d. and b.

[signature]

Lieut.Colonel,
General Staff,
12th Division.

Copies to :-

G.O.C.	O.C., 12th Div. Signal Coy., R.E.
C.R.A., 25th Division.	18th Division.
C.R.E.	47th Division.
35th Infantry Brigade. (4)	58th Division.
36th Infantry Brigade.	III Corps (2 copies).
37th Infantry Brigade.	5th Brigade R.A.F.
12th Bn. Machine Gun Corps.	10th Tank Battalion.

appx. V

SECRET.

12th Division No. GX.3378.

7th August, 1918.

Correction No. 1
to
12th Division G.X.3331 of 6th Aug. - ARTILLERY ARRANGEMENTS
with reference to 12th Division Order No. 271.

Delete para 3 and substitute the following :-

3.   At Zero plus 120 intense bombardment of trench K.8.a.0.7. to K.2.c.0.8., of selected trenches, and of railway bends in E.26.d., K.2.b. and K.2.d.

At Zero plus 124 mins.   lift off trench K.8.a.0.7. to K.2.c.0.8. and on more Easterly of two railway bends in K.2.b.

"   "   " 129   "   lift off trench running from K.8.a.25.75. - K.8.a.00.10. and thence southwards, on to protective barrage East of this trench.

"   "   " 134   "   lift off trenches West of Westerly railway bend in K.2.d. and b. and on to easterly railway.

"   "   " 140   "   lift off Western railway and trenches West of the N. and S. line through K.2.b.6.5.

"   "   " 150   "   lift on to protective barrage on a N. and S. grid line through E.27.central and K.3.central.

"   "   " 180   "   slow down to bursts of fire, until ordered to stop.

Major
for
A.Ryan
Lieut.Colonel,
General Staff,
12th Division.

To all recipients of 12th Division No. G.X.3331.

Appx. VI.

SECRET.

12th Division No. G.X. 3380.

7th AUGUST, 1918.

ADDITION TO 12th DIVISION ORDER No. 271.

1. The objective of the 35th Infantry Brigade has been extended Southwards to include the trench from junction of CULGOA and CLONCURRY at K.13.b.2.8 - K.7.d.9.0 - K.8.a.0.0 - K.8a.2.7.
Artillery fire will lift off this trench at Zero plus 128 minutes.

2. Two Companies, 5th Northamptonshire Regt. (Pioneers) will dig a communication trench from our present front line to the new front line about K.2.central during night 8th/9th inst. under orders issued by G.O.C., 35th Infantry Brigade.

3. North of the grid line through K.13. and 14. the Division on our right is holding BURKE LINE as far North as K.7.c.6.3 thence to CULGOA TRENCH.

The Northern objective of that Division is CLONCURRY TRENCH as far South as K.13.d.5.8, thence along trench running East through K.14.c and d

4. On the completion of the relief to-night by the 132nd (American) Regt. the 37th Infantry Brigade will place 1 Battalion at the disposal of the 35th Infantry Brigade. Details to be arranged mutually between Brigadiers concerned.

CARyan
Major for
Lieut.Colonel,
General Staff,
12th Division.

Copies to all recipients of 12th Division Order No. 271.

Appdx. VII

SECRET.

Addendum and Corrigendum No. 1 to 12th Division Order No. 272.
----

1. Para. 1 and serials A. and C. of the move table are cancelled. The 36th Infantry Brigade will move in accordance with orders issued separately to all concerned.

2. With reference to para. 4 (c), the 5th Northamptonshire Regt. (Pioneers) on night of 7th/8th instant will move to the area of the Support Battalion, 35th Infantry Brigade, in accordance with instructions to be issued by 35th Infantry Brigade.
   They will be under the orders of B.G.C. 35th Infantry Brigade tactically from midnight 7th/8th instant, but will not be used except for defensive purposes.

3. In Move Table, Serial E, column 5, for BEHENCOURT read IBARTS FARM.

C.A.Ryan
Major for Lieut.Colonel,
General Staff,
12th Division.

6th August, 1918.

Copies to all recipients of 12th Division Order No. 272.

SECRET.
Copy No.

12th DIVISION ORDER No. 274.

Sheet 62.D. N.E. 1:20,000.   12th AUGUST, 1918.

1. At Zero on the 13th August the 36th Infantry Brigade will capture the trench running from K.5.b.5.3. through E.29.d.3.0. - E.29.d.0.1. - E.29.c.2.5. and will joint it up to the present line on both flanks.

2. The line to be consolidated will be from railway crossing K.5.d.7.8. along the above mentioned trench to our present front line at about E.23.c.9.5.

3. Artillery will open at Zero on the objective and on trench line from E.29.a.4.0. to E.17.d.5.5.: trenches at E.29.a.0.0. in E.29.a. and b.: old gun pits in E.30.c. and K.6.a. and b.; and Sunken Road in E.23.b. and d. and E.24.a.

   At Zero plus   Artillery fire will lift off the objective and on to protective barrage, where it will continue for one hour.

4. Dumps of wire and consolidating materials will be formed tonight close to the present front line, for the use of the infantry in their new positions.

5. The line, as detailed in para. 2., and the present Front Line from E.28.c.9.5. to the RIVER ANCRE will be wired and thoroughly organized as a defensive line.
   The Brigades in the Front Line will be responsible for this work.

   Brigades in line will be responsible for constructing a system of defences on this line consisting of a Front and Support Line. Each line will be wired and the system made as strong as possible, to be held at all costs as a defensive flank to the Fourth Army.

B. Belgrave
Lieut-Colonel,
General Staff,
12th Division.

Issued at 5.30 p.m.

Distribution over.

P.T.O.

Copies to :-
1. 35th Infantry Brigade.
2. 36th Infantry Brigade.
3. 37th Infantry Brigade.
4. C.R.A., 25th Division.
5. C.R.E.
6. A.D.M.S.
7. 5th Northamptonshire Regt. (Pioneers).
8. 12th Battn. M.G.C.
9. 12th Div. Signals.
10. "Q".
11. III Corps.
12. 47th Division.
13. 18th Division.
14.) War Diary.
15.)
16 - 22. G.S. and Records.

MESSAGES AND SIGNALS.

Prefix	Code	Words	Charge			
				This message is on a/c of:	Recd. at ___ m.	
Office of Origin and Service Instructions.		Sent			Date	
Secret		At ___ m.		___ Service	From	
		To		(Signature of "Franking Officer.")	By	
		By				

TO: ~~Royal 2 Bde~~ CRA 12 SW — 47 DW
~~BLGU~~ 36 " 12 Bn MGC — 18 DW
~~BLGU~~ 37 " 3rd Corps

Sender's Number	Day of Month	In reply to Number	
S.170	12		AAA

Addendum No 1 to 12 Dvn
Order No 274 aaa Zero
hour will be 4.55 a.m
AAA acknowledge ✓

From 12 Dw
Place
Time

C. A. Ryan
Major G
12 DW

35th Inf. Bde.
C.R.A.
18th Division.
47th Division.
58th Division.

SECRET.

12th Division No. 52

12th AUGUST, 1918.

MACHINE GUN ARRANGEMENTS
with reference to
12th DIVISION ORDER No. 274.
==

18 guns in battery positions will fire on S.O.S. lines from Zero to Zero plus 3 minutes

'E' Battery, 4 guns, in E.15.c. will fire on work and trenches E.29.a.0.0. to E.29.a.3.3. from Zero to Zero plus 3 minutes: lift to work E.29.a.central and trench North of same, from Zero plus 3 mins. to Zero plus 60 mins.

'D' Battery, 4 guns, in E.20.b.1.2. will fire on work E.29.a.0.0. to E.29.a.3.3. from Zero to Zero plus 60 mins.

ARTILLERY ARRANGEMENTS.
=============================

Reference para 3.

At Zero plus 3 mins., all Heavy and Field Artillery will lift off objective except one R.F.A. Brigade, which will continue firing on trench from K.5.b.5.6. to E.29.c.8.2. till Zero plus 6 minutes and will then lift. Remainder of Artillery remains on the targets given in para. 3 for one hour.

B. Belgrave
Lieut-Colonel,
General Staff,
12th Division.

Appdx. IX

SECRET.

12th DIVISION WARNING ORDER No. 275.

1. In conjunction with the Division on our right, the 12th Division may be ordered to attack at Zero Hour on Z Day to capture the general line shown on the map, and form a defensive flank to the Fourth Army.

2. The first objective, shown in blue on the map, will be taken by the 36th Infantry Brigade attacking on the right and 37th Infantry Brigade on the left.

   35th Infy. Brigade will then pass through 36th Infantry Brigade and will take the second objective shown on the map in red.

3. The outside boundary of the Division is shown by a dotted blue line on the map. The boundary between 36th and 37th Infantry Brigades is shown by a dotted green line.

4. First objective :- A Trench from F.25.a.6.1. through F.19.B.0.4 to Southern end of cutting at E.24.d.0.8 - thence to road junction E.23.d.6.6.

   37th Infantry Brigade :- Road junction E.23.d.6.6 - Eastern end of bank at E.23.c.4.8 - road junction E.22.b.5.3 - thence to River ANCRE at E.22.a.8.5.

   Second objective :-

   35th Infantry Brigade : Bend in road F.20.b.3.8 - trench F.13.d.3.7 to F.19.d.4.7 - old strong point at F.19.c.6.0 - junction of tank in trench at F.19.a.3.5 - Southern end of cutting E.24.d.0.8.

   It will be noted that on the above definite points easily recognised on the ground have been given, to which troops can be marched before making posts to right and left of them.

5. The line to be consolidated and wired is shown on the map by a continuous green line.

   Boundary between 35th and 36th Infantry Brigades :- trench at F.19.c.0.4.

   Boundary between 36th and 37th Infantry Brigades :- trench at E.29.b.2.7.

6. Artillery barrage will open at Zero and will move forward at the rate of 100 yards in 3 minutes until it is 300 yards beyond first objective.

   There will then be a pause of from 1 to 2 hours.

   Barrage will then creep forward at the rate of 100 yards in 3 minutes to 300 yards beyond the second objective, where it will form a protective barrage.

   A protective barrage will be maintained throughout to cover the left flank.

   Note. These arrangements are liable to alteration to fit in with the Division on our right.

/7. ....

7. Tanks will co-operate.

   One intelligent Infantry soldier with good eyesight will be detailed to go in each tank, for watching the infantry and keeping the tank informed of their movements.

   Each fighting tank will carry 5,000 rounds of S.A.A. for the use of the Infantry. This will be dumped in the line to be consolidated.

   Further details will be notified later.

8. Machine guns from positions in E.15.c. and E.20.b. will form a protective barrage on the left flank and will deal with visible targets.

   Further arrangements will be notified later.

   1 Section, detailed by O.C., 12th Bn. M.G. Corps, will be under the orders of the G.O.C. of each Infantry Brigade for consolidation.

9. C.R.E. will detail 2 Sections Field Company R.E. to be under the orders of each Infantry Brigade.

10. Flares, tin discs, and the signal with three rifles will all be used by troops in front line to show their position to contact aeroplanes.

    Hours at which contact aeroplanes will fly over will be notified.

11. Signal Communications, Medical and Administrative Arrangements will be issued separately.

12. Shelters for two Brigade Headquarters are being made at quarry in K.9.b.2.8.

    Advanced Divisional Headquarters will remain as at present.

                                              B. Belgrave
                                              Lieut.Colonel,
                                              General Staff,
13th August, 1918.   12th Division.

        Copies to :-   35th Infantry Brigade.
                        36th Infantry Brigade.
                        37th Infantry Brigade.
                        C.R.A.
                        C.R.E.
                        12th Bn. M.G. Corps.
                        47th Division.
                        10th Tank Battn.
                        III Corps.

SECRET.
Copy No. 18.

12th DIVISION—ORDER NO. 276.

Ref: Sheet 62.D.N.E.
15th AUGUST, 1916.

1. 35th Infantry Brigade will relieve 36th Infantry Brigade in the Right Subsector of the Divisional Front on the night 16th/17th inst., under arrangements made by the Brigade Commanders concerned.

2. The boundary between Brigades in the line will be the track running from the Front Line at E.26.c.8.8., to road junction F.3.b.4.8., thence along road to junction with Grid Line at L.3.c.4.8., thence along Grid Line between K.1 and K.7.
   The Left Brigade will be responsible for the defence of these roads and tracks, but they will be used by both Brigades for traffic.
   Battalions of Brigades in line will be accommodated in areas as above.

3. The 36th Infantry Brigade, on relief, will occupy the area in the BENDIGO – BALLARAT Line now occupied by 2 Battalions 35th Infantry Brigade. The third Battalion will be in trenches and shelters South of PERICOURT L'ABBE, if there is sufficient accommodation; if not, in DERWENT and TASMANIAN Trenches.

4. THORPE'S Group, R.F.A., will be affiliated to 35th Infantry Brigade.

5. C.R.E. will detail one Field Coy., R.E., (less 2 Sections), for work in each subsector of the Divisional line under the orders of G.O's.C. Brigades.

6. Brigades in the line will be responsible for the construction and upkeep of the Front Line and Support Line.
   The present Front Line and the line of posts in front of it, will be adapted under Brigade arrangements to form a Front and Support Line, not less than 200 yds. apart.
   The Front Line will be sited to provide observation, the Support Line with a view to the best fire effect.
   Arrangements as to construction and wiring of these two lines will be made forthwith.

7. Work on the Reserve line will be carried out under Divisional arrangements.

8. Completion of relief will be reported by the Code word "COOK." G.O.C. 35th Infantry Brigade will take over command of the Subsector on completion of relief.

9. ACKNOWLEDGE.

Belgrave
Lieut-Colonel,
General Staff,
12th Division.

Issued at 9.30 p.m. SDR to 35 & 36 Bdes.

/Distribution over ...

Issued to :-

1. C.R.A. 25th Div.
2. C.R.E.
3. 35th Infantry Brigade.
4. 36th Infantry Brigade.
5. 37th Infantry Brigade.
6. 12th Battn. M.G.C.
7. 5th Northamptonshire Regt.
8. 12th Div. Signal Coy., R.E.
9. 12th Div. Train.
10. A.D.M.S.
11. D.A.D.V.S.
12. A.P.M.
13. "Q"
14. III Corps.
15. 18th Division.
16. 47th Division.
17. 58th Division.
18.)
19.)War Diary.
20. G.O.C.
21 - 24.   G.S. and Records.

SECRET.

Copy No.

12th DIVISION WARNING ORDER No. 277.

1. The operations now in progress may result in a withdrawal of the enemy across the old SOMME battlefield.

   It is important, therefore, that the earliest information regarding the enemy's intentions and moves should be obtained.

2. Vigorous patrolling will be carried out along the whole front.

3. If it is found that the enemy has withdrawn, the Division will be ordered to move forward.

4. On receipt of the message "Division will move as in Warning Order No. 277".

   (a) The Brigade holding the Right Sub-Sector will relieve the Battalion of the Brigade holding the Left Sub-Sector, and take over responsibility for the defence of the present Divisional line.

   (b) The advanced guard to the Division will be formed as follows:

   At present.

Advanced guard Commander — (G.O.C., Left Brigade)	Brigadier-General A.B.E. WEBBER, D.S.O.
One troop, Corps Cavalry.	Troop, Northumberland Hussars.
One Brigade, R.F.A.	110th Brigade, R.F.A.
One Field Company, R.E.	70th Field Coy. R.E.
Left Infantry Brigade.	37th Infantry Brigade.
One Company, Divnl. M.G. Battn.	A. Coy. 12th Bn. M. G. C.
One Section, Tank Battalion.	One Section, 6th Tank Battn.
Bearer Sub-Division, Field Ambce.	Bearer Sub-Division, 38th Field Ambulance.

   On receipt of the order to move each of the above units will send an officer to report for orders at Headquarters, 37th Infantry Brigade.

   The detachments Corps Cavalry now with Brigades will be sent to report to their Troop leader at Headquarters, 37th Infantry Bde.

   (c) The advanced guard will move forward and will occupy the spur F.14.c. and a. and F.8.c. and b.

   The advanced guard will be responsible for clearing the villages of MEAULTE and BECORDEL-BECOURT and all ground within the Divisional boundaries, and for keeping touch with Divisions on the flanks.

5. The Southern Divisional boundary will be :-
   Present front line at K.5.d.6.9 - cross-roads F.25.b.8.8 - thence along the road through F.20.c. and a. - F.14.d. and b. and F.9.c. and a. to the stream at F.9.a.6.9.

/ The Northern.......

(2).

The Northern Divisional boundary will be :-
River ANCRE and stream through E.16.d. - E.17.a. and b. - E.11.d. - E.12.c. and d. - F.7.a. and b. - F.8.a. and b. to F.9.a.6.9 (stream exclusive), where 12th Division is squeezed out by the Divisions on either flank, and comes into reserve.

6. Two horse drawn 60 pdr. Batteries or one 60 pdr. and one horse drawn 6" Howitzer Battery are being allotted by G.O.C., R.A., III Corps to 12th Division. These will work under orders of the C.R.A.

7. Three Whippet Tanks, 6th Tank Battalion, are allotted to the Division, and will come under orders of G.O.C., advanced guard.

8. The MEAULTE - FRICOURT - MARICOURT Road will be repaired as the advance progresses, under arrangements to be made by the C.R.E.

9. Prior to the advance all ranks will be warned of the danger of collecting trophies and of occupying evacuated dugouts.

The enemy is employing many and various ruses to cause loss to our troops, by means of hidden gas shell, mines, etc. Parties to search for such traps will be detailed by the C.R.E.

No dug-out will be occupied until it has been thoroughly examined and a notice board erected to the effect that it is safe. C.R.E. will arrange for the preparation and erection of these boards.

10. The rapidity of an advance will depend largely on the maintenance of communications. No Brigade will move its Rear Headquarters forward until its Advanced Headquarters have been opened and the Division informed.

Infantry Brigade Headquarters will be alongside Headquarters of affiliated Artillery Brigades.

Visual signalling will be organized.

Mounted orderlies will be used. Brigades will consider the possibility of organizing mounted orderlies from the grooms and horses on the establishment of Brigade Headquarters and Battalions. Mounted officers of units will keep their horses in locations from which these can be brought up quickly to their present Headquarters.

All units will put out ground signal sheets and strips at their Headquarters.

Men will carry flares and discs for communication with aeroplanes, and the signal with three rifles will be used.

Pack transport trains, as at present organized, will be used by Brigades.

Divisional units will be prepared to utilize pack transport if necessary.

/11. .....

(3).

11. All outposts and advanced posts will be dug in and wired. This will be practised by the Brigade in reserve as part of its training, and instructions will be given in siting and general design of posts.

12. The question of the transport of Stokes Mortars requires consideration.
    Brigades will forward suggestions on this point as soon as possible.

13. C.R.E. will arrange for the opening up of wells and the supply of water in the area occupied. All water must be tested by a Medical Officer before being used for drinking or cooking.

14. Every opportunity will be taken by units in the line as well as in reserve of giving instruction in map reading and the use of the compass.

15. The imperative necessity of good march discipline and of discipline at all times will be specially impressed on all concerned.

16. G.234 is cancelled.

17. A C K N O W L E D G E.

B. Belgrave
Lieut.Colonel,
General Staff,
12th Division.

15th August, 1918.

Copies to :-
No.	
1.	35th Inf. Bde.
2.	36th Inf. Bde.
3.	37th Inf. Bde.
4.	C.R.A., 25th Division.
5.	C.R.E.
6.	5th Northamptonshire Regt.
7.	12th Bn. M.G. Corps.
8.	12th Div. Signal Coy. R.E.
9.	A.D.M.S.
10.	A.P.M.
11.	"Q".
12.	18th Division.)
13.	47th Division.) (For information).
14.	III Corps.)
15.	6th Tank Battn.

S E C R E T

<u>12th Division No. G.X.3622.</u>

18th AUGUST, 1918.

<u>AMENDMENT TO 12th DIVISION WARNING ORDER No. 277.</u>

    Reference 12th Division Warning Order No.277, dated 15th August, 1918.

Para. 4 (b)

    For "one Troop Corps Cavalry ...... Troop Northumberland Hussars

read "   "   " (less 2 Sections)"   "   (less 2 Sections)

    Two Sections, Northumberland Hussars, will remain with Divisional Headquarters.

                                           C.A. Ryan
                                               Major

                                      for Lieut-Colonel,
                                          General Staff,
                                          12th Division.

Issued to all recipients of 12th Division Warning
       Order No. 277.

D.R.L.S.

35th, 36th & 37th Inf. Bdes. G. 12th Div.
13th Bn. M.G.C., 5th Northants Regt.
Signals, A.D.M.S., A.P.M. "Q". 18th & 47th
Division, III Corps, 6th Tank Battn.

G. 265   16

Reference	12th	Division	Warning
Order	No.277	para.	4(b)
A.M.	From	11 a.m.	17th
Company	15th	Battn.	M.G.C.
detailed	for	A.G.	will
be	"G"	Company	12th
Battn.	M.G.C.		

12th Division.

D.R.L.S. 8.15 a.m.

Belgrave
Lt.Col.
G.S.

SECRET.

Copy No. 16

12th DIVISION ORDER No.278

Ref: Sheet 62.D. N.E.   19th AUGUST, 1918.

1.   36th Infantry Brigade will relieve 37th Infantry Brigade in the Left Subsector on the night 20th/21st inst. under arrangements to be made by Brigades concerned.

2.   On the completion of relief, the 37th Infantry Brigade will be in Divisional Reserve and will be disposed as follows:-

    Headquarters

    Two Battalions in BALLARAT and BENDIGO Trenches, South of the R. ANCRE.

    One Battalion in TASMANIAN LINE, North of the R. ANCRE.

3.   The 37th Infantry Brigade will place 1 Battalion at the disposal of the 35th Infantry Brigade at a date to be notified later.

4. (a)   Completion of the relief will be reported by the Code word "ALIEN".

   (b)   Command of the Left Subsector will pass to the B.G.C., 36th Infantry Brigade on the completion of relief.

                                                            Major for A.P.Ryan
                                                            Lieut-Colonel,
                                                            General Staff,
                                                            12th Division.

Issued at 3.30 p.m.

Copies to:-

    1.   G.O.C.
    2.   "Q"
    3.   C.R.A.
    4.   C.R.E.
    5.   35th Inf. Bde.
    6.   36th Inf. Bde.
    7.   37th Inf. Bde.
    8.   12th Battn. M.G.C.
    9.   5th Northampton-
          shire Regt.
   10.   12th Div. Signal Coy., R.E.
   11.   A.D.M.S.
   12.   III Corps.
   13.   18th Division.
   14.   47th Division.
   15)   War Diary.
   16)   "
   17 - 21.   G.S. and Records.

"C" FORM.
MESSAGES AND SIGNALS.

Army Form C. 2123.

Prefix	Code	Words	Received.	Sent, or sent out	Office Stamp
	£ s. d.		From	At	
Charges to Collect			By		
Service Instructions				To	
				By	

Handed in at .... Office .... m. Received .... m.

TO 3rd Corps

*Sender's Number.	Day of Month.	In reply to Number.	AAA
G371	21		

Reference OO278 aaa Complete

FROM PLACE & TIME 12 Div ... 1.30 am

*This line should be erased if not required.

S E C R E T

12th Division No. G.X.3665.

19th August, 1918.

ADDENDUM TO 12th DIVISION ORDER No. 278.

Para 2. after "Headquarters".   add "J.9.b.8.2."

[signature]
Major for
Lieut-Colonel,
General Staff,
12th Division.

Copies to all recipients of
12th Division Order No.278.

"A" Form
MESSAGES AND SIGNALS.

Army Form C. 2121 (in pads of 100).

Prefix	Code	m.	Words	Charge	This message is on a/c of:		Recd. at	m.
Office of Origin and Service Instructions.			Sent				Date	
SECRET			At	m.		Service	From	
D.R.L.S.			To					
			By		(Signature of "Franking Officer.")		By	

35th, 36th & 37th Inf.Bdes., 12th Bn.M.G.C., 5th
Northamptonshire Regt., 12th Div.Signals,
25th D.A., C.R.E., A.D.M.S.

Sender's Number.	Day of Month	Corps, In reply Number. 47th DIVS.
G.296.	19	AAA

Confirmation of verbal arrangements AAA
37th Inf. Bde. will take over tonight 18/19th
inst. left Battn. front of 35th Inf. Bde, all
arrangements to be made between Bdes. concerned
AAA Boundary between Brigades E.28.d.7.0. -
K.4.b.5.9. - level crossing K.4.a.9.3. -
thence track through K.4.a. - K.3.b. to
CRUCIFIX K.3.c.4.7. inclusive to left Brigade
AAA 37th Infantry Brigade will vacate area
K.1.b. and d. which will be available for
Reserve Battalion 35th Infantry Brigade AAA
Addsd. 35th and 37th Inf. Bdes., reptd.
remainder of List "X" and A.D.M.S.

From: **12th Division.**
Place:
Time: 7.30 a.m. D.R.L.S.

C.A.Ryan.
Maj.

The above may be forwarded as now corrected. (Z)
Censor. Signature of Addressor or person authorised to telegraph in his name.
† This line should be erased if not required.
(18965.) Wt. W12952/M1294. 187,500 Pads. 1/17 McC. & Co., Ltd. (E. 813.)

Appdx XI

SECRET.

Copy No. 23

12th DIVISION ORDER No. 279.

Ref: Sheet 62.d. N.E.   21st August, 1918.

1. The attack will take place to-morrow in accordance with 12th Division Instructions already issued.

2. One Battalion, 37th Infantry Brigade, will be under the orders of G.O.C. 35th Infantry Brigade from 5 p.m. today.

3. In case of counter-attack, the attacking Brigades will be responsible for the maintenance of our new front. 37th Infantry Brigade will be responsible for the defence of the present front line and of the trench K.5.b.5.0. - E.29.d.0.1. - E.29.c.2.5.

4. A Divisional O.P. has been established at E.27.d.75.30.

5. 37th Infantry Brigade will have a direct telephone line to a balloon, and will forward reports received from it to all concerned, and will transmit messages to it.

6. ACKNOWLEDGE by WIRE.

J. Belgrave
Lieut-Colonel,
General Staff,
12th Division.

Issued at

Copies to :-

1. G.O.C.
2. G.S.O.1.
3. 35th Infantry Brigade.
4. 36th Infantry Brigade.
5. 37th Infantry Brigade.
6. C.R.E.
7. A.D.M.S.
8. 12th Battn. M.G.Corps.
9. 12th Div. Signal Coy., R.E.
10. 5th Northamptonshire Regt. (Pioneers).
11. A.A. & Q.M.G.
12. C.R.A., 25th Division.
13. III Corps.
14. 47th Division.
15. 18th Division.
16. 4th Tank Battn.
17. Troop, Northumberland Hussars.
18.) War Diary.
19.)
20 - G.S. and Records.

10/

appdx. X

SECRET.
12th Division No. G.X. 3657.
Copy No. 19

NOTES ON THE ATTACK - No. 1.
(With reference to a Conference held by the Divisional Commander at Advanced Divisional Headquarters on 18th instant.)

1. It is important that matters discussed at this Conference and information regarding future operations be only disclosed to those for whom it is absolutely essential. It should be kept from the troops as long as possible.

2. Boundaries and objectives are as shown on attached map.

3. (a) The attack will be carried out by the 35th Infantry Brigade (with 1 Battalion 37th Infantry Brigade attached) on the right, and 36th Infantry Brigade on the left. 37th Infantry Brigade (less 1 Battalion) will be in reserve. Tanks will co-operate.

   (b) Headquarters will be as follows :-

   35th Infantry Brigade. - K.9.b.25.55.
   36th Infantry Brigade. - K.9.b.30.75.
   37th Infantry Brigade. - J.5.d.80.50, moving to K.4.b.3.8 if a move becomes necessary.

4. Artillery Creeping Barrage.

   (a) The Artillery creeping barrage will start at Zero and make the first lift at Zero plus 4 minutes, moving subsequently at 100 yards in 3 minutes until Zero plus 28 minutes, and then at 100 yards in 4 minutes until Zero plus 100 minutes, at which time it will reach the line covering the first objective.

   (b) There will be a pause of 10 minutes on this line from Zero plus 100 minutes to Zero plus 110 minutes, at which time the barrage will lift and move forward at 100 yards in 4 minutes to the line of the final protective barrage.

   (c) A tracing showing the creeping Barrage will be issued later to all concerned.

   (d) The Artillery are firing 1 smoke shell to 15 Shrapnel throughout the barrage, and 1 thermite shell every 2 minutes on the Southern Divisional boundary and also on the Inter-Brigade boundary.

   (e) Special arrangements are being made with regard to the attack of the 36th Infantry Brigade on MEAULTE, and these will be notified later.

5. Royal Engineers and Pioneers.

   (a) The C.R.E. will arrange to place 2 Sections R.E. and 1 Coy. 5th Northamptonshire Regt. at the disposal of each of the 35th and 36th Infantry Brigades.

   (b) The remainder of the R.E. with 1 Coy. 5th Northamptonshire Regt., 180th Tunnelling Coy. R.E. and attached Infantry will be available under the C.R.E. for work on roads and consolidation.

   (c) The 5th Northamptonshire Regt. (Pioneers) will arrange for each man to carry up a coil of concertina barbed wire which will be put out in front of the BLUE LINE before any work on digging is commenced.

/ 6. Consolidation.......

6. **Consolidation.**

(a) The line to be consolidated is the BLUE LINE in the attached map. This will be taped out as soon as possible after its capture under arrangements to be made by Brigades.

(b) After the capture of the objective the consolidation will be carried out as follows:-

Line of Posts   by leading Battalions of attacking Brigades.

BLUE LINE   by support Battalions of attacking Brigades with 1 Coy. of 5th Northamptonshire Regt. (Pioneers) in each Brigade Sub-Sector working under the orders of the Brigadiers concerned.

(c) The C.R.E. will arrange to dig three strong points in rear of the BLUE LINE, marked with a cross on the attached map. For this work he will have at his disposal such R.E. personnel as are not employed on roads or with attacking Brigades, and the third Company of 5th Northamptonshire Regt. (Pioneers) after they have put out their wire in front of the BLUE LINE.

7. Further Notes will be issued in due course.

8. ACKNOWLEDGE by wire.

Belgrave
Lieut.Colonel,
General Staff,
12th Division.

19th August, 1918.

Copies to :-

No.
1. G.O.C.
2. G.S.O. 1.
3. 35th Infantry Brigade.
4. 36th Infantry Brigade.
5. 37th Infantry Brigade.
6. C.R.E.
7. A.D.M.S.
8. 12th Bn. M. G. Corps.
9. 12th Div. Signal Coy. R.E.
10. 5th Northamptonshire Regt. (Pioneers).
11. A.A. Q.M.G.
12. C.R.A. 25th Division.
13. III Corps.
14. 47th Division.
15. 18th Division.
16 & 17. War Diary.
18 - 23. G.S. and Records.

SECRET.
12th Division No. G.X. 3658
Copy No. 1

NOTES ON THE ATTACK - No. 2.

1. The following establishments of special stores are suggested per Brigade :-

Tin Discs.		300.
Flares.		500.
Message Rockets.		30. (if available).
S.O.S. Rockets.		60.
Wire Cutters. (Additional to establishment)	long	30.
	short	30.

2. Brigades will report by wire or by last D.R. tonight, 19th instant, the number of the above stores they require to make up to the above establishments.

If stores are required in excess of the amounts quoted in para. 1, a note to that effect should be added.

"Success signals" have not been included, but can be obtained if required.

C. Ryan
Major
for
Lieut.Colonel,
General Staff,
12th Division.

19th August, 1918.

Copies to :-   No.
1. G.O.C.
2. G.S.O. 1.
3. 35th Infantry Brigade.
4. 36th Infantry Brigade.
5. 37th Infantry Brigade.
6. "Q".
7 & 8. War Diary.
9 to 14. G.S. and Records.

SECRET.
12th Division No. G.X. 3709.

Copy No. 116

12th DIVISION INSTRUCTIONS FOR ATTACK No. 3.

1. Reference 12th Division No. G.X. 3657 and G.X. 3658.

   Amend title to read "INSTRUCTIONS FOR ATTACK Nos. 1" and "No. 2" respectively.

   No. 1. para. 4 : delete (a) and (b). (See para 9 below).

   No. 1. para. 5 (c): Delete "in front of the BLUE LINE" and add at end of sub-para "by them".

   No. 1. para. 6 (c): Delete from "after" to end of sub-para.

   The third Company with their wire will be available for strong points in the BROWN LINE.

2. In map issued with Instructions No. 1 some blue crosses were marked on the second objective - these were intended to indicate suitable places for strong points.

3. The objective when captured will be consolidated and troops organized at once in depth.

   Consolidation will consist in the first instance in the construction of a series of strong points, which will be connected up later to form a continuous trench system.

   The BROWN LINE will be consolidated by 1 Field Company R.E. (less 1 Section) and 1 Company 5th Northamptonshire Regt. (Pioneers).

   If 7th Infantry Brigade is not ordered to send a battalion forward to exploit success, the Brigade will be prepared to send forward a battalion to assist in consolidating the BROWN LINE.
   A guide from this battalion will be at the level crossing in K.4.a.9.3 from 5 p.m. onwards to meet an officer of the 87th Field Coy. R.E. and take him to Battalion Headquarters.
   This officer will carry the instructions for the work to be done by the battalion on the BROWN LINE and the time at which they will be required to commence work.

4. An advanced guard to the Division constituted as below will be prepared to move forward through our troops on the final objective to exploit success, on receipt of orders from Divisional Headquarters.

   Advanced Guard Commander - Brigadier-General A.E.T.WEBBER, D.S.O.
   Commanding 37th Infantry Brigade.
   each of 1 N.C.O. and 4 men
   One troop, Northumberland Hussars (less 3 Sections; one Section with Divisional Headquarters, one Section with 35th Infantry Brigade, and one Section with 36th Infantry Brigade).

87th Field Coy. R.E.

37th Infantry Brigade (less 1 Battalion).

B. Company, 12th Battn. M. G. Corps.

Bearer Subdivision, 38th Field Ambulance.

The above units will be in position one and a half hours after zero as follows :-

37th Infantry Brigade (less 1 Battalion) in present front line.

179th Army Brigade, R.F.A. - West of MARETT WOOD (Headquarters J.6.c.5.3.)

87th Field Coy. R.E. - in area K.1.

B. Coy. 12th Battn. M. G. Corps. - in area N. of SOLITARY TREE.

Bearer Subdivision, 38th Field Ambulance - at A.D.S. about D.29.d.2.8 BUIRE.

These troops will keep in close touch with G.O.C. 37th Inf. Bde. sending liaison officers to report to his Headquarters.

5. Corps Cavalry and Whippet Tanks are being employed immediately the GREEN LINE has been captured, to exploit as far as the high ground extending from the GREAT BEAR F.23.a. via F.16.central to BOIS FRANCAISE, F.9.d.

Should the Cavalry find that the above high ground is unoccupied, they have been ordered to occupy it and to inform the supporting infantry.

Troops from the 47th Division have been ordered to take over the ground gained as soon as they can be brought up.

The 12th Division Advanced Guard will be prepared to push forward infantry in F.14.a and b., to prolong the left flank of these troops of the 47th Division.

Rapidity and close co-operation are essential for the above operation.

The Advanced Guard Commander will keep in touch with the situation and with the advanced guard 47th Division. (Headquarters 140th I.B. J.11.d.5.5), as well as with the 35th and 36th Brigades, by means of liaison officers, mounted orderlies, patrols, visual signalling, etc.

6. Traces showing machine gun barrages and the positions of machine guns during and after the battle have been issued.

O.C., 12th Bn. M.G. Corps will detail one Section to be under the orders of the G.O.C. of each of the attacking Brigades.

S.O.S. Barrage will be arranged between the M.G. Group Commanders at Brigade Headquarters in accordance with the situation and reported at once to all concerned.

/7. ....

7. Tanks.

Routes for tanks are shown on tracing already issued.

7 Tanks will operate in 36th Brigade zone of attack, and 3 in 35th Brigade zone.

Each tank will carry at least 5,000 rounds S.A.A. for the use of the infantry. These will be dumped in the GREEN LINE.

One intelligent infantry soldier with good eyesight will be detailed to go in each tank, for watching the infantry and keeping the tank informed of their movements.

A wireless tank will be in the vicinity of Brigade Headquarters in K.9.b. at Zero, and will be available for forwarding any urgent operation messages.
This tank will probably move up towards the present front line, and Brigade Headquarters should keep in touch with it.

Three supply tanks are allotted to the Division.
These will take tools, wire, ammunition and water up to the line during the night after the attack, under Divisional arrangements, but they cannot be absolutely relied on as they are not in firstrate order.

One Supply Tank will come up with each Company of Pioneers.

8. A contact aeroplane will fly over at Zero plus 3 hours 15 minutes, when Infantry will burn flares and show their discs and rifle signals when called for by this aeroplane.

There will be three aeroplanes constantly in the air from the Corps Squadron - 1 contact aeroplane, 1 counter-attack aeroplane, and 1 Artillery aeroplane.

Ammunition will not be dropped at fixed points, but will be dropped by aeroplanes in any place where a "V" Signal is put out.

Aeroplanes will drop smoke bombs on the high ground in X.26.d. and about the 120 contour in F.23.a. between Zero plus 2 hours and Zero plus 4 hours.

There will be a special attack on hostile balloons, but if a hostile balloon is seen in the air it should be at once reported to Divisional Headquarters, as the R.A.F. is making arrangements to deal with balloons as soon as they are reported.

9. Reference Instructions No. 1 para. 4 (a) and (b).
The Artillery creeping barrage will start at Zero and will make the first lift at Zero plus 4 minutes.
It will move at a uniform rate of 100 yards in 4 minutes till it is 300 yards in advance of the first objective, i.e. the BROWN LINE shown on the map. It will pause there [until Zero plus 118 minutes] and will then move forward at the rate of 100 yards in 4 minutes till it is 300 yards beyond the second objective, i.e. the GREEN LINE, where it will form a protective barrage for approximately half an hour. It will then lift again to let the Cavalry and Whippets/through
move

/10.......

(4).

10. A Liaison officer will be sent by 36th Infantry Brigade to the Brigade of 18th Division on their left.

Brigades on Right of 35th Infantry Brigade will be 141st Infantry Brigade up to first objective, then 142nd Infantry Brigade, 47th Division. Headquarters of both, J.14.b.2.2.

Brigade on Left of 36th Infantry Brigade will be 54th Infantry Brigade, 18th Division. Headquarters E.15.central.

Brigades will detail special parties to gain touch with troops of Divisions on right and left as follows :-

35th Infantry Brigade at road junction E.30.c.9.0, road F.25.a.2.1, road F.19.d.4.0 (FILIFORM TREE), BROWN LINE, GREEN LINE.

36th Infantry Brigade at junction of road with railway E.17.a.6.6, BROWN LINE, cross roads E.11.d.8.5, GREEN LINE.

11. The following Code Words will be used :-

First objective taken................... JOHN

Second objective taken.................. BULL

12. If orders are received by the Division that the attack will not take place, the following code message will be sent :-
"CAPTAIN COOK AAA ACKNOWLEDGE"

13. A C K N O W L E D G E.

(signed) Belgrave
Lieut.Colonel,
General Staff,
12th Division.

20th August, 1918.

Copies to :-

No.
1. G.O.C.
2. G.S.O. 1.
3. 35th Infantry Brigade.
4. 36th Infantry Brigade.
5. 37th Infantry Brigade.
6. C.R.E.
7. A.D.M.S.
8. 12th Bn. M. G. Corps.
9. 12th Div. Signal Coy. R.E.
10. 5th Northamptonshire Regt. (Pioneers).
11. A.A.Q.M.G.
12. C.R.A. 25th Division.
13. III Corps.
14. 47th Division.
15. 18th Division.
16. & 17. War Diary.
18. 4th Tank Battalion.
19 - 24. G.S. and Records.

Identification Trace for use with Artillery

SECRET

Superimpose on
1:20000 Map

TANK ROUTES
From map references...

E F
K L

14   20
17 Méaulte   19   25
16   29   5
       4

Identification Trace for use with Artillery Maps.

REFERENCE

Final Objective	——————
Intermediate Objective	— · — · —
18 pr. Creeper	———————
18 pr. protector	- - - - - -

Ref. Sh. 62ª N.E.   1/20,000   TRACING "J"

SECRET.

12th Division No. G.X. 3736

Copy No. 19.

12th DIVISION INSTRUCTIONS FOR ATTACK No.4.

1. At Zero on 'Z' day 'D' Special Coy., R.E. will fire 50 drums of burning oil into the head of the valley in E.29.a. from their present emplacements about K.4.a.5.4.

2. Troops must be warned to put on gas masks on the slightest indication of gas shelling. It is the duty of any Commander in an area which is being, or has been shelled, with gas to post sentries to warn men entering the area.

3. Eight pigeons are allotted to each Brigade.

4. Compasses will be carried by all Officers and as many N.C.O's. and men as possible.

5. Watches will be synchronised by a Divisional Staff Officer at Brigade Headquarters - 35th Infantry Brigade at 6.45 p.m.: 36th Infantry Brigade at 7.15 p.m.

6. ACKNOWLEDGE by WIRE.

J. B. Belgrave
Lieut-Colonel,
General Staff,
12th Division.

31st August. 1918.

Copies to :-

1. G.O.C.
2. G.S.O.1.
3. 35th Inf. Bde.
4. 36th Inf. Bde.
5. 37th Inf. Bde.
6. C.R.E.
7. A.D.M.S.
8. 12th Battn. M.G.C.
9. 12th Div. Signal Coy., R.E.
10. 5th Northamptonshire Regt.
11. A.A.Q.M.G.
12. C.R.A. 25th Division.
13. III Corps.
14. 47th Division.
15. 18th Division.
16. 4th Tank Battn.
17 & 18. War Diary.
19 - 24. G.S. and Records.
25. 58th Division.

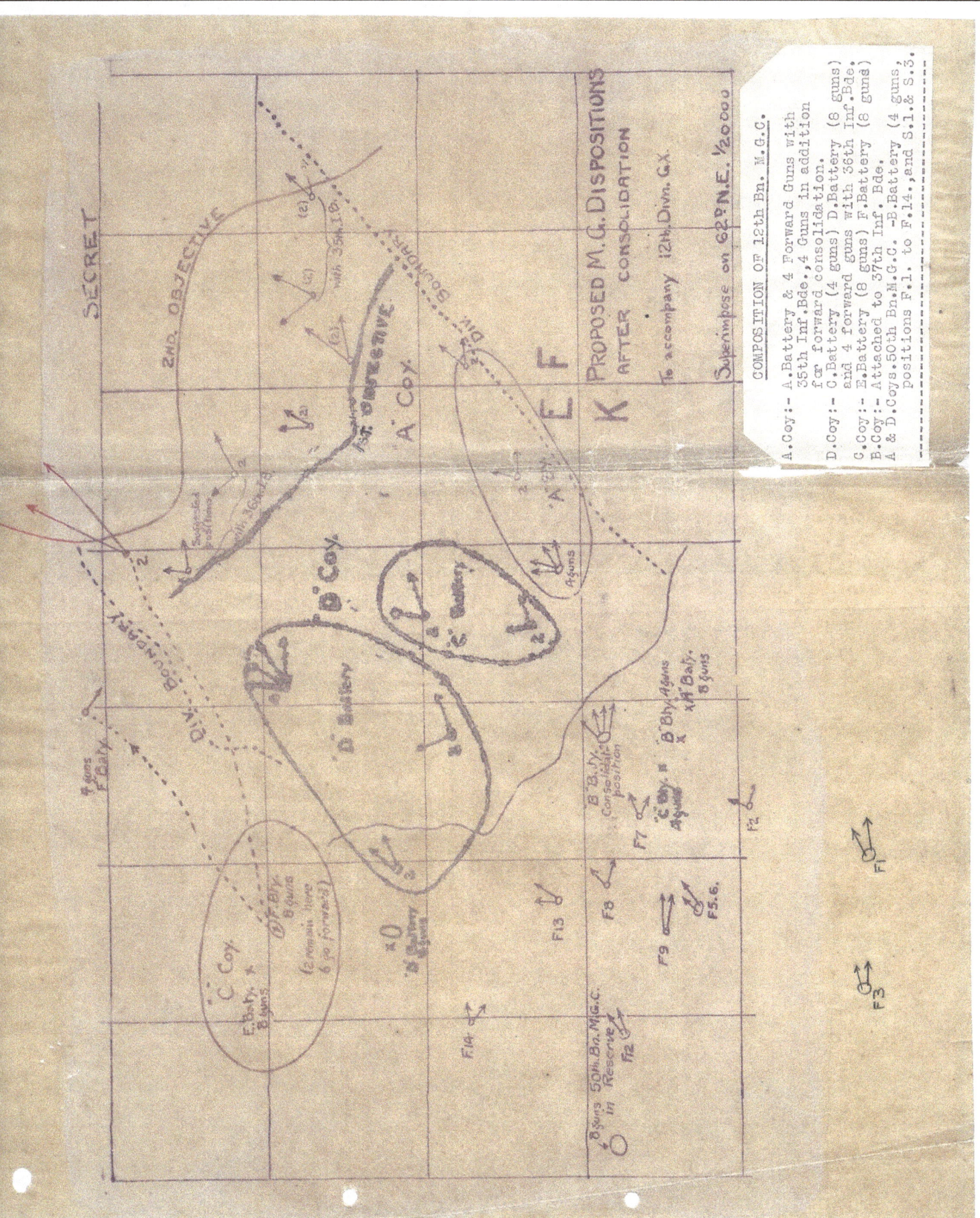

SECRET.

12th Division No. G.X.3745.

21st AUGUST, 1918.

35th Inf. Bde.
36th Inf. Bde.
37th Inf. Bde.
25th Divnl. Artillery.
12th Bn. M.G. Corps.
5th Northamptonshire Regt. (Pioneers)
"Q".

Reference Instructions for the Attack.

1. 175th Brigade 58th Division is moving from BOIS ESCARDONNEUSE at Zero hour on Z day to positions of assembly in rear of old British Front Line W. of MORLANCOURT.

2. The 58th Division is in III Corps Reserve.

3. A C K N O W L E D G E.

A. Ryan
Major
for
Lieut.Colonel,
General Staff,
12th Division.

12th BN. M.G.C.
Ref. Sh. 62D N.E.

0 to +10 G

G
+10 to +40

17

23

29

x
G. Battery
4 guns

E

SECRET

To accompany 12" Div. N° 6x.

M.G. Barrage.
12ᵀᴴ Bn. M.G.C.

Superimpose on 1/20000 map.
62ᵈ N.E.

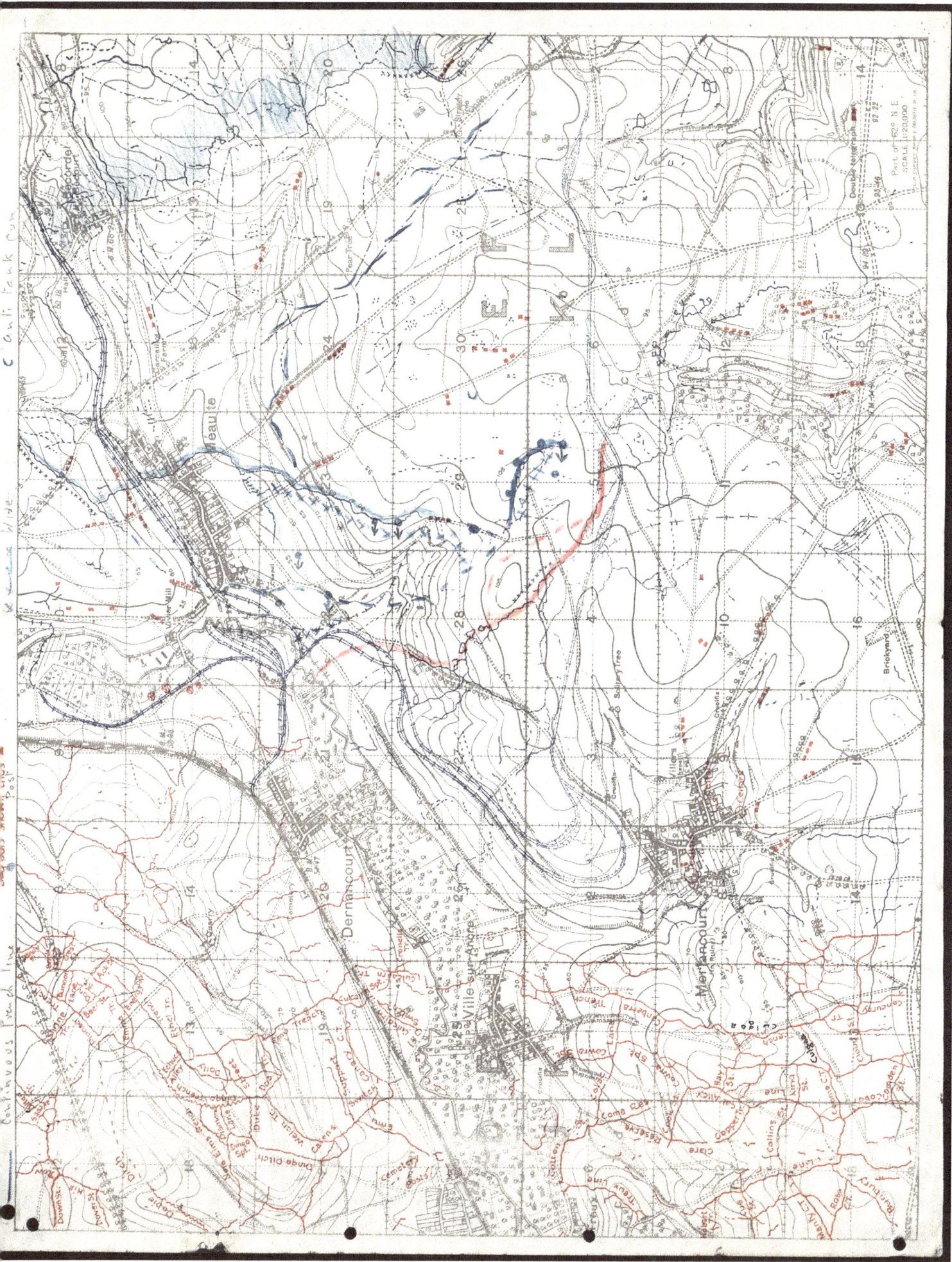

MESSAGE FORM.

_____ Division

1. I am at _____
2. I am at _____ and am consolidating
3. I am at _____ and have consolidated
4. Am held up by M.G. at _____
5. I need:
   - Ammunition
   - Bombs
   - Rifle Grenades
   - Water
   - Verey Lights
   - Stokes Shells
6. Counter-attack forming up at _____
7. I am in touch with _____ on Right _____ on Left _____
8. I am not in touch on Right _____
9. Am being shelled from _____
10. I estimate my present strength at _____ Rifles
11. Hostile Battery _____ active at _____
    Machine Gun
    Trench Mortar

Time _____ Name _____
                      Platoon _____
Date _____ Company _____
                      Battalion _____

Intelligence Map (handwritten annotation)

SECRET.

12th Division No. G.X. 3657.
Copy No.

INSTRUCTIONS FOR ATTACK No 1

~~NOTES ON THE ATTACK No. 1.~~
(With reference to a Conference held by the Divisional Commander
at Advanced Divisional Headquarters on 18th instant.)

1. It is important that matters discussed at this Conference and information regarding future operations be only disclosed to those for whom it is absolutely essential. It should be kept from the troops as long as possible.

2. Boundaries and objectives are as shown on attached map.

3. (a) The attack will be carried out by the 35th Infantry Brigade (with 1 Battalion 37th Infantry Brigade attached) on the right, and 36th Infantry Brigade on the left. 37th Infantry Brigade (less 1 Battalion) will be in reserve. Tanks will co-operate.

   (b) Headquarters will be as follows :-

35th Infantry Brigade.	K.9.b.25.55.
36th Infantry Brigade.	K.9.b.30.75.
37th Infantry Brigade.	J.5.d.80.50, moving to K.4.b.3.8 if a move becomes necessary.

4. Artillery Creeping Barrage.

   (a) The Artillery creeping barrage will start at Zero and make the first lift at Zero plus 4 minutes, moving subsequently at 100 yards in 3 minutes until Zero plus 28 minutes, and then at 100 yards in 4 minutes until Zero plus 100 minutes, at which time it will reach the line covering the first objective.

   (b) There will be a pause of 10 minutes on this line from Zero plus 100 minutes to Zero plus 110 minutes, at which time the barrage will lift and move forward at 100 yards in 4 minutes to the line of the final protective barrage. *See I No 3/para 9*

   (c) A tracing showing the creeping Barrage will be issued later to all concerned.

   (d) The Artillery are firing 1 smoke shell to 15 Shrapnel throughout the barrage, and 1 thermite shell every 2 minutes on the Southern Divisional boundary and also on the Inter-Brigade boundary.

   (e) Special arrangements are being made with regard to the attack of the 36th Infantry Brigade on MEAULTE, and these will be notified later.

5. Royal Engineers and Pioneers.

   (a) The C.R.E. will arrange to place 2 Sections R.E. and 1 Coy. 5th Northamptonshire Regt. at the disposal of each of the 35th and 36th Infantry Brigades.

   (b) The remainder of the R.E. with 1 Coy. 5th Northamptonshire Regt., 180th Tunnelling Coy. R.E. and attached Infantry will be available under the C.R.E. for work on roads and consolidation.

   (c) The 5th Northamptonshire Regt. (Pioneers) will arrange for each man to carry up a coil of concertina barbed wire which will be put out ~~in front of the BLUE LINE~~ before any work on digging is commenced *by Kem.*

/ 6. Consolidation.......

6. **Consolidation.**

(a) The Line to be consolidated is the BLUE LINE in the attached map. This will be taped out as soon as possible after its capture under arrangements to be made by Brigades.

(b) After the capture of the objective the consolidation will be carried out as follows :-

Line of Posts by leading Battalions of attacking Brigades.

BLUE LINE by support Battalions of attacking Brigades with 1 Coy. of 5th Northamptonshire Regt. (Pioneers) in each Brigade Sub-Sector working under the orders of the Brigadiers concerned.

(c) The C.R.E. will arrange to dig three strong points in rear of the BLUE LINE, marked with a cross on the attached map. For this work he will have at his disposal such R.E. personnel as are not employed on roads or with attacking Brigades, and the third Company of 5th Northamptonshire Regt. (Pioneers) after they have put out their wire in front of the BLUE LINE.

7. Further Notes will be issued in due course.

8. ACKNOWLEDGE by wire.

A. Belgrave

Lieut.Colonel,
General Staff,
12th Division.

19th August, 1918.

Copies to :-

No.
1. G.O.C.
2. G.S.O. 1.
3. 35th Infantry Brigade.
4. 36th Infantry Brigade.
5. 37th Infantry Brigade.
6. C.R.E.
7. A.D.M.S.
8. 12th Bn. M.G. Corps.
9. 12th Div. Signal Coy. R.E.
10. 5th Northamptonshire Regt. (Pioneers).
11. A.A. Q.M.G.
12. C.R.A. 25th Division.
13. III Corps.
14. 47th Division.
15. 18th Division.
16 & 17. War Diary.
18 - 23. G.S. and Records.

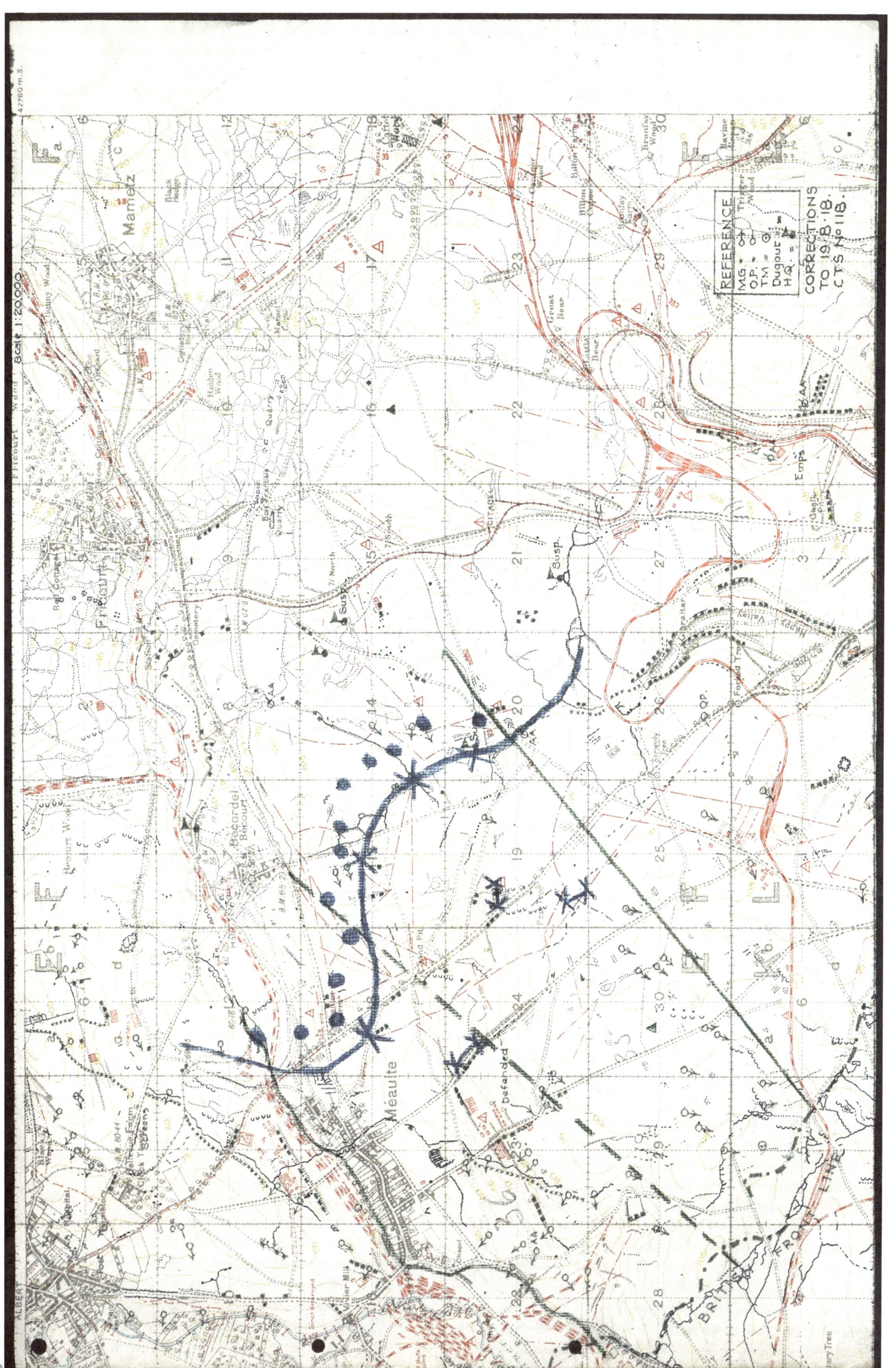

LEGEND MAP A.

DIVL BOUNDARIES	————
INTER-BRIGADE BOUNDARY	— — —
PRESENT FRONT LINE	▬▬▬
LINE OF CONSOLIDATION	▬ ▬ ▬
POSTS	● ●
" "	● ●
STRONG POINTS (TO BE)	✕ ✕
DUG UNDER C.R.E. }	

SECRET

ISSUED WITH
N.2 Dn No GX 3657

"A" Form
MESSAGES AND SIGNALS.

Army Form C. 2121
(In pads of 100.)

No. of Message............

Prefix......Code......m	Words	Charge	This message is on a[cut]	Recd. at......m
Office of Origin and Service Instructions	Sent		......Service.	Date......
147TH	At ...?.....m.			From ......
C BRIGADE	To			
PRIORITY.	By		(Signature of "Franking Officer")	By......

TO	~~~~~	~~~~~	"Q"	47th Div.
		JRTS	Signals.	12th Div.
Sender's Number.	Day of Month.	In reply to Number.		56th Div.
G.129.	25		AAA	

12th Division will carry out an operation
tonight at a zero hour which will be
communicated later in conjunction with the
47th Division on right to advance to the
general line F.20.central - F.14.central -
to junction with 18th Division about F.7.b.8.8
and 37th Inf. Bde. will advance on the right
~~at the time~~ the 36th Inf. Bde. on the left
AAA G.O.C. 37th Inf. Bde. will take over
command of the right brigade front at 11 p.m.
at which hour the 6th Buffs will come under
his orders AAA Dividing lines will be as
follows AAA Between 47th and 12th Divisions
~~railway from~~ F.13.d.70 to ~~road at~~
F.20.c.5.2. AAA Between 12th and 18th Divns.
Railway from N.12.a.9.5 to F.7.b.8.7. AAA
37th Inf. Bde. will form up on South side of
road running through F.19.c. and d.
Between trenches known from SAND PIT to
N.13.central thence to F.9.c.6.0 with their
right in touch with 140th Inf. Bde. 47th Divn.
Extending on their right AAA

From			
Place			
Time			

The above may be forwarded as now corrected. (Z)

Censor. Signature of Addressor or person authorised to telegraph in his name
* This line should be erased if not required.

Order No. 1625. Wt. W3253/ P 511. 27/2 H. & K., Ltd. (E. 2634).

"A" Form.
MESSAGES AND SIGNALS.

Army Form C. 2121.
(In pads of 100.)

No. of Message:...........

Prefix............Code............ m | Words. | Charge. | This message is on a/c of: | Recd. at.........m.
Office of Origin and Service Instructions. | Sent | | | Date..........
.... | At..........m. | | ....Service. | From..........
.... | To.......... | | |
.... | By.......... | | (Signature of "Franking Officer.") | By..........

TO

Sender's Number. | Day o Month. | In reply to Number. | **A A A**

Objective AAA 57th Inf. Bde will capture
and consolidate line between P.6.c.5.5.
and P.14.a.5.5. AAA One platoon under an extra
officer will be specially detailed to gain
touch with the 47th Divn. on the front line
at P.20.c.5.5. AAA 50th Inf. Bde will capture
and consolidate the line shown in blue on map
from P.14.c.5.5. to P.7.b.5.7. AAA One
platoon will be specially detailed to
establish touch with the 16th Divn. on this
line AAA The Artillery barrage 57th Divn.
will open 100 yards in front of the road
running through P.8.b. AAA The barrage
who will be continued by 12th Divn. from
19.d.5.5. to P.10.c. control - P.13.d.5.5.
- P.14.a.0.0. - P.13.b.5.7. - B.7.c.0.0. -
B.7.c.0.0. where it will remain for four
four minutes AAA It will then move forward
at the rate of 100 yards in four minutes
until it is 300 yards beyond the
objective line given at the beginning of this
message where it will halt AAA In addition
at Zero a crash will be put down on the
area P.8.a. and 19.c. outside the above
barrage line AAA

From..........
Place..........
Time..........

The above may be forwarded as now corrected. (Z)

....
Censor. | Signature of Addressor or person authorised to telegraph in his name.

* This line should be erased if not required.

"A" Form.
MESSAGES AND SIGNALS.

Army Form C. 2121.
(In pads of 100.)

No. of Message..............

Prefix......Code........m	Words.	Charge.	This message is on a/c of :	Recd. at ....m.
Office of Origin and Service Instructions.	Sent		............Service.	Date............
....	At..........m.			From ....
....	To............			By ....
....	By............		(Signature of "Franking Officer.")	

TO				

| * | Sender's Number. | Day of Month | In reply to Number. | A A A |

Brigade attacking on the right of the AAA
Wir I.f. 340 will be 140th Bde. with
Headquarters at K.17.a.5.2. AAA ACKN WLDGE
Add : Bdes. R.A. Reptd all concerned.

From ....
Place ....
Time ....

The above may be forwarded as now corrected. **(Z)**

.... Censor. Signature of Addressor or person authorised to telegraph in his name.

* This line should be erased if not required.

(3198.) Wt. W 12952/M1294. 575,000 Pads. 1/17. H. W. & V., Ld. (E. 818.)

Appdx. XIII

35th Inf. Bde: 36th Inf. Bde: 37th Inf. Bde.
C.R.A. 12th Bn. M.G.C. 5th Northants. 12th
Signals. A.D.M.S. C.R.E. A.P.M. "Q" 22nd
Corps Cav. 22nd Corps Cyclists. 3rd Corps.
18th Division. 58th Division.

G. 98   27th

12th Division will attack tomorrow 28th inst.
at 4.55 a.m. AAA 36th Bde. will attack on
the Right 35th Bde. on the Left AAA The
boundary between Brigades will be junction of
trench with road at A.4.d.4.1 - 100 yards N.
of FAVIERES WOOD - road A.12.b.9.5 AAA
Objective the general line A.18.b.7.1 -
CLAPHAM FARM inclusive to 12th Division -
B.13.a.2.7 - Eastern outskirts of HARDECOURT
- cross roads A.12.b.9.3 - Eastern edge of
MAITZ HORD FARM ENCLOSURE at A.6.b.2.3 AAA
Artillery barrage will start at Zero on the
N. and S. grid line between A.5. and 6. and
A.11. and 12. where it will remain for thirty
minutes AAA It will then move forward at
the rate of 100 yards in four minutes until
it reaches a line 300 yards beyond the
objective where it will remain for 30 minutes
after which there will be bursts of fire on
the same line for 30 minutes AAA It will
then stop and touch will be gained with the
enemy AAA 36th Bde. will detail 1 Platoon
to move on the left of the 58th Division and
be   /behind....

behind the barrage of the 58th Division to
CLAPHAM FARM A.18.b.7.2 and gain touch with
its own Battn. at the S.E. corner of
HARDECOURT AAA This Platoon will establish
an international post at about CLAPHAM FARM
AAA 35th Inf. Bde. will detail 1 Platoon
to gain touch with the 18th Divn. at the
North Eastern corner of MAITZ HORN FARM
at A.6.b.2.3 AAA Advanced H.Q. of 35th
and 36th Inf. Bdes. will be established
at APPLE TREES A.1.b. AAA As soon as
35th and 36th Inf.Bdes. have established
themselves on their objectives 37th Inf.Bde.
will move under orders of 12th Divn. and will
concentrate about A.9. and will be prepared
to either counter-attack or occupy the
general line MACHINE GUN WOOD - THE
FLECHE - A.3.c.0.5 - S.27.c.8.0 AAA
The general line of consolidation for the
35th and 36th Inf. Bdes. will be A.12.c.1.0 -
A.12.a.4.5 - A.6.d.0.0 - A.6.c.7.5 -
MAITZ HORN FARM AAA This line will be the
main line of resistance AAA The objective line
will be held as a line of observation AAA

(3).

ACKNOWLEDGE BY WIRE AAA Addressed 3 Bdes.
repeated C.R.A. 12th Bn. M.G.C. 5th Northants.
12th Signals. A.D.M.S. C.R.E. A.P.M.
"Q" 22nd Corps Cav. 22nd Corps Cyclists.
3rd Corps. 18th Division. 58th Division.

12th Division.

8.45 p.m.

D. Belgrave

General Staff.

Appx. XIV

SECRET.

12th Division No. 37.

29th AUGUST, 1918.

35th Inf. Bde.	12th Div. Signals.
36th Inf. Bde.	5th Northants Regt.
37th Inf. Bde.	"Q"
C.R.A.	A.P.M.
C.R.E.	12th Div. Train.
12th Battn. M.G.C.	

WARNING ORDER

1. The Division (less Artillery) will be relieved by the 47th Division (less Artillery) tonight 29th/30th inst.

2. On relief the Division will be responsible for the defence of the RIDGE LOOP STATION (F 27) - BECORDEL (F.8.) which will be held by the 36th Infantry Brigade on the right and the 35th Infantry Brigade on the left, with the 37th Infantry Brigade in support, disposed in the old AMIENS DEFENCES.

3. Brigades will be relived as follows :-

   35th Infantry Brigade by   142nd Infantry Brigade

   36th Infantry Brigade by   141st Infantry Brigade.

   37th Infantry Brigade by   140th Infantry Brigade.

   Brigadiers commanding Brigades of 47th Division are visiting this morning Headquarters of 12th Division Brigades, they will relieve, to arrange details.

4. ACKNOWLEDGE by WIRE.

A. Ryan
Major for

Lieut-Colonel,
General Staff,
12th Division.

Copy to :-
    47th Division.

Fourth Army No. G.S.2/9.

III Corps.
───────────

I desire to place on record my appreciation of the part played by the III Corps in the battle of August 8th.

The plans for the Corps offensive were interfered with by the hostile attack which took place S.W. of MORLANCOURT on August 6th. The assembly of the troops and tanks, as well as the placing of the artillery for the barrage, were, for this reason, rendered difficult. Notwithstanding this the assault was launched on the morning of the 8th with commendable vigour, and, after heavy fighting, the first objective and portions of the second objective were won. During the 9th and 10th fighting continued until, in spite of vigorous opposition, the front was finally established on the line of the old AMIENS defences.

The 12th, 18th and 58th Divisions, which were all heavily engaged, succeeded in winning the several objectives allotted to them, and I desire to convey to them my warm thanks for their gallantry and determination during a period of no little difficulty.

The progress made on the flanks by the 58th and 12th Divisions in face of determined opposition reflects high credit on the leadership and drive of these two divisions, for the enemy met them with vigorous counter-attacks on several occasions, and, in the case of the 58th Division, succeeded in temporarily regaining possession of the CHIPILLY spur.

The Staff work of the Corps, as well as of the Divisions, and the skill with which the mobile artillery was worked forward, are points on which I desire to express my special admiration.

In protecting the left flank of the Fourth Army the Corps were given a difficult task, which was carried out with a determination and gallantry beyond all praise, and I offer to all ranks my warmest thanks and my sincere appreciation of their hard fought victory.

H. Rawlinson

General,
Commanding Fourth Army.

H.Q., Fourth Army,
16th August, 1918.

"C" Form.
MESSAGES AND SIGNALS.　No. of Message............
Army Form ....
(In books of 100.)

Prefix...... Co...... Words.........	Received....... Sent, or sent out.	Office Stamp.
£ s. d.	From...... JL	At............m.
Charges to Collect	Bm	To............
Service Instructions.	By........	
............JL............	............Office 11.30 /..m.	Received 11.48/..m.

Handed in at

TO　Mojo

Sender's Number	Day of Month	In reply to Number	AAA
Gx 498	24		

Cancel Gx 3809 of 24.8.18

SEEN BY:-
G.O.C. ....
G.S.O.I ....
G.S.O.II ....
G.S.O.III ....

CL×
11.50/

FROM　　　　Jel　　　11.10 pm
TIME & PLACE　　12 Divn

*This line should be erased if not required.
C. & R. 7800　Wt. W14832/M1523　100,000.　3/17.　(E930)　Forms C/2123

"A" Form
MESSAGES AND SIGNALS.

Army Form C. 2121
(In pads of 100.)

SECRET.

BUVU BUJU BUZU WURA JEHE MOWE FOQI A.P.M.
TO A.D.M.S. "Q". ROVU III Corps.
~~18th Divn. 47th Divn. 58th Divn.~~
XXII Corps Cavalry XXI Corps Cyclists.

Sender's Number.	Day of Month.	In reply to Number.	AAA
C.4/7/6	24		

Reference G.X.3805 of 23rd inst., Zero hour will be 2.30 a.m. 25th inst. AAA Acknowledge by wire AAA Addsd. all recipient of G.X. 3805.

From
Place JELE
Time 40 p.m. (Z)

SDR

Major
G. S.

"A" Form
MESSAGES AND SIGNALS.

Army Form C. 2121
(In pads of 100.)

Prefix....Code....m.	Words	Charge	This message is on a/c of:	Recd. at......m.
Office of Origin and Service Instructions	Sent		....................Service.	Date............
	At ....m.			From ....
	To			
	By		(Signature of "Franking Officer")	By...............

TO 35th Inf. Bde. 36th Inf. Bde. 37th Inf. Bde. ... G.O.C. 5th Northants Regt. 12th Bn. M.G. Corps ... M.S. "C" 22nd Corps Cavalry 12th Corps Cyclist. D.C. 12th Div. Signals.

AAA 58th Divn.

Sender's Number	Day of Month	In reply to Number
G. 458	24	

Reference 12th Division No. G.X. 58.5 dated 23rd August, 1918. AAA Unless otherwise notified Z~~ero~~ hour for operation ~~today~~ 24th will be 4 pm. aaa acknowledge

From
Place 12th Division.
Time

J. Belgrave Lt Col.

G.S.

"C" Form.				Army Form C. 2123. (In books of 100.)
MESSAGES AND SIGNALS.				No. of Message ....
Prefix M Code Words 34	Received. From GHQ By Ers	Sent, or sent out. At .... m. To .... By		Office Stamp.
£ s. d. Charges to Collect				
Service Instructions				
.... Handed in at YL		Office 3-0 m. Received 3-23 m.		

TO 58 Div

* Sender's Number	Day of Month.	In reply to Number	AAA
G 482	24		
Ref	GX 2805	of	23rd
August	road	in	720B
21A	15C	will	be
inclusive	to	you	and
exclusive	to 58Div	MOSO	army
aaa	added	Bugu	rpts
mejs			

FROM 12 Div
PLACE & TIME 2·50 pm

* This line should be erased if not required.

SECRET.

12th Division No. O.X.3605.

23rd AUGUST, 1918.

35th Inf. Bde.
36th Inf. Bde.
37th Inf. Bde.
C.R.A.
C.R.E.
5th Northampton-
  shire Regt.(Pioneers).
12th Battn.M.G.C.
A.D.M.S.
"Q".

III Corps.
18th Division.
47th Division.
58th Division.
XXII Corps Cavalry.
XXII Corps Cyclists.
12th Div.Signal Coy.,R.E.

12th Division will be prepared to advance at Zero hour on the 24th inst. to the general line F.17.c.5.5., F.9.d.9.5., F.3.c.3.0. AAA 58th Division will be advancing on right and 18th Division on left of 12th Division AAA Advance will be carried out by 37th Infantry Brigade on right and 36th Infantry Brigade on left with 35th Infantry Brigade in Reserve AAA Dividing line between 58th and 12th Divisions will be F.20.b.0.6. road junction F.15.d.2.5., road junction F.16.d.6.7., cross roads F.13.c.6.3. AAA Between 12th and 18th Divisions is line of the stream running South of FRICOURT and North of BECORDEL - BECOURT inclusive to 12th Division AAA Dividing line between Brigades through F.9.c.0.0. thence to road at F.10.c.8.0. AAA After operations tonight Brigades will reorganize in depth with a view to the advance tomorrow from the positions held at daylight AAA For this purpose the line must be held as lightly as possible and the bulk of the troops kept under cover in positions where they can receive orders AAA The advance will be carried out under creeping barrage which will open at Zero hour on the S.O.S. line, will make first lift at Zero plus four minutes and will move forward at the rate of 100 yards in four minutes AAA Five whippet tanks will co-operate in the advance one section in the zone of each Brigade AAA C.R.E. will detail one section Field Company R.E. to be under orders of each attacking Brigade AAA Remainder of R.E. and Pioneers will be under C.R.E. AAA Orders regarding Machine Guns will follow AAA 37th Infantry Brigade will send a liaison officer to Headquarters 173rd Infantry Brigade K.14.b.2.2. by 12 noon AAA 36th Infantry Brigade will send a liaison officer to report to right Brigade 18th Division by 12 noon AAA As soon as the advance takes place conditions approximating to open warfare will be reached and units will push on without expecting to be in close touch on their flanks AAA Units will, however, always safeguard their flanks and will gain touch with units on the flanks on the objective AAA 37th Infantry Brigade will detail a special platoon to gain touch with 173rd Infantry Brigade at road junction F.15.d.2.4. and F.16.d.7.6. AAA 36th Infantry Brigade will detail a special Platoon to gain touch with 18th Division at bend of stream F.2.d.1.0., and on the objective AAA As soon as the objective is reached the line will be consolidated covered by an outpost line AAA One squadron 22nd Corps Cavalry and 1 Coy. 22nd Corps Cyclists will be sent forward under Divisional orders when the objective has been reached to keep touch with the enemy and exploit success and will rendezvous at Divisional Headquarters D.26.b.8.5. by 2 p.m. AAA 35th Infantry Brigade will concentrate under cover in front of the old AMIENS Defence Line and move forward at Zero hour 1 Battalion to the front system vacated by the attacking Brigades and 2 Battalions to the BROWN LINE where they will be in Divisional Reserve

Lieut-Colonel,
General Staff,

12th Division No.G.X.3809.

24th AUGUST, 1918.

35th Inf. Bde.   III Corps.
36th Inf. Bde.   18th Division.
37th Inf. Bde.   47th Division.
C.R.A.   58th Division.

Reference 12th Division G.X.3805; 3 whippet tanks will rendezvous in valley F.19.a. and b. by 3.30 a.m. and will move on F.13.d. and b., F.8.c., F.14. and will assist in clearing the valley F.15.c. and d. and/F.8. and 9. They will cross the front line at Zero plus 10 minutes. If Infantry require their help, they will put their helmets on their bayonets and hold them up.

Cancelled
12 Div. G.498.

Lieut-Colonel,
General Staff,
12th Division.

SIGNALS.

Secret

TO Z 58 DW

Sender's Number: 158 | Day of Month: 12 | AAA

Ref O.O. 274 aaa Zero hour will be 4.55 am 13th inst (four fifty five)

Acknowledge by wire

From: 12 DW
Time: 11.30 p.m.

36th Inf. Bde.
C.R.A.
18th Division.
47th Division.
58th Division.

SECRET.

12th Division No. 52

12th AUGUST, 1918.

MACHINE GUN ARRANGEMENTS
with reference to
12th DIVISION ORDER NO. 274.
================================

18 guns in battery positions will fire on S.O.S. lines from Zero to Zero plus 3 minutes

'E' Battery, 4 guns, in E.15.c. will fire on work and trenches E.29.a.0.0. to E.29.a.3.3. from Zero to Zero plus 3 minutes: lift to work E.29.a.central and trench North of same, from Zero plus 3 mins. to Zero plus 60 mins.

'D' Battery, 4 guns, in E.20.b.1.2. will fire on work E.29.a.0.0. to E.29.a.3.3. from Zero to Zero plus 60 mins.

ARTILLERY ARRANGEMENTS.
=========================

Reference para 3.

At Zero plus 3 mins., all Heavy and Field Artillery will lift off objective except one R.F.A. Brigade, which will continue firing on trench from K.5.b.5.6. to E.29.c.8.2. till Zero plus 6 minutes and will then lift. Remainder of Artillery remains on the targets given in para. 3 for one hour.

B.Belgrave

Lieut-Colonel,
General Staff,
12th Division.

BUVU   WUR.   A.D.M.S.   ROVU/
BUJU   FOGI   D.A.D.V.S. 3rd Corps.
BUZU   JEHE   A.P.M. "Q" 18th, 47th &
                                58th Divns.

G.141   28

The Division will remain in its present
position tonight and will consolidate on the
main line of resistance given in G.98 AAA
The present front line in front of HARDECOURT
and the MALTZ HORN FARM-ridge will be
organized tonight as a line of strong points
AAA In particular good strong points will
be made on the flanks at CLAPHAM FARM and
at MALTZ HORN FARM and by each front line
Brigade to cover their junction AAA Strong
patrols will be sent forward to raid and
harass the enemy in co-operation with machine
gun groups AAA The Reserve Brigade will be
disposed in the best positions to rest the
men while carrying out the role ordered in
G.125 AAA Dispositions for 29th will be
reported as soon as possible and maps forwarded by 12 noon shewing Companies AAA Artill-
ory will carry out harassing fire, but all
artillery fire, except S. O. S., will be east
of the N. & S. KXMXGrid line between B1 and 2.
except as arranged by Brigade Commanders
with their affiliated artillery brigades

G.141 (cont)
AAA Harassing fire will not be within
3000 yards of the front line after 2 a.m.
to allow fighting patrols to Mipush out and
gain touch with the enemy AAA 22nd Corps
Cavalry and Cyclists will be in a position
of assembly about valley in F.12. and KMM
A.7.by 7 a.m. and will send an officer to
Headquarters of each Inf. Bde. in the line
by that hour to keep in touch with the
situation AAA Addsd. Divl. Units, reptd.
Corps and Flank Divns.

ACKNOWLEDGE AAA

JELE
8.15 p.m.

35th Inf. Bde: 36th Inf. Bde: 37th Inf. Bde.
C.R.A. 12th Bn. M.G.C. 5th Northants. 12th
Signals. A.D.M.S. C.R.E. A.P.M. "Q" 22nd
Corps Cav. 22nd Corps Cyclists. 3rd Corps.
18th Division. 58th Division.

G. 98   27th

12th Division will attack tomorrow 28th inst.
at 4.55 a.m. AAA 36th Bde. will attack on
the Right 35th Bde. on the Left AAA The
boundary between Brigades will be junction of
trench with road at A.4.d.4.1 - 100 yards N.
of FAVIERES WOOD - road A.12.b.9.5 AAA
Objective the general line A.18.b.7.1 -
CLAPHAM FARM inclusive to 12th Division -
B.13.a.2.7 - Eastern outskirts of HARDECOURT
- cross roads A.12.b.9.3 - Eastern edge of
MAITZ HORN FARM ENCLOSURE at A.6.b.2.3 AAA
Artillery barrage will start at Zero on the
N. and S. grid line between A.5. and 6. and
A.11. and 12. where it will remain for thirty
minutes AAA It will then move forward at
the rate of 100 yards in four minutes until
it reaches a line 300 yards beyond the
objective where it will remain for 30 minutes
after which there will be bursts of fire on
the same line for 30 minutes AAA It will
then stop and touch will be gained with the
enemy AAA 36th Bde. will detail 1 Platoon
to move on the left of the 58th Division and
be   /behind....

behind the barrage of the 58th Division to
CLAPHAM FARM A.18.b.7.2 and gain touch with
its own Battn. at the S.E. corner of
HARDECOURT AAA This Platoon will establish
an international post at about CLAPHAM FARM
AAA 35th Inf. Bde. will detail 1 Platoon
to gain touch with the 18th Divn. at the
North Eastern corner of MAITZ HORN FARM
at A.6.b.2.3 AAA Advanced H.Q. of 35th
and 36th Inf. Bdes. will be established
at APPLE TREES A.1.b. AAA As soon as
35th and 36th Inf.Bdes. have established
themselves on their objectives 37th Inf.Bde.
will move under orders of 12th Divn. and will
concentrate about A.9. and will be prepared
to either counter-attack or occupy the
general line MACHINE GUN WOOD - THE
FLECHE - A.3.c.0.5 - S.27.c.8.0 AAA
The general line of consolidation for the
35th and 36th Inf. Bdes. will be A.12.c.1.0 -
A.12.a.4.5 - A.6.d.0.0 - A.6.c.7.5 -
MAITZ HORN FARM AAA This line will be the
main line of resistance AAA The objective line
will be held as a line of observation AAA

(3).

ACKNOWLEDGE BY WIRE AAA Addressed 3 Bdes.
repeated C.R.A.   12th Bn. M.G.C. 5th Northants.
12th Signals. A.D.M.S. C.R.E. A.P.M.
"Q" 22nd Corps Cav. 22nd Corps Cyclists.
3rd Corps. 18th Division. 58th Division.

12th Division.   *B. Belgrave*
8.45 p.m.
                           General Staff.

"A" Form
MESSAGES AND SIGNALS.

Army Form C. 2121
(in pads of 100).
No. of Message..........

Prefix......Code......m.	Words	Charge	This message is on a/c of:	Recd. at......m.
Office of Origin and Service Instructions.				Date...........
....	Sent		..................Service	From...........
....	At ......m.			
....	To..........			
....	By..........	(Signature of "Franking Officer")	By...........

TO { | 12 | DIV | Q | |

Sender's Number	Day of Month	In reply to Number	AAA
* 9.565.	2	Q151	

arranged

From 3 SRA

Place

Time

The above may be forwarded as now corrected. (Z)

Censor.   Signature of Addresser or person authorised to telegraph in his name.

* This line should be erased if not required.
(7700.) Wt. W492/M1647 110,000 Pads. 5/17. G.&R. Ltd. (E. 1187.)

"C" FORM.
MESSAGES AND SIGNALS.

Prefix	Code	Words 29	Received	Sent, or sent out	Office Stamp
	£ s. d.		From YK	At	ARMY SIGNALS
Charges to Collect			By Hady	To	
Service Instructions				By	

Handed in at J.X (12h15) Office 2.28 m. Received 3.4to m.

TO 3d Corps G

Sender's Number	Day of Month	In reply to Number	
Q151	2	G1117	AAA

Two busses required VIGNACOURT church 8.00 3rd inst aaa none arrived today ref Q104 dated 1st aaa Kindly confirm

(m/37)

FROM PLACE & TIME 12 Div Q

"A" Form
MESSAGES AND SIGNALS.

Army Form C. 2121 (in pads of 100).

TO	12th	DIV	Q	
Sender's Number	Day of Month	In reply to Number	AAA	
S.557	1	Q 103		
and	Q 104	AAA	losses	
arranged	as	requested	AAA	
losses	not	lorries	available	

From: 3 CORPS
Time: 4 20

```
12th. Division.      A.D. Signals.
18th. Division.      D.D.M.S.
47th. Division.      "Q"
58th. Division.      "I"
III Corps H.A.       C.E.
25th. D.A.           C.M.G.O.
G.O.C., R.A.         A.P.M.
```

Secret

III Corps No. G.O.1117.

WARNING ORDER.

1. On night 1st/2nd August, 58th Division will take over from 18th Division (Right Divisional Sector) as far South as where HAY STREET cuts Front Line in K.7.d.0.8., HAY STREET, COPPER STREET, CUE STREET to remain inclusive to Right Division.

2. On nights 31st July/1st August and 1st/2nd August, the 25th Divisional Artillery will relieve the 58th Divisional Artillery in Centre Divisional Sector.

3. On nights 2nd/3rd and 3rd/4th August, 12th Division, from VIGNACOURT - PERNOIS Area (H.Q.VIGNACOURT), will relieve 58th Division (H.Q. BEAUCOURT CHATEAU) in Centre Divisional Sector on III Corps Front.
   Relief will be carried out - Personnel by Bus, Transport by March Route.
   58th Division, on relief, will move to area vacated by 12th Division.

4. Busses required by 12th Division for Advance and Reconnaissance parties should be applied for to this office 24 hours in advance.

5. Acknowledge.

[signature]

B.G.G.S., III Corps.

III Corps H.Q.
30th July, 1918.

Buses & lorries for
advance parties, 12th Div
a. 2/8/18

2. HQ. 35th Bde. CAMARLES
2. — 36th — VIGNACOURT
4. — 37th — BERTEAUCOURT
1. Div Headqrs VIGNACOURT

all at 8 a.m.

Also for reconnoitring
party of 36th Bde

2. at VIGNACOURT CH.

8.30 a.m

Wrie 12 DW
Busses arranged
as asked for

"C" FORM.
MESSAGES AND SIGNALS.

Prefix	Code	Words	57		Received		Sent, or sent out	Office Stamp
Charges to Collect	£ s. d.				From		At	
					By		To	
Service Instructions	12 Divn						By	

Handed in at .... Office 10.50 a.m. Received 10.56 a.m.

TO 2nd Corps G

*Sender's Number.	Day of Month.	In reply to Number.	AAA
Q 103	1		
Lorries	required	2nd	inst
convey	advance	parties	forward
aaa	Two	at	HQ
35	Bde	CANAPLES	two
at	HQ	36	Bde
VIGNACOURT	four	at	HQ
37	Bde	BERTEAUCOURT	one
at	Div	HQ	VIGNACOURT
aaa	all	at	8
am	aaa	Kindly	confirm
early			
		N/9	

FROM 12 Division Q
PLACE & TIME

*This line should be erased if not required.

"C" FORM.
MESSAGES AND SIGNALS.

Prefix.... Code.... Words.... Received. Sent, or sent out. Office Stamp.
Charges to Collect   From....   At....
Service Instructions   By....   To....
                    12 Divn   By....

Handed in at.................... Office 10.50 a.m. Received 11.1 a.m.

TO 3rd Corps G.

Sender's Number	Day of Month	In reply to Number
Q104	1	G0111/7

AAA

Two buses required VIGNACOURT
church 8.30 am 2nd
inst kindly confirm

M/10

FROM 12 Div Q
PLACE & TIME

SECRET

12th Division No. G.X.3205.

31st JULY, 1918.

WARNING ORDER.

Ref: Maps LENS 1:100,000.
and Sheet 62.D. N.E. 1:20,000.

1. (a) The Division (less Artillery) will take over the Centre Sector, III Corps, from the 58th Division (less Artillery) on the nights of the 2nd/3rd and 3rd/4th August.

   (b) Personnel will move by bus and transport by march route.

2. (a) The 58th Division, Headquarters BEAUCOURT, has two Brigades in line and one in reserve, as follows :-

   173rd Inf. Bde.   Right Subsector, H.Q. D.26.b.9.3.
   175th Inf. Bde.   Left Subsector, H.Q. D.21.b.5.2.
   174th Inf. Bde.   Reserve, H.Q. BEAUCOURT.

   (b) Infantry reliefs will be carried out as follows :-

   173rd Inf. Bde. by 35th Inf. Bde.
   175th Inf. Bde. by 37th Inf. Bde.
   174th Inf. Bde. by 36th Inf. Bde.

   (c) Heads of Administrative Services, A.D.M.S., C.R.E., O.C., 12th Bn. M.G.Corps, O.C., 12th Divl. Signal Coy. and Divl. Gas Officer will get into touch with similar officers of the 58th Division and make preliminary arrangements for the relief.

3. (a) A car will be put at the disposal of the B.G.C., 35th Inf. Bde. and another at the disposal of the B.G.C. 37th Inf. Bde. to-day, 31st inst., and will be at their Headquarters at 10. 0 a.m. The former will arrange to pick up the O.C., 12th Battn. M.G.Corps at FLESSELLES, and the latter the C.R.E. at VIGNACOURT about 10.15 a.m.

   (b) Cars can proceed almost up to both Brigade Headquarters in the line.

4. (a) Arrangements will probably be made for two lorries per Brigade Group for reconnaissance to-morrow, 1st prox., and seven lorries per Brigade Group on 2nd prox. to take up Advance parties. Further details will be issued later.

   (b) B.G's. C. 35th and 37th Inf. Bdes. will complete the details to-day regarding reconnaissance to be carried out by units of their Brigade Groups tomorrow 1st prox.

.. 1 ..   /(5) A full issue..

5. A full issue of Maps will be made this evening. A few copies of 62 D. N.E. 1:20,000 are enclosed for Officers visiting Units of the 58th Division to-day.

6. Acknowledge

C.A. Ryan.

Major,
General Staff,
12th Division.

Copies to :-

"Q".
C.R.A.
C.R.E.
35th Inf. Bde.
36th Inf. Bde.
37th Inf. Bde.
12th Battn. M.G.C.
12th Div. Signals.
5th Northampton-
   shire Regt.

A.D.M.S.
D.A.D.V.S.
12th Divl. Train.
S.S.O.
A.P.M.
D.A.D.O.S.
214th Empl. Coy.
12th Divl. Recpn. Camp.
Camp. Comdt.
Divl. Gas Officer.
III Corps.
58th Division.

"A" Form
MESSAGES AND SIGNALS.

Army Form C. 2121
(In pads of 100.)

No. 166

Prefix....Code....m.	Words	Charge.	This message is on a/c of:	Recd. at....m.
Office of Origin and Service Instructions	Sent			Date..........
	At ....m.		........Service.	From ....
	To			
	By	(Signature of "Franking Officer")	By........

TO— 35th Inf. Bde. 36th Inf. Bde. 37th Inf. Bde.

Sender's Number.	Day of Month.	In reply to Number.	AAA
C. 450	24th		

Reference 12th Division No. G.S. 256 dated
26th August 1915. AAA Unless otherwise
ordered move hour for operation today
24th at 1. 4 pm. aaa acknowledge

From
Place 12th Division.
Time

The above may be forwarded as now corrected.   (Z)
....
Censor.   Signature of Addressee or person authorised to telegraph in his name
* This line should be erased if not required.

Order No. 1625. Wt. W3253/   P 511. 27/2. H. & K., Ltd. (E. 2634).

SECRET.
12th Division No. G.X. 3995.

23rd AUGUST, 1918.

35th Inf. Bde.
36th Inf. Bde.
37th Inf. Bde.
C.R.A.
C.R.E.
5th Northamptonshire
  Regt. (Pioneers).
12th Dn. M.G.Corps.

A.D.M.S.
"Q".
III Corps.
18th Division.
47th Division.
58th Division.

12th Division will be prepared to advance at Zero hour on the 24th instant to the general line F.17.c.5.5, F.9.d.9.5, F.3.c.3.0 AAA 58th Division will be advancing on right and 18th Division on left of 12th Division AAA Advance will be carried out by 37th Infantry Brigade on right and 36th Infantry Brigade on left with 35th Infantry Brigade in Reserve AAA Dividing line between 58th and 12th Divisions will be F.22.b.0.6, road junction F.15.d.8.5, road junction F.16.d.6.7, cross roads F.18.c.6.3 AAA Between 12th and 18th Divisions is line of the stream running South of BEHENCOURT and North of BECORDEL-BECOURT inclusive to 12th Division AAA Dividing line between Brigades through F.9.c.9.0 thence to road at F.10.c.8.0 AAA After operations tonight Brigades will reorganise in depth with a view to the advance tomorrow from the positions held at daylight AAA For this purpose the line must be held as lightly as possible and the bulk of the troops kept under cover in positions where they can receive orders AAA The advance will be carried out under creeping barrage which will open at Zero hour on the S.O.S. line, will make first lift at Zero plus four minutes and will move forward at the rate of 100 yards in four minutes AAA Five whippet tanks will co-operate in the advance one section in the zone of each Brigade AAA C.R.E. will detail one section Field Company R.E. to be under orders of each attacking Brigade AAA Remainder of R.E. and Pioneers will be under C.R.E. AAA Orders regarding machine guns will follow AAA 37th Infantry Brigade will send a liaison officer to Headquarters 173rd Infantry Brigade K.14.b.2.2 by 12 noon AAA 36th Infantry Brigade will send a liaison officer to report to right brigade 18th Division by 12 noon AAA As soon as the advance takes place conditions approximating to open warfare will be reached and units will push on without expecting to be in close touch on their flanks AAA Units will however always safeguard their flank and will gain touch with units on the flanks on the objective AAA 37th Infantry Brigade will detail a special Platoon to gain touch with 173rd Infantry Brigade at road junction F.15.d.2.4. and F.16.d.7.0. AAA 36th Infantry Brigade will detail a special Platoon to gain touch with 18th Division at bend of stream F.2.d.4.0, and on the objective AAA As soon as the objective is reached the line will be consolidated covered by an outpost line AAA One squadron 22nd Corps Cavalry and 1 Company 22nd Corps Cyclists will be sent forward under Divisional orders when the objective has been reached to keep touch with the enemy and exploit success and will rendezvous at Divisional Headquarters D.26.b.8.3. by 2 p.m. AAA 35th Infantry Brigade will concentrate under cover in front of the old AMIENS Defence Line and move forward at Zero hour 1 Battalion to the front system vacated by the attacking Brigades and 2 Battalions to the BROWN LINE where they will be in Divisional Reserve.

Lieut.Colonel,
General Staff,
12th Division.

Prefix	Code	Words	Received. From	Sent, or sent out. At ___ m.	Office Stamp.
Charges to Collect £ s. d.			By	To ___	
Service Instructions				By	

Handed in at ___ Office ___ m. Received ___ m.

TO: 3rd corps

*Sender's Number	Day of Month.	In reply to Number	A A A
G.119	23		

12th Division will carry out an operation tonight at an hour about which will be communicated later. operation will ... 7.30 ... F14 ... to ... with 18th ... about E7 B9 ... 37th Inf Bde will advance ... the right 36th Inf Bde ... the left aaa GOC 37 Inf Bde will take ... of the

FROM
PLACE & TIME

* This line should be erased if not required.

Prefix	Code	Words		Received.	Sent, or sent out.	Office Stamp.
		£ s. d.		From	At m.	
Charges to Collect				By	To	
Service Instructions					By	

Handed in at _____ Office _____ m. Received _____ m.

TO: 3rd Corps (3)

*Sender's Number	Day of Month	In reply to Number	A A A
G 229	23		

right Brigade front at 11 pm at which hour the 6th Buffs will come under his orders aaa dividing lines will be as follows aaa Between 47th and 12th Divns F.19.d.2.0 to F.20.a.5.2 aaa Between 12th and 15th Divns Railway from E.10.c.0.5 to F.7.b.3.9 aaa Between Brigades Track from SAND PIT to F.13.... and to F.9.c.0.0 aaa 37th Inf Bde will form up on South side of Road

FROM
PLACE & TIME

"C" Form.
MESSAGES AND SIGNALS.

Army Form C. 2123.
(In books of 100.)

No. of Message _____

Prefix _LO_ Code _11_ Words ____
Received From _MR_
By _Isali_
Sent, or sent out. At ____ m. To ____
Office Stamp.

Charges to Collect ____
Service Instructions _urgent operat Pk_
By ____

Handed in at _12 Div advd_ Office _8.45_ m. Received _9.20_ m.

TO _3 Bde_ (3)

*Sender's Number	Day of Month.	In reply to Number	A A A
G429	23		

running through F19C and D with
their right in touch
with 140th Inf Bde
47th Divn attacking on
their right aaa Objective
aaa 37th Inf Bde
will capture and consolidate
line between F20A5.2 and
F14A5.5 aaa One platoon
under an officer will
be specially detailed to
gain touch with the
47th Div on the
front line at F20A5.2
aaa 36th Inf Bde
will capture and consolidate
the line shown in

FROM
PLACE & TIME

* This line should be erased if not required.

"C" Form.
MESSAGES AND SIGNALS.

Army Form C. 2123.
(In books of 100.)

Prefix O Code Words
Received. From 41R By [sig]
Sent, or sent out. At ___ m. To ___ By ___
Office Stamp.

Service Instructions: wrt op Pty

Handed in at 12 Div Adv Office 8 4 m Received 9 20 m

TO 3 bps (4)

Sender's Number	Day of Month	In reply to Number	A A A
G429	23		

Place on map from F14A55 to F7B8·7 aaa One platoon will be specially detailed to establish touch with the 18th Divn on this line aaa The artillery barrage 47th Divn will open 100 yards in front of the road running through F25B aaa The Barrage line will be continued by 12th Divn from F19D·5·2 to F19B butt — F13D60 — F14A00 — F13B67 — E7C82 E7C00 where it will remain for four minutes

FROM
PLACE & TIME

"C" Form.
MESSAGES AND SIGNALS.

Army Form C. 2123.
(In books of 100.)

No. of Message _____

Prefix _____ Code _____ Words _____
£   s.   d.

Received.
From _____
By _____

Sent, or sent out.
At _____ m.
To _____
By _____

Office Stamp.

Charges to Collect _____

Service Instructions _____ Urgent Opn Pty

Handed in at _____ Office 8.11 m. Received 9.20 m.

TO _____ 3 Gp _____ (5)

*Sender's Number	Day of Month.	In reply to Number	A A A
G 239			

aaa it will then
move forward at the
rate of 150 yards
per minute until
it is 300 yards
beyond the objective and
gives at the beginning
of the message when
it will halt aaa
in halt aaa in
addition at Zero a
smoke will be put
down on the area
720A and 19B until
the above barrage line
aaa Brigade attacking on
the right of the

FROM
PLACE & TIME _____

* This line should be erased if not required.

"C" Form.
MESSAGES AND SIGNALS.

Army Form C. 2123.
(In books of 100.)

No. of Message _____

| Prefix | Code | Words | Received. From JR By | Sent, or sent out. At ___ m. To ___ By | Office Stamp. |

Charges to Collect

Service Instructions

Handed in at _Urgent Op Pty_ _13 Div_ adsd Office 8.46 m. Received 9.27 m.

TO _3 Gps_ (6)

*Sender's Number	Day of Month.	In reply to Number	A A A
G439	23		

37th Inf Bde will be 140a Bde with Headquarters at K17A5 8 aaa acknowledge aaa Added Bdes Ra rptd all concerned

FROM PLACE & TIME 12 Div 6 pm

* This line should be erased if not required.

"A" Form
MESSAGES AND SIGNALS.

Army Form C. 2121 (in pads of 100).

G.O 1528

Prefix....Code....m.	Words.	Charge.	This message is on a/c of:	Recd. at.....m.
	Sent			Date
Office of Origin and Service Instructions. D.R.L.S.	At......m. To...... By......		............Service (Signature of "Franking Officer.")	From By

35th, 36th & 37th Inf. Bdes., 12th Bn. M.G.C., 5th
N'hamptonshire Regt., 12th Div. Signals,
25th D.A., C.R.E., A.D.M.S.

III Corps, 18th & 47th Divs.

| Sender's Number. | Day of Month. | In reply to Number. | AAA |
| * G.296. | 19 | | |

Confirmation of verbal arrangements AAA
37th Inf. Bde. will take over tonight 18/19th
inst. left Battn. front of 35th Inf. Bde., all
arrangements to be made between Bdes. concerned
AAA Boundary between Brigades E.28.d.7.0. -
K.4.b.5.9. - level crossing K.4.a.9.3. -
thence track through K.4.a. - K.3.b. to
CRUCIFIX K.3.c.4.7. inclusive to left Brigade
AAA 37th Infantry Brigade will vacate area
K.1.b. and d. which will be available for
Reserve Battalion 35th Infantry Brigade AAA
Addsd. 35th and 37th Inf. Bdes., reptd.
remainder of List "X" and A.D.M.S.

From: 12th Division.
Place:
Time: 7.30 a.m. D.R.L.S.

C.A.Ryan.
Maj. GS

The above may be forwarded as now corrected. (Z)

Censor. Signature of Addresser or person authorised to telegraph in his name.

* This line should be erased if not required.
(18965.) Wt. W12952/M1294. 187,500 Pads. 1/17 McC. & Co., Ltd. (E. 819.)

SECRET.

12th Division No.G.X. 3598

17th AUGUST, 1918.

Reference 12th Division Warning Order No.275 and 12th Division Order No.276, from completion of relief 35th Infantry Brigade will be prepared to carry out role allotted to 36th Infantry Brigade in Warning Order No. 275 and 36th Infantry Brigade that allotted to 35th Infantry Brigade. 48 hours notice will probably be given of action in accordance with Warning Order No.275.

B. Belgrave
Lieut-Colonel,
General Staff,
12th Division.

Addressed all recipients of
12th Division Warning Order No.275.

"C" FORM.
MESSAGES AND SIGNALS.

From	Code	Words 15	Received	Sent, or sent out	Office Stamp
Charges to Collect			From Div²	At	
Service Instructions			By	To	
1/R 3adds				By	

Handed in at ...... Office ...... Received ......

TO 3 Corps

Sender's Number	Day of Month	In reply to Number	AAA
320	20		

Ref Gx3625 PEAR aaa
added recipients of above

FROM 12 Div
PLACE & TIME 1.45 am.

"C" Form.

MESSAGES AND SIGNALS.

| Prefix Im Code Da Words 41 | Received From YRR By Chili | Sent, or sent out At To By | Office Stamp. |

Charges to Collect

Service Instructions 10 f 3 adds

Handed in at 12 Divn Ad Office 4.5 h Received 4.40 p.m.

TO 3rd Corps

Sender's Number	Day of Month	In reply to Number	AAA
9290	18 12 noon		
Reference	Jehe	GX 3625	of
18°	aaa	Postponed	for
24	hours	aaa	Addressed
Jehe	Buvu	Buju	Buzu
Joqi	mowe	Repeated	3rd
Corps	D.	Special	Coy
RE	18°	Divn	47
Divn	Div	Gas	Officer

FROM PLACE & TIME 12° Div 4pm

This line should be erased if not required.

(No. 1515)

S E C R E T.

12th Division No.G.X.3625.

18th AUGUST, 1918.

C.R.E.
35th Inf. Bde.
37th Inf. Bde.
12th Battn. M.G.C.
5th Northampton-
    shire Regt.(Pioneers).

1.(a)   'D' Special Coy., R.E. will discharge projectors tonight, 18th/19th inst., from K.4.a.4.5. on to the area around E.29.a.15.40. provided the wind is favourable.

(b)   Zero hour will be .... 12.30 am

2.(a)   The C.R.A. will arrange to search the head of the valley in E.29.a. with bursts of fire from Zero plus 1 to Zero plus 10.

(b)   Correct time will be given to 'D' Special Coy., R.E. and 25th Divl. Artillery by telephone at 6 p.m. to day.

3.   The attached trace (to Units of 12th Div. only) shows :-

(a)   Area to be cleared completely by Zero minus 10 minutes.
(b)   Area which need not be cleared, but in which box respirators must be worn from Zero minus 10 minutes to Zero plus 10 minutes.

4.   As soon as the flash of the discharge has taken place, troops wearing box respirators may commence to reoccupy the area vacated.   Box respirators can be removed in this area at Zero plus 10 minutes.

5.   'D' Special Coy. R.E. will have an officer at the Headquarters 7th Battn. The Norfolk Regt. at K.4.a.15.50. during the operation, and Brigades will arrange for trained gas personnel to be forward with companies in time to make certain the trenches are free from gas at Zero plus 10 minutes.

6.(a)   The following Code words will be used in connection with the operation :-

    APPLE   = Operation will take place tonight.
    ORANGE = Operation will NOT take place tonight.
    PEAR   = Operation completed.

(b)   The wind limits for the projection will be S.S.W. to W. through S.W.

A C K N O W L E D G E by wire.

A. Ryan
Major for
Lieut-Colonel,
General Staff,
12th Division.

Copies to :-
    III Corps.   47th Divn.
    'D' Special Coy.R.E. 36th Inf. Bde.
    18th Divn.   D.G.O.

Prefix...Code...m.	Words.	Charge.	This message is on a/c of:	Recd. at......m.
O...of O...in and ...rvice Instructions. Sent				Date......
SECRET At......			G.1405 ...Service.	From......
To......				
By......		(Signature of "Franking Officer.")		By......

TO
- BUVU — C.R.A. C.R.E. M.G.Battn. A.D.M.S.
- BUJU — 12th Div. Signals. 5th Northampton Regt
- BUZU — III Corps. 47th Divn. 18th Divn.

Sender's Number.	Day of Month.	In reply to Number.	
G.163	12		AAA

36th Infantry Brigade will take over tonight 12/13th inst. the portion of the front now held by 37th Inf. Bde. from the Southern Divisional boundary to track at E.28.c.80.85. exclusive. AAA Boundary between Brigades track E.28.c.80.85. to road in E.3.b. -a. - c. all inclusive to 37th Inf. Bde. but available for traffic to both AAA Bde. Hdqrts. will be established as follows AAA 35th Inf. Bde. at J.9.b.3.3., 36th Inf. Bde. at J.11.a.central, 37th Inf. Bde. no change, at J.5.d.8.5. AAA Dispositions of Reserve (i.e.35th) Bde. will be 2 Battns. BALLARAT LINE 1 Battn. K.14.a. - b.

AAA Details to be arranged between Bdes. concerned AAA Situation maps giving exact dispositions

From			
Place			
Time			
The above may be forwarded as now corrected.	(Z)		
	Censor.	Signature of Addressor or person authorised to telegraph in his name.	

*This line should be erased if not required.

"A" Form
MESSAGES AND SIGNALS.

Army Form C. 2121 (in pads of 100).

TO

— 2 —

by Coys and Bn Hdqrs will be forwarded to reach this office by 12 noon to-morrow 13th inst AAA Bn. of 36th Inf. Bde. (5th R.Berks) in K.1.b. & d. and Bn. of 37th Inf. Bde. (6th Buffs) K.9.d. K.10.c. need not be moved until to-morrow night 13/14th inst unless Brigades wish to do so. AAA ACKNOWLEDGE AAA Addsd 3 Bdes reptd remainder of List X plus A.D.M.S.

From: 12 Div.
Place: JELE
Time: P.M.

G.S. 12 Div

SECRET.

12th Division No. G.X.3362.

7th AUGUST, 1918.

ARRANGEMENTS WITH REGARD TO GAS AND SMOKE.

GAS.

1. If the wind is favourable, Gas will be fired between Zero and Zero plus 30 minutes from Sunken Road K.1.d.1.3 to K.1.d.2.7, with targets in MORLANCOURT and trenches which have been selected in consultation with G.O.C. 35th Infantry Brigade.

2. Os.C. Special Companies have guaranteed that there will be no Gas on or West of the line K.8.c.0.5 - K.8.a.0.0 - K.2.d.0.0 - K.2.central - K.26.central at or after Zero plus 2 hours.

    Patrols will be able to enter MORLANCOURT without respirators at Zero plus 2 hours, but must be warned not to enter cellars or deep dug-outs without putting their respirators on.

3. The wind limits for the operation are W.N.W. through W. to W.S.W., and of a velocity exceeding 4 miles per hour.

4. If at any time up to Zero minus 2 hours it becomes certain that the wind will be unfavourable, the gas operation will be cancelled by a message from Divisional Headquarters.

    The following code will be used :-

    Operation will not take place ... ... VESLE.

    On receipt of this message, Brigade will inform the officer of Special Company, who will be at their Headquarters. This officer will then be responsible for stopping the gas operation. This does not affect the responsibility of the officers in charge of each group of emplacements for deciding whether or not the wind at Zero is safe for discharge.

SMOKE.

Stokes Mortars will fire smoke from Zero plus 120 minutes, under arrangements which have been made direct between O.C. Stokes Mortars and G.O.C. 35th Infantry Brigade, with a view to neutralizing the machine guns in K.2.d. and b.

J.D. Belgrave
Lieut.Colonel,
General Staff,
12th Division.

Copies to :-

G.O.C.	O.C., 12th Div. Signal Coy., R.E.
C.R.A., 25th Division.	18th Division.
C.R.E.	47th Division.
35th Infantry Brigade.(4)	58th Division.
36th Infantry Brigade.	III Corps (2 copies).
37th Infantry Brigade.	5th Brigade R.A.F.
12th Bn. Machine Gun Corps.	10th Tank Battalion.

SECRET.

12th Division No. GX.3378.

7th August, 1918.

Correction No. 1
to
12th Division G.X.3331 of 6th Aug. - ARTILLERY ARRANGEMENTS
with reference to 12th Division Order No. 271.

Delete para 3 and substitute the following :-

3.   At Zero plus 120 intense bombardment of trench K.8.a.0.7. to K.2.c.0.8., of selected trenches, and of railway bends in E.26.d., K.2.b. and K.2.d.

At Zero plus 124 mins.   lift off trench K.8.a.0.7. to K.2.c.0.8. and on more Easterly of two railway bends in K.2.b.

"   "   " 129 "   lift off trench running from K.8.a.25.75. - K.8.a.00.10. and thence southwards, on to protective barrage East of this trench.

"   "   " 134 "   lift off trenches West of Westerly railway bend in K.2.d. and b. and on to easterly railway.

"   "   " 140 "   lift off Western railway and trenches West of the N. and S. line through K.2.b.6.5.

"   "   " 150 "   lift on to protective barrage on a N. and S. grid line through E.27.central and K.3.central.

"   "   " 180 "   slow down to bursts of fire, until ordered to stop.

Major
for
             Lieut.Colonel,
             General Staff,
             12th Division.

To all recipients of 12th Division No. G.X.3331.

TABLE 'B'. All Batteries EXCEPT C/110, B/110, B/232.

BTY.	I.	II.	III.	IV.	V.	VI.	VII
A/232. 375 Bty. 377 Bty. C/232.	0 to plus 4.	Plus 4 to plus 50.	Plus 50 to plus 124.	Plus 124 to plus 134.	Plus 134 to plus 140.	Plus 140 to plus 156.	Plus 150 till ordered to stop.
	Put down Barrage on first barrage line in Zone.	Comb backwards and forwards to a distance of 800 yards.	Bombard trenches and wire and Red Railway in areas marked.	Same as Column III.	Green Railway in Group Zone.	Green Railway in Group Zone.	Blue Protective Barrage in Group Zone.
A/110.	ditto.	ditto.	ditto.	Lift to Green Railway cuttings	Same as Col. IV.	ditto.	ditto.
376 Bty. 378 Bty.	ditto.	ditto.	ditto.	Same as Col.III.	Same as Col.III.	ditto.	ditto.
C/112. D/112. E/112.	ditto.	ditto.	ditto.	ditto.	ditto.	ditto.	ditto.

Rates of Fire.
I. 1 r.p.m.
II. ½ r.p.m.
III. 1 r.p.m.
IV. ½ r.p.m.
V. ½ r.p.m.

Zero to plus 4.
plus 4 to plus 120.
Plus 120 to plus 125.
Plus 125 to plus 130.
plus 130 till further orders show.

THIS TABLE IS TO BE SUBSTITUTED FOR THE TABLE 'B' ISSUED WITH 25th DIVISIONAL ARTILLERY INSTRUCTIONS No.1.

M.M.Tart
Major. R. A.
Brigade Major,25th Div. Arty.

7th August. 1919.

Tracing "B"

Identification Trace for use with Artillery Maps.

D E

OBJECTIVE
FIRST BARRAGE
PROTECTIVE BARRAGE
S.O.S. BARRAGE
SMOKE BARRAGE

SMOKE
D113 D112
ZERO to 240 mins

LEFT GROUP — A112, B112, C112

E K

RIGHT GROUP — 378, 379, A110, C232, 377

ZERO to 240 mins
8 Div   D110   SMOKE

PROTECTIVE BARRAGE
S.O.S.

376
A232
TOVEY'S GROUP — B110, B232, C110

FINAL OBJECTIVE 18 DIV
1ST OBJECTIVE

NOTE.—(1). These tracings are intended to facilitate the communication of information as to the position of targets, which have been located on a squared map.
(2). Two squares on this trace are 500 yards in length on the 1/10,000 scale, 1,000 yards in length on the 1/20,000 scale, and 2,000 yards in length on the 1/40,000 scale.
(3). The squares on this trace are fitted to the squares of the map showing the targets, which are then drawn on the trace. Sufficient letters and numbers must also be added to enable the recipient to place the trace in the correct position on his own map. A little detail may also be traced, but this is not essential. The name and scale of the map to which the trace refers must be always given. The trace can be used for the 1/10,000, 1/20,000, or 1/40,000 scale.

G.S.G.S. 3025.

Tracing taken from Sheet 62D N E
of the 1/20,000 map of
Signature   Date 6.8

SECRET.

12th Division No. G.X. 3362.

7th AUGUST, 1918.

ARRANGEMENTS WITH REGARD TO GAS AND SMOKE.

GAS.

1. If the wind is favourable, Gas will be fired between Zero and Zero plus 30 minutes from Sunken Road K.1.d.1.3 to K.1.d.2.7, with targets in MORLANCOURT and trenches which have been selected in consultation with G.O.C. 35th Infantry Brigade.

2. Os.C. Special Companies have guaranteed that there will be no Gas on or West of the line K.8.c.0.5 - K.8.a.0.0 - K.2.d.0.0 - K.2.central - K.26.central at or after Zero plus 2 hours.

   Patrols will be able to enter MORLANCOURT without respirators at Zero plus 2 hours, but must be warned not to enter cellars or deep dug-outs without putting their respirators on.

3. The wind limits for the operation are W.N.W. through W. to W.S.W., and of a velocity exceeding 4 miles per hour.

4. If at any time up to Zero minus 2 hours it becomes certain that the wind will be unfavourable, the gas operation will be cancelled by a message from Divisional Headquarters.

   The following code will be used :-

   Operation will not take place ... ... VESLE.

   On receipt of this message, Brigade will inform the officer of Special Company, who will be at their Headquarters. This officer will then be responsible for stopping the gas operation. This does not affect the responsibility of the officers in charge of each group of emplacements for deciding whether or not the wind at Zero is safe for discharge.

SMOKE.

Stokes Mortars will fire smoke from Zero plus 120 minutes, under arrangements which have been made direct between O.C. Stokes Mortars and G.O.C. 35th Infantry Brigade, with a view to neutralizing the machine guns in K.2.d. and b.

J.D. Belgrave
Lieut.Colonel,
General Staff,
12th Division.

Copies to :-

G.O.C.	O.C., 12th Div. Signal Coy., R.E.
C.R.A., 25th Division.	18th Division.
C.R.E.	47th Division.
35th Infantry Brigade. (4)	58th Division.
36th Infantry Brigade.	III Corps (2 copies).
37th Infantry Brigade.	5th Brigade R.A.F.
12th Bn. Machine Gun Corps.	10th Tank Battalion.

S E C R E T.

12th Division No. G.X. 2677

18th AUGUST, 1918.

35th Inf. Bde.
36th Inf. Bde.
37th Inf. Bde.

1. Herewith / copies of map showing lines of resistance likely to be encountered in an advance.

2. The dotted line through 9, 16, 22, and 28 denotes probable line of our posts.

3. [illegible]

4. [illegible]

5. [illegible]

Major General,
Commanding,
12th Division.

SECRET

Possible Line of Exploitation

2ND. OBJECTIVE
GREEN LINE

1ST OBJECTIVE
LINE 24

BROWN

To superimpose on 1/20,000 map

247 R.I.R
246 R.I.R } 54ᵀᴴ R.D.
——— Approx. Div. Boundary
248 R.I.R.

448 I.R
449 I.R. } 233 DIV.
450 I.R.

——— Approx. S. Boundary (Div.)

MESSAGE FORM.

To _____

Map Reference or Mark on Map at Back.

1. I am at _____
2. I am at _____
3. I am at _____ and am consolidating
4. Am held up by M.G. at _____ and have consolidated
5. I need:
   - Ammunition
   - Bombs
   - Rifle Grenades
   - Wire
   - Verey Lights
   - Stokes Shells
6. Counter-attack forming up at _____
7. I am in touch with _____ on Right at _____ Left at _____
8. I am not in touch on Right
9. Am being shelled from _____
10. I estimate my present strength at _____ rifles.
11. Hostile Machine Gun active at _____ Trench Mortar _____ Battery _____

Name _____
Platoon _____
Company _____
Battalion _____

Time _____
Date _____

M3.de Instructors

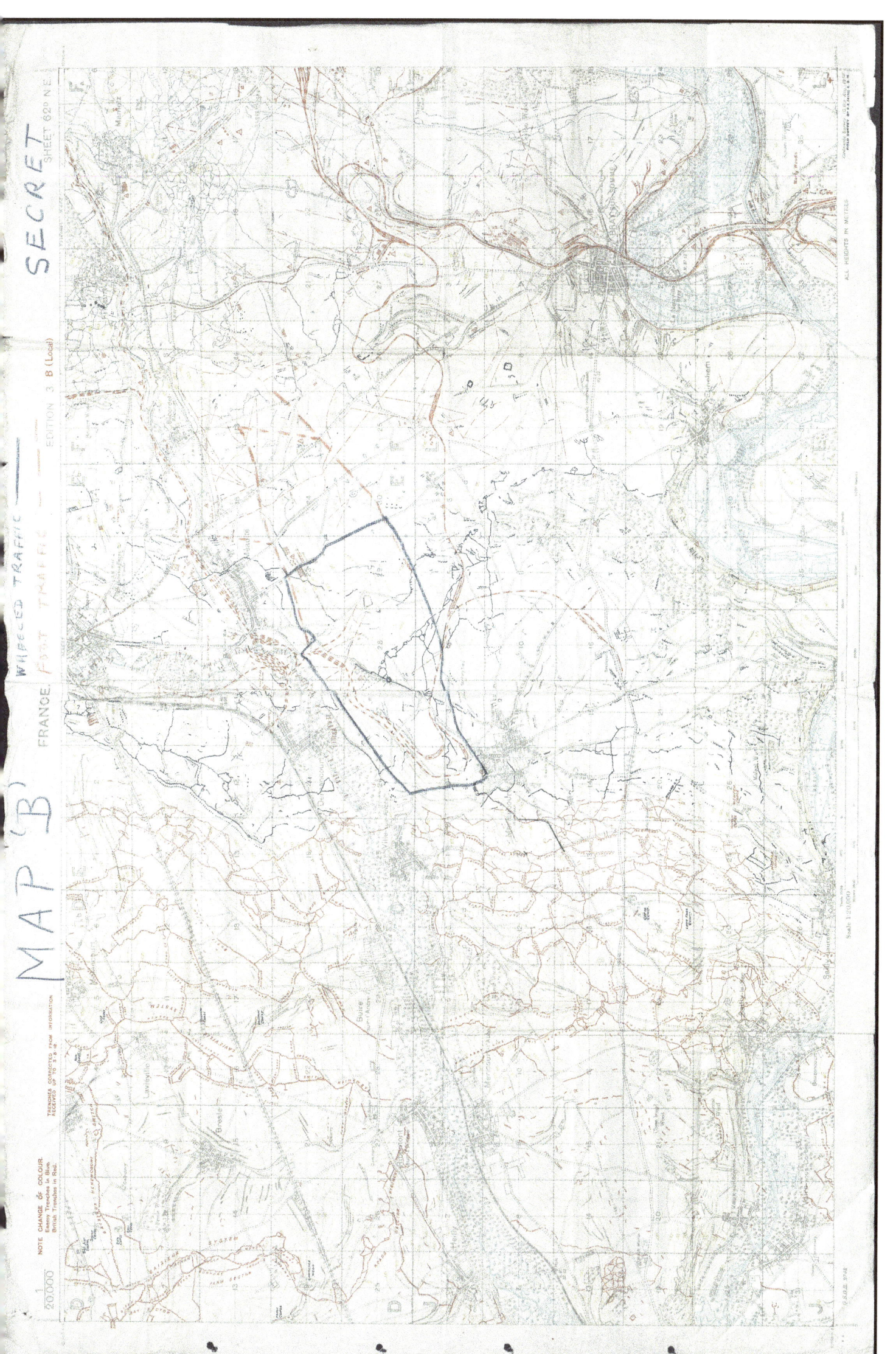

12th Division
August 1915

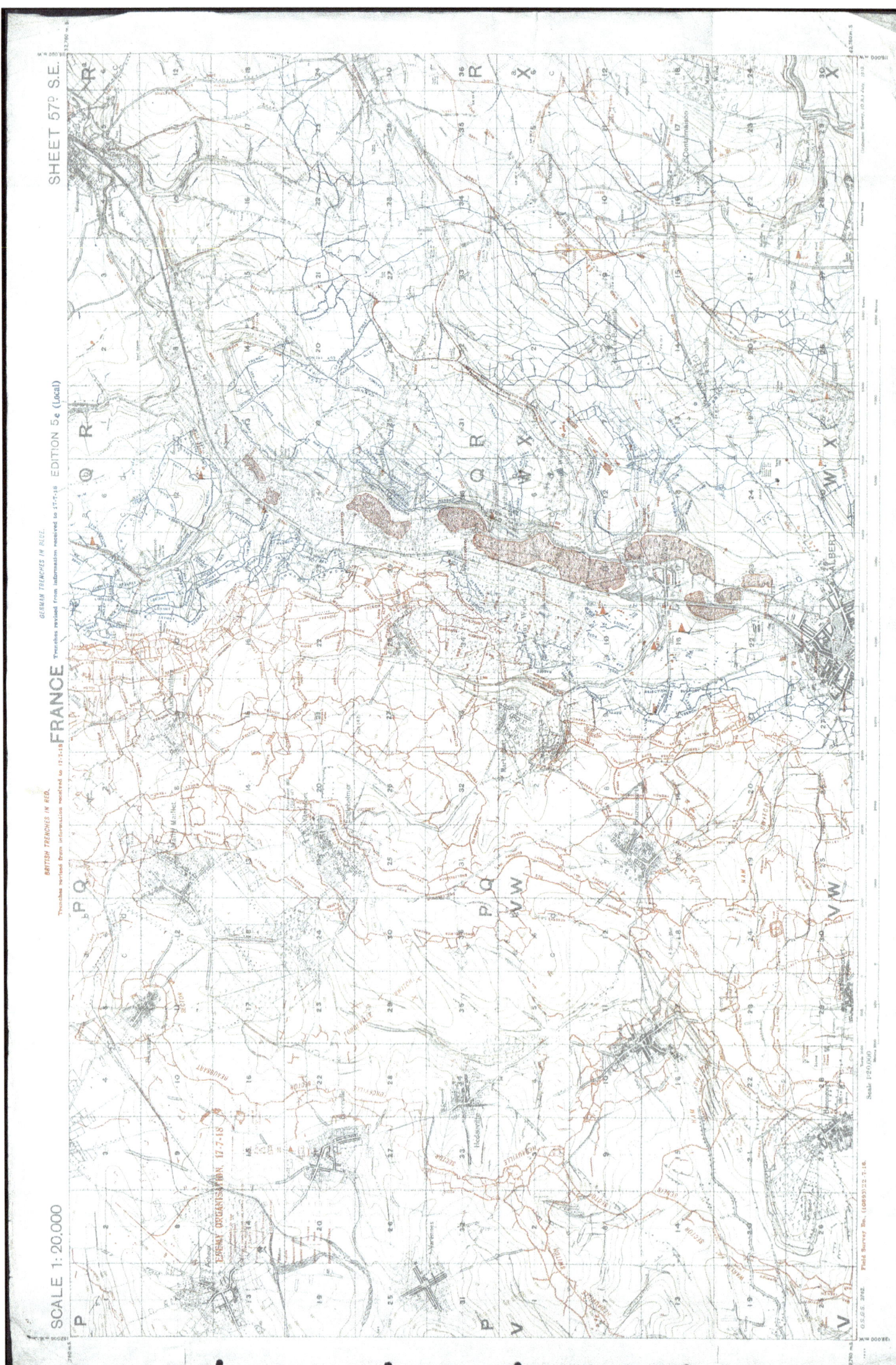

5 yP S.F

34° S.W

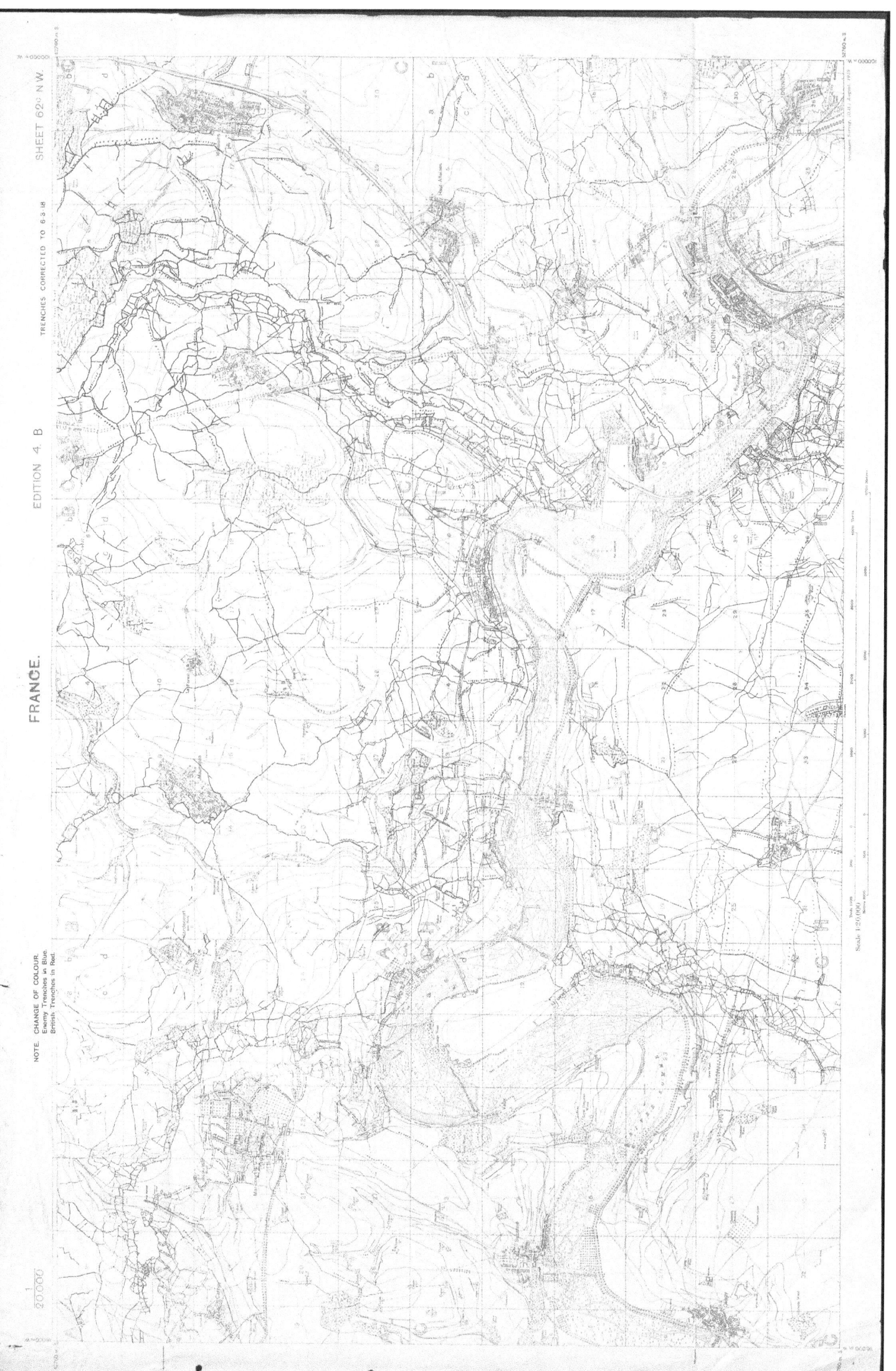

52c
N.W

5Y.C.5.F

62° NE

GENERAL STAFF,

12th DIVISION,

SEPTEMBER, 1918.

NARRATIVE OF OPERATIONS

and

MAP SHOWING ADVANCE OF DIVISION

from 8th Aug. to 30th Sept. 1918

IN SEPARATE COVER

Army Form C. 2118.

12th DIVISION WAR DIARY
September 1918.
INTELLIGENCE SUMMARY.
(Erase heading not required.)

Instructions regarding War Diaries and Intelligence Summaries are contained in F. S. Regs., Part II. and the Staff Manual respectively. Title pages will be prepared in manuscript.

Places	Date	Hour	Summary of Events and Information	Remarks and references to Appendices
HIDDEN WOOD	1/9/18.		Day spent re-organising and resting.	Reference attached maps
"	2/9/18.		do.	
"	3/9/18.		36 Bde in reserve to 47 Div. - in area B.10 and 11.	
"	4/9/18.		On night of 4th/5th, 35 Bde and 36 Bde relieved 53rd Bde and 55th Bde, 18th Div. on line of TORTILE RIVER in vicinity of RIVERSIDE and VAUX WOODS - relief was difficult on account of the extreme darkness and the heavy gas shelling of the woods in the valley of the River.	
COMBLES.	5/9/18.		At 6.45 a.m. 35 and 36 Bdes advanced to attack NURLU and the trench system of it. They were held up in the trench system W. of the village. At 7.30 p.m. the Bdes co-operated in an attack on the village. Little progress was made, the enemy making a strong bombing attack on their left flank, which had become exposed. Change in weather to wet and stormy at intervals. Divisional Headquarters opened at COMBLES at 8 a.m.	
"	6/9/18.		At 8 a.m. troops of the 35 and 36 Bdes attacked again, with complete success - posts were pushed out in V.29.a.9.1. and V.23.central, and during the afternoon 36th Inf. Bde. pushed out to the line LIERAMONT CEMETERY - SOREL WOOD, and 1/1st Cambs. maintained touch with 62nd Inf. Bde. S. of SOREL LE GRAND. Touch maintained with 47 Div. on right. Divisional Headquarters moved to VAUX-WOOD (U.29.a.3.8.) at 7 p.m.	
VAUX WOOD	7/9/18.		At 8 a.m. 37 Bde passed through line held on previous evening. The advance was made on a two Bn front. Hostile M.Gs were active, particularly at the commencement of the attack. At 1.30 p.m. our troops had reached line of Road W.28.a. and c. and E.4.a. and c. The attack was held up on the right by heavy M.G. fire from E.5.a. and c. An enemy aeroplane was brought down by L.G. fire, and crew (2) taken prisoners. The Advance was continued at 8 p.m., and despite heavy opposition from enemy M.Gs, the line at midnight ran as follows :- W.29.a. and c. E.5.a. and c. with posts in front.	
"	8/9/18.		At 7.30 a.m. 174 Bde commenced to pass through 37 Bde, and command of Sector passed to G.O.C. 38th Div. Division passed into Corps Reserve with :-	

Army Form C. 2118.

12th DIVISION.
WAR DIARY
September 1918.
INTELLIGENCE SUMMARY.

(Erase heading not required.)

Instructions regarding War Diaries and Intelligence Summaries are contained in F.S. Regs., Part II. and the Staff Manual respectively. Title pages will be prepared in manuscript.

Place	Date	Hour	Summary of Events and Information	Remarks and references to Appendices
VAUX WOOD.	8/9/18.		Contd., 35 Bde in vicinity of RIVERSIDE WOOD. 36 Bde Area west of NURLU. 37 Bde in VAUX WOOD. Divisional Headquarters remained in VAUX WOOD Area.	
,,	9/9/18.		Resting and re-organising - Weather wet with intervals of sunshine.	
,,	10/9/18.		Resting and reorganising - Weather unsettled.	
,,	11/9/18.		Precautionary Order issued from Corps for Division to be prepared to man the TINCOURT WOOD - NURLU Line - 12th Divisions Instructions for Defence No. 2 issued and the necessary reconnaissances carried out.	
,,	12/9/18.		Conference at Corps H.Q. at 3.15 p.m. followed by one at Divisional H.Q. at 7.15 p.m. at which Bde Cmmdrs attended.	
,,	13/9/18.		Corps Conference held at 12th Divisional H.Q. at 6 p.m. Fine night, in consequence of which enemy aeroplanes active; two enemy aeroplanes were brought down in flames about 10.30 p.m.	
,,	14/9/18.		12th Division Order No. 282 issued relative to an attack which was to be made on a large front and in which the Division was to take part.	App 2
,,	15/9/18.		Division engaged in training.	
,,	16/9/18.		Division Order No. 282, and subsequent instructions were cancelled, and Order No. 283 issued giving the detailed order for the attack. Zero day and hour to be 5.20 a.m. on 18th instant. The task of the 12th Division to be the capture of EPEHY and objective lines beyond it, as shown on the plan of attack on Map "A".	App 3
EPINETTE WOOD	17/9/18.		On the night of the 17th/18th the Bdes moved up to assembly positions between GUYENCOURT and the existing front line. The Bdes allotted to the capture of the GREEN LINE, i.e., the first objective, were the 35 Bde. on the left, and the 36 Bde. on the right. The capture of the village of EPEHY wsallotted to the 35 Bde, 36 Bde. attacking from the Railway in F.2.c.	

Army Form C. 2118.

12th DIVISION.
WAR DIARY
September 1918

INTELLIGENCE SUMMARY.
(Erase heading not required.)

Place	Date	Hour	Summary of Events and Information	Remarks and references to Appendices
EPINETTE WOOD.	17/9/18.		Contd., when the area between the front line and the Railway had been cleared up.	
,,	18/9/18.		Rain fell heavily from about midnight to an hour after daylight. This, combined with a very heavy mist, made it quite impossible to see any landmarks. The attack, as arranged, took place. Considerable opposition was encountered by the 35 Bde in EPEHY. Parties of Germans who hid themselves in the numerous cellars in the town gave a great deal of trouble and the village was not entirely mopped up until late in the afternoon. In consequence of this, the first objective (GREEN LINE) was only reached at its southern end by the 9th R.F., the line held by and the dispositions of the Division at the close of the day's fighting being as shown on attached Map "B".	App 4
		11.55 p.m.	Divisional Order No. G. 164 issued, ordering an attack to be carried out at 11 a.m. on the next day by the 37th Inf. Bde on the right and the 35th Inf. Bde on the left. The objectives to be BRAETON POST – BIRD TRENCH – MULE TRENCH – X.28.c.0.0. – OCKENDEN TRENCH – ROOM TRENCH. During the night the Royal Berks advanced to the general line of :- F.2.central, eastern edge of TETARD WOOD – X.26.c.7.1. – CHESTNUT AVENUE to X.26.a.5.0. where a block was made. Left Brigade reported that they still had some East Kents in RIDGE RESERVE, between MAY COPSE and MALASSISE FARM.	App 5
,,	19/9/18. 11.30 a.m.		Divisional Order G. 181 issued relative to action of 36th Inf. Bde after 37th Inf. Bde has passed through it.	App 6
		11.45 a.m.	Report from Divisional Observers timed 11.10 a.m. stated that enemy barrage came down at 11.3 a.m. MALASSISE FARM was heavily shelled and that at 11.10 a.m. barrage was still heavy in vicinity of TETARD WOOD.	
		12.10 p.m.	37th Inf. Bde reported their troops in OLD COPSE, and still advancing. Considerable opposition was experienced by our troops from ROOM and OCKENDEN TRENCHES which were strongly held by the enemy.	
,,	20/9/18.		The attack was continued today, the objectives being to establish the RED LINE. Fighting continued during the day, considerable local opposition being encountered on various parts of the Divisional Front, especially from BRAETON and HEYTHORPE POSTS in F.5.a. and F.4.b.	

Army Form C. 2118.

12th DIVISION.
WAR DIARY
September 1918.
INTELLIGENCE SUMMARY.
(Erase heading not required.)

Instructions regarding War Diaries and Intelligence Summaries are contained in F. S. Regs., Part II. and the Staff Manual respectively. Title pages will be prepared in manuscript.

Place	Date	Hour	Summary of Events and Information	Remarks and references to Appendices
EPINETTE WOOD.	20/9/18.	3.0 p.m.	Contd.; The 36 and 37 Inf. Bdes ordered to attack at 5.40 a.m. on the 21st., in which the 18th Div. would co-operate. The object of the attack was to make good the general line of the Trench system from F.5.c.6.0. HEYTHORPE POST, HEYTHORPE LANE and MULE TRENCH. An Artillery barrage was arranged.	Appdx Y
		5.0. p.m.	At this time 35 and 36 Bdes., held ROO and OCKENDEN TRENCHES in their entirety, and the 37th Bde held the line of ST PATRICK'S AVENUE, thence east to outskirts of LEMPIRE, where it was in touch with the Bde. on its flank. The situation slightly improved during the night.	
,,	21/9/18.		The assembly for and start of the attack went successfully. Heavy opposition was encountered from enemy M.Gs. The enemy by a counter attack, forced back the 18th Division on the right to POMPONIOUS LANE and reoccupied TOMBOIS FARM. MULE TRENCH and its junction with DEELISH AVENUE was captured by our troops. Considerable casualties were inflicted on the enemy in the course of the day's fighting. Another attack was ordered to be carried out at 1215 a.m. on the 22nd by 37 and 36 Inf. Bdes on right and left respectively, the objectives to be the same as for the attack today.	
,,	22/9/18.	2.0. a.m.	The Left Bde reported their objectives gained, but that they were being heavily enfiladed from KILDARE POST, and that they were not in touch on their left. Divisional Order No. 234 issued, - additional frontage being taken over by the Division on night 23rd/24th.	
		4.15. a.m.	Left Bde reported that they were in touch with Right Bde at F.4.d.9.9. and that HEYTHORPE POST was in our hands. Subsequent reports confirmed that we had taken all our objectives.	
,,	23/9/18.		The line stabilised during the day, and apart from shelling of our forward positions nothing of any import occurred. On the night 23rd/24th the 56th Inf. Bde relieved 175th Inf. Bde up to the new Northern Divisional Boundary, viz:- E. and W. Grid Line between X.20 and 26, and including EADOS LANE and STONE LANE.	
,,	24/9/18.		At 11.30 a.m. the enemy attacked from KILDARE POST, southwards, after a heavy artillery bombardment, but was driven off by our Artillery and Stokes Mortar fire. O.O.C. 35th Inf. [illegible] posts out in front of LITTLE PRIEL, put it immediately under	

Army Form C. 2118.

12th DIVISION.
WAR DIARY
September 1918.

INTELLIGENCE SUMMARY.
(Erase heading not required.)

Instructions regarding War Diaries and Intelligence Summaries are contained in F. S. Regs., Part II. and the Staff Manual respectively. Title pages will be prepared in manuscript.

Place	Date	Hour	Summary of Events and Information	Remarks and references to Appendices
EPINETTE WOOD	24/9/18.		Contd.; Artillery fire. After the attack was repulsed our posts east of the Farm were re-established. Elements of the enemy succeeded, however, in occupying DADOS LANE and LOOP between about X.22.d.3.4. and X.22.d.6.0.	
"	25/9/18.		On night 25th/26th, a Gas Projector shoot on enemy's positions in vicinity of S.29.d. was successfully carried out. Situation normal during the day. A minor operation carried out by the left Brigade with the object of recapturing DADOS LOOP and LANE was not successful owing to heavy enfilade M.G. fire and counter bombing attacks made by the enemy. At 4.45 a.m. the enemy made an unsuccessful attempt to capture BRAETON POST: estimated strength of attacking party was four Coys. The enemy was repulsed, leaving 13 dead in the Post, and one unwounded prisoner in our hands. From the prisoner's statement, his Bn. (1st Bn. 153 I.R., 8th Div.) had been ordered to capture and hold the trench at all costs.	App. A.8
"	26/9/18. 4.30 a.m.		The Left Brigade again attacked DADOS LOOP and LANE, and it was reported at 4.20 a.m. that the LOOP had been occupied and that DADOS LANE was believed to be cleared. Posts were established at X.22.d.8.5. and X.22.d.8.6.	
	6.10 a.m.		Report received that enemy had counterattacked at DADOS, and that fighting was still in progress. Later reports received stated that owing to the heavy opposition encountered by the 33rd Div. on our left, and their consequent failure to come up on our left, our troops had to come back to their original positions. Divisional Order No. 432 and supplementary Order G. 456 issued, relative to attack by 27th American Division, in which the Division would co-operate. During the afternoon blocks were established in DADOS LOOP at X.22.d.8.5. and in STONE LANE X.22.d.9.3.	
"	27/9/18.		At the 27th American Division attacked the Line QUENEMONT FARM – GILLEMONT FARM – THE KNOLL. The Division co-operated by pushing out patrols for reconnaissance, and also to capture points of tactical advantage, if possible. The Americans were forced back from the KNOLL by heavy enemy counter attacks. Our patrols found the QUARRIES and LARK POST strongly held. We advanced our post in DADOS LOOP, but a counter bombing attack made by the enemy with Gas Hand Bombs, forced us back.	

(A099). Wt. W16930/M1293 75,000 4/17. D. D. & L., Ltd. Forms/Cam814.

Army Form C. 2118.

12th DIVISION.
WAR DIARY
September 1918.
INTELLIGENCE SUMMARY.
(Erase heading not required.)

Place	Date	Hour	Summary of Events and Information	Remarks and references to Appendices
ENINETTE WOOD.	28/9/18.		Divisional Order No. 286 issued relative to an attack to be carried out on Z day. Orders were received from the Corps that the Division would probably be withdrawn from the line on the night 29th/30th, and entrain on the 1st October, for another Army front. During the night 28th/29th our Artillery gassed enemy trenches in vicinity of LARK POST and the QUARRIES. Notification received that the 29th inst., would be Zero day.	
	29/9/18.		The big attack was launched at 5.50 a.m. By the evening of the same day the Division had made good the following line TOMBOIS SUPPORT, A.1.d; TINO SUPPORT, as far north as X.30.c.5.6. - TINO TRENCH F.6.a. - LARK TRENCH - QUARRIES in X.29.d. GATELET TRENCH was also captured and touch was maintained with the 18th Div on the Right. During the afternoon the enemy attempted to make a counter attack up GATELET VALLEY. This was completely repulsed by our fire. 150 prisoners were captured in the vicinity of the QUARRIES.	
	30/9/18. 10.15 a.m.		R.W.K's attacked DADOS LOOP but met with strong resistance. Continued pressure, however, was exerted, and the enemy was forced to evacuate his positions. At this time our troops were in possession of DADOS LOOP, STONE LANE and trench south of STONE LANE, FALCON TRENCH, BIRD CAGE and practically the whole of KILDARE TRENCH.	
	12.00 noon		BELOW TRENCH reported captured. R.W.Ks and Essex kept pushing on and occupied HAWK TRENCH, N. and S. of OSSUS WOOD, and established posts at X.24.c.9.1. and 9.6.	
	5.25 p.m.		Divisional Order G.61 issued relative to relief of 37 Bde. night 30th/1st by 53rd Bde. 18th Division.	
	7.40 p.m.		37 Bde. reported on line of CANAL.	
			During the day, 4 prisoners, numerous M.Gs and one 77 m.m. gun were captured.	

Casualties for month ending
31st Sept. 1918.
Officers K. 15 W. 41 M. 4
O.R.s 444 2244 408

H.B. Higginson
Major-General,
Commanding, 12th Division.

S E C R E T.

Copy No.

12th DIVISION ORDER No. 280.

4th September

1. The 12th Division will relieve the 18th Division in the Left Sector of III Corps front on the night 4th/5th instant.

2. The Divisional boundaries will be as follows :-
Southern boundary - an East and West line through C.11.a.0.6.
Northern boundary - an East and West line through U.17.c.0.0.
The boundary between Brigades at present is an East and West line through U.30.c.0.0.

3. 36th Infantry Brigade will relieve 55th Infantry Brigade on the Right: 35th Infantry Brigade will relieve 53rd Infantry Brigade on the Left.
The line will be taken over as held, and adjustments will be made during the night 5th/6th instant for the attack.
37th Infantry Brigade will relieve 54th Infantry Brigade in the line of trenches running North and South through the Western end of FREGICOURT.
Headquarters of 54th Infantry Brigade is at S.30.a.9.6.

4. One Company of 12th Battn. M.G. Corps will remain attached to each Infantry Brigade as at present.

5. One Section, Field Company R.E. will be attached to each Infantry Brigade.

6. Buses have been arranged as follows :-
35th Brigade Group. (35th Infantry Brigade with attached M.G. Company and Section R.E.).
Busses facing N., head at BRIQUETERIE, A.4.b.3.3., on MARICOURT - BERNAFAY WOOD Road, at 3.30 p.m.
Route. GUILLEMONT - COMBLES - FREGICOURT - U.14.c.0.0.

37th Brigade Group (37th Brigade with attached M.G. Coy. and Section R.E. and Reserve Machine Gun Company).
Busses facing N., head at BRIQUETERIE, A.4.b.3.3., on MARICOURT) BERNAFAY WOOD Road, about 6 p.m.

7. Command of the line will pass from G.O.C. 18th Division to G.O.C. 12th Division at 9 a.m. on the 5th instant, at which hour 12th Divisional Headquarters will open at B.4.a.2.7.

8. A C K N O W L E D G E.

Issued at 4 a.m.

Lieut.Colonel,
General Staff,
12th Division.

Copies to :-
1. G.O.C.
2. G.S.O.1.
3. 35th Infantry Brigade.
4. 36th Infantry Brigade.
5. 37th Infantry Brigade.
6. C.R.A.
7. C.R.E.
8. 12th Bn. M.G.C.
9. 12th Div. Signal Coy. R.E.
10. 5th Northants Regt.
11. A.A. & Q.M.G.
12. III Corps.
13. 6th Division.
14. 18th Division.
15. 47th Division.
16. 58th Division.
17. 74th Division.
18. 35th Sqdn. R.A.F.
19. Troop, Northd. Hussars
20 & 21. War Diary.
22 - 27. G.S. & Records.

"C" Form
MESSAGES AND SIGNALS.

Army Form C. 2123.

| Prefix | Code | Words | Received From ECO Oliver | Sent, or sent out At ... m. To ... By | Office Stamp. |

Charges to collect

Service Instructions.
Urgent ops pty

Handed in at .... Office 2.15 m. Received 5.10 p.m.

TO 35 Divn

Sender's Number	Day of Month	In reply to Number	AAA
G254	4		

Warning Order aaa In the event of enemy continuing his retirement and the occupation of the NURLU TRENCH system by 18th Divn troops tonight BUSU group will form the advanced guard tomorrow and will pass through RUHA at Dawn aaa VUQU and two troops 22nd corps cavalry will be attached to BUSU group and will be under orders of GOC BUSU aaa objective of advanced guard will be Trench system GUYENCOURT (inclusive) HEUDECOURT station N16d aaa BUVU group with VUSU affiliated will be in

FROM

PLACE & TIME

"C" Form
MESSAGES AND SIGNALS.
Army Form C. 2123.
(In books of 100.)
No. of Message..........

Prefix......Code......Words......	Received	Sent, or sent out	Office Stamp.
£ s. d.	From......	At......m.	
Charges to collect	By......	To......	
Service Instructions.		By......	

Handed in at........................Office........m. Received........m.

TO ②

*Sender's Number	Day of Month	In reply to Number	AAA

Support prepared to form a defensive flank with one battalion and two sections machine guns on the spurs in W20 — W20 — W13 aaa BUZU camps with an Arty Bde affiliated concentration in reserve prepared to move to assembly positions in the Valley SW of SORREL LE GRAND or to occupy the NURLU defenses within the Divl boundaries aaa Divl signal Coy will lay a cable through GOVERNMENT FM — MANANCOURT — NURLU — HEUDECOURT aaa acknowledge aaa addsd Bdes WURA FONI repld all comsd

	G.S.O. 1
FROM	G.S. 12 Bde
	G.
PLACE & TIME 12 Div 3.20 p	G.S.O. 4

3.20 p

* This line should be erased if not required.

"A" Form
MESSAGES AND SIGNALS.

Army Form C. 2121
(In pads of 100.)

TO: 35th Inf. Bde. 36th Inf. Bde. 37th Inf. Bde. C.R.A.
C.R.E. 12th Bn. M.G.C. A.D.M.S. A. & M. "B" Sqdn.
New Zealand Cav. Coy. New Zealand Cyclists. Signals.

Sender's Number: G.1. Day of Month: 5 In reply to Number: Sqdn. R.A.F.
AAA

35th Inf. Bde. will attack on the 5th September and capture trench system East and West of NURLU AAA Objective trench D.10.a.9.6 – D.4.c.9.7 – D.4.b.9.4 – V.29.a.8.6 – V.?.b.9.9 AAA Barrage will open on a North and South grid line between V.20. and V.21 and will remain on this line from 6.45 a.m. till 7.5 a.m. AAA It will then move forward at the rate of 100 yards in 4 minutes until it reaches a protective barrage line 300 yards beyond the objective where it will remain for half an hour and then stop AAA The Southern limit of this barrage will be on East and West line through V.27.c.0.8 AAA Heavy artillery and Field Hows. will open a bombardment at 6.45 a.m. on NURLU and the trench system in the neighbourhood of NURLU also on trench in D.3.d. and V.27.c. AAA This bombardment will be kept far enough South to be safe for a man walking along the East and West grid line through V.27.central and there will be no fire South of an East and West line through D.3.d.0.8 AAA This bombardment will cease at 8.5 a.m. in order to allow troops of 35th Inf. Bde. to clear up NURLU and the trench system as far South as the dvnl. boundary and also the valley in D.5.a. and D.5.c. AAA 36th Inf. Bde. will hold its present front with 1 battalion AAA The Advance Guard consisting of 36th Inf. Bde. (less 1 Battalion) C. Coy. 12 h Bn. M.G.C.

"A" Form
MESSAGES AND SIGNALS.

Army Form C. 2121
(In pads of 100.)

No. of Message............

Prefix.........Code.........m.	Words	Charge.	This message is on a/c of :	Recd. at......m.
Office of Origin and Service Instructions				
....	Sent		........................Service.	Date............
....	At .... m.			From ....
....	To			
....	By		(Signature of "Franking Officer")	By...................

TO

(2)

M.G.C. 1 Section 70th Field Coy. R.E. 1 Troop New
Zealand ~~Cavalry and Platoon New Zealand Cyclists and~~
Bearers of a Field Ambulance will assemble about V.25.
b. and d. ready to move under orders of Division
~~through 35th Inf. Bde. with furthest objective the~~
trench system running from Eastern outskirts
GUYENCOURT to HEUDECOURT Station in W.16.c. AAA
Battalion 36th Inf. Bde. holding the line will be
available for the Advance Guard as soon as the Advance
Guard ~~scanner~~ has moved forward AAA Troop N.Z. Cav.
and Platoon New Zealand Cyclists will report at
Headquarters 36th Inf. Bde. at U.26.c.3.7 on main road
North of RANCOURT at 6 a.m. AAA Brigades must be
careful to safeguard their flanks and will detail
special liaison platoons to gain touch with units of
Divisions on either flank AAA 37th Inf. Bde. with
attached Machine Gun Coy. and Section R.E. will be
in reserve ready to move at half an hours notice AAA
Reserve Coys. of Machine Gun Battalion will be ready
to move at half an hours notice AAA R.E. and
Pioneers will receive instructions from the C.R.E.

| G.S.O.1 |
| G.S.O.2 |
| G.S.O.3 |
| G.S.O.4 |

From
Place 12th Division.
Time

The above may be forwarded as corrected. (Z) Lieut.Colonel,
General Staff.

Censor. Signature of Addressee or person authorised to telegraph in his name
* This line should be erased if not required.

"C" FORM.
MESSAGES AND SIGNALS.

Army Form C. 2123.
(In books of 100.)
No. of Message.........

Prefix......Code......Words 41	Received. From......	Sent, or sent out. At.........m	Office Stamp.
Charges to Collect	By......		
Service Instructions		To............	
West April Pb		By	

Handed in at...VKR......Office 2.0 a.m. Received 2.17 a.m.

TO — 38 Div

*Sender's Number.	Day of Month.	In reply to Number.	AAA
GS	5		

Ref G1 the northern limit of the barrage will be an east and west line through V 20 central aaa There will be no fire in the S ers D 3 or D 2 without further orders

FROM PLACE & TIME	12 Divn 1.35 am

This line should be erased if not required.

"C" Form.
MESSAGES AND SIGNALS.

Army Form C. 2123.
(In books of 100.)

Handed in at ... Office ... m. Received ... 29 ... m.

TO: 3t Divn.

Sender's Number: 96
Day of Month: 5th

GOC. 12th Divn has assumed Command of Left Sector

(10·36 am)

FROM PLACE & TIME: 12 Div 9·0 am

"O" FORM.
MESSAGES AND SIGNALS.

Army Form C. 2123.
(In books of 100.)

Prefix	Code	Words	Received.	Sent, or sent out.	Office Stamp.
			From	At......m.	
Charger Collect			By		
Service Instructions			To......m.		
			By		

Handed in at.............Office.............m. Received.............m.

TO 35 Div

* Sender's Number.	Day of Month.	In reply to Number.	AAA
114	3		
35	Inf	Bde.	will
not	advance	their	left
until	the	situation	on
their	left	flank	is
more	definite	aaa	36
Bde	will	be	prepared
to	move	on	a
one	battalion	front	up
the	spur	in	D8a
and	B	D3c	to
take	NURLU	from	the
south	west	and	mop
past	the	village	and
the	spur	north	east
of	NURLU	in	V23
forming	a	flank	facing
N E	in	conjunction	with

FROM
PLACE & TIME

* This line should be erased if not required.

"O" FORM.   Army Form C. 2123.
MESSAGES AND SIGNALS.   No. of Message..........

Prefix......Code......Words.......... | Received. | Sent, or sent out. | Office Stamp.
                    £ s. d. | From................ | At................m. |
Charges to Collect | By.................. | |
Service Instructions | | To................ |
                                      | | By................ |

Handed in at....................Office..........m. Received..........m.

TO

* Sender's Number.	Day of Month.	In reply to Number.	AAA
35	Bde	asa	Retard
35	and	36	Bdes
and	RA	rptd	3Rd
Corps	and	flank	Divn

114 told   12.54 pm   G.S.O.1
                                        G.S.O.2
                                        G.S.O.3
                                        G.S.O.4

FROM   12 Div
PLACE & TIME   12.5 pm

"O" Form.
MESSAGES AND SIGNALS.

Prefix	Code	Words	Received. From ECO By	Sent, or sent out. At ... in. To ... By	Office Stamp.

Charges to Collect
Service Instructions

Handed in at **9f pty** Office **9.14** m. Received **9.35** m.

TO **38 Div**

Sender's Number.	Day of Month.	In reply to Number.	AAA
438	5		

If	NURLU	is	not
taken	tonight	the	attack
will	be	continued at	
8	am	6th	inst
aaa	BUJU	on	right
BUVU	on	left	aaa
DIVIDING	line	between	Brigades
trench	running	E.	and
W.	through	V28	central
aaa	objective the		trench
system	from	D10a9.6	along
the	eastern	edge	of
NURLU	to	V29a5.6	thence
along	road	to	V23c4.1
— Trench	V22b6.2	— Trench	V16c4.0
aaa	If the		Division
on	our	left	advances

FROM
PLACE & TIME

"C" FORM.
MESSAGES AND SIGNALS.

Army Form C. 2123.
(In books of 100.)

Prefix......Code......Words.........	Received.	Sent, or sent out.	Office Stamp.
£ s. d.	From...RCO	At...............m.	
Charges to Collect	By...........		
Service Instructions		To...............	
		By...........	

Handed in at......7/1......Office......9.0...m. Received......9......m.

TO ②

* Sender's Number.	Day of Month.	In reply to Number.	AAA

to line of trenches in V16d and V22B junction will be in trench at V22B6.0 aaa patrols will be pushed forward immediately after the protective barrage lifts to establish and maintain touch with the enemy followed by companies to make good ground gained as far as the line D11a5.6 — D5B5.0 — V29B2.0 V22B6.2 aaa CRE will arrange for batteries to move tonight to the east of the canal to

FROM
PLACE & TIME

"C" Form.
MESSAGES AND SIGNALS.

Army Form C. 2123
(In books of 100.)

Prefix	Code	Words		Received.	Sent, or sent out.	Office Stamp.
		£ s. d.		From..........	At..........m.	
Charge to Collect				By..........	To..........	
Service Instructions					By..........	

Handed in at.......4/4..........Office.....8.10....m. Received..........m.

TO ③

* Sender's Number.	Day of Month.	In reply to Number.	AAA

support a further advance aaa the attack will be made under a barrage details of which will be forwarded later aaa Brigade commanders will forward as soon as possible the line west of which artillery cannot fire aaa addsd all concerned

(9·50 pm)

| G.S.O. 1 |
| G.S.O. 2 |
| G.S.O. 3 |
| G.S.O. 4 |

FROM
PLACE & TIME   12 Div   7.55 pm

"O" FORM.
MESSAGES AND SIGNALS.

Army Form C. 2123.
(In books of 100.)

| Prefix AA | Code | Words 57 | Received From 2Cu By Olive | Sent, or sent out. At .... m. To .... By .... | Office Stamp. |

Charges — Collect
Service Instructions

Handed in at JL OO .... Office 4.51 m. Received 6.48 m.

TO   38 Div

*Sender's Number.	Day of Month.	In reply to Number.	AAA
139	5		

The nothern boundary between
Divs now runs through
Y21c04 — Y22a02 Y23a00 — W72c00
thence due east aaa.
Southern boundary between Divs
remains the same ie
east and west line
through D8a06 aaa added
Bdes CRA CRE mly
Bn Pioneers signals Q
adms aPm 47 Div
38 Div 21 Div
Anthony
10.0 lu   G.S.O.1 ✓
            G.S.O.
            G.S.O.
            G.S.O.

FROM
PLACE & TIME   12 Div
                  8·30 pm

*This line should be erased if not required.

"C" Form
MESSAGES AND SIGNALS.

Army Form C. 2123.
(In books of 100.)

No. of Message..................

Prefix......Code.......Words......	Received	Sent, or sent out	Office Stamp.
£ s. d.	From..................	At.................m.	
Charges to collect	By.....................	To..................	
Service Instructions.		By..................	

Handed in at.................. Office........... m. Received 6.45 m.

TO ....

*Sender's Number	Day of Month	In reply to Number	AAA

37 Bde group forming the advance guard will contain the advance convoys and will pass through the field by 96th and 25th Bde groups in E1 and E25 at ??? ??? ??? ??? Northumberland Hussars will be attached to the advance guard for the day and will report at Headquarters 37th Inf Bde V28.b2.5 NURLU one hour before zero aaa first objective the trench system eastern edge of GUYENCOURT to W22.d.4.0 aaa Second objective high ground E10.b3 — E4D — JACQUENNE COPSE aaa Third

FROM
PLACE & TIME

* This line should be erased if not required.

"C" Form.
MESSAGES AND SIGNALS.

Army Form C. 2123.
(In books of 100.)
No. of Message

Prefix	Code	Words		Received, From	Sent, or sent out. At m.	Office Stamp.
	£	s.	d.			
Charges to Collect				By	To	
Service Instructions					By	

Handed in at		G.S.O. 1	m. Received. m.
TO	(2)	G.S.O. 2	
		G.S.O. 3	
Sender's Number	Day of Month	G.S.O. In reply to Number	AAA
7121			

objective eastern outskirts of EPEHY and railway east of PEIZIERE aaa Touch will be maintained with the Divs on either flanks by special troops detailed for the purpose aaa Details of artillery fire will be issued later aaa acknowledge aaa Added Bdes WULA Northumberland Hussars reptd Corps flank Divns 5 Sqdrn RAF and all units concerned

6/11

FROM	12 Div
PLACE & TIME	5.0 Pm

*This line should be erased if not required.
(27802) Wt. W14832/M1523. [E 930] 100,000 Pads 3/17. M.R.Co.,Ltd. Forms C/2123.

SECRET.

Copy No. 19

12th Division Instructions for Defence No. 2.

1. As a precautionary measure the Division will be prepared to occupy the line of defences from the Southern Corps boundary at J.12.b.9.0 via TINCOURT WOOD D.20.b., D.16.d. and b., NURLU, to V.16.a.9.0 and to be in occupation of this line 6 hours after the order has been received at Divisional Headquarters.

2. On receipt of the order "MAN NURLU LINE" 35th Inf. Bde. will occupy the Southern portion of the line between the Corps Southern boundary (an East and West line through J.10.central) and the present boundary between Divisions (the East and West grid line between E.7. and E.13.). 36th Inf. Bde. will occupy the Northern portion of the line, between the East and West grid line between E.7. and E.13. and the Northern Corps boundary (an East and West line through V.16.d.9.0).
37th Inf. Bde. will be in Divisional Reserve assembled about D.7. and D.13.

3. 12th Machine Gun Battalion will be prepared to place 3 Companies in positions for the defence in depth of the whole of the above line with one Coy. in Divisional Reserve assembled about D.7. and D.13.

4. Reconnaissance will be carried out forthwith for the occupation of this line, and schemes for occupation forwarded to Divisional Headquarters.

5. The five Field Artillery Brigades in Corps Reserve will be available for covering this line, under the command of C.R.A. 12th Division, under orders which will be issued by G.O.C., R.A., IIIrd Corps.

6. Messages will be prepared at Divisional, Infantry Brigade, Artillery Brigade and Battalion Headquarters ready for signature, giving the order "MAN NURLU LINE", and arrangements will be made to ensure that the line will be occupied without delay on receipt of these messages.

7. All Infantry and M.G. posts will be marked with notice boards, and positions of command posts from platoons upwards.
No work will be done on the line at present, nor will any ammunition be dumped.

8. Infantry Brigade Commanders and the O.C. Machine Gun Battn. will arrange that the troops under their command will stand to on their positions as soon as the dispositions have been decided upon.
Range tables for all Machine Gun and Lewis Gun positions will be prepared.

Lieut.Colonel,
General Staff,
12th Division.

11th September, 1918.

/Copies to ......

Copies to :-

1. G.O.C.
2. G.S.O.1.
3. C.R.A.
4. C.R.E.
5. 35th Infantry Brigade.
6. 36th Infantry Brigade.
7. 37th Infantry Brigade.
8. 5th Northamptonshire Regt. (Pioneers).
9. 12th Battn. M.G. Corps.
10. 12th Div. Signal Coy. R.E.
11. A.D.M.S.
12. D.A.D.V.S.
13. A.P.M.
14. "Q".
15. III Corps.
16. 18th Division.
17. 21st Division.
18. 46th Division.
19. 58th Division.
20 & 21. War Diary.
22 - 26. G.S. and Records.

"C" Form.
MESSAGES AND SIGNALS.
Army Form C. 2123
(In books of 100.)

No. of Message..........

Prefix.........Code........Words........ Received From .... Sent, or sent out........ Office Stamp.

Charges to Collect

Service Instructions.

Handed in at .... Office .... m. Received .... m.

TO 58 Div

*Sender's Number	Day of Month	In reply to Number	
J68	12		AAA

Ref 12th Div Instructions for Defence no 2 Para 1 line 4 for 11oa 9.0 read 1/16 29.0

SEEN BY :-
G.O.C.
G.S.O.1
G.S.O.11
G.S.O.111

890
2.5p

FROM: 12 Div
TIME & PLACE: 1.15 pm

SECRET.
Copy No.

12th Division Order No. 282.

14th September, 1918.

1. At Zero hour on Z Day, 12th Division will take part in an attack which is being made on a wide front.

2. 18th Division is attacking on the right of the 12th Division, and a Division of the V Corps on the left.

3. 35th Infantry Brigade will attack on the Right, 36th Infantry Brigade on the Left, passing through troops of the 58th Division now in the line.
When those Brigades have captured the first objective, 37th Infantry Brigade will pass through and attack the second objective.

4. Boundary lines of the zone of attack of 12th Division are shown in green ink on the attached map.
Boundary line between 35th and 36th Infantry Brigades is as follows :- Bend in trench at E.6.b.6.2 - South Eastern corner of FISHERS KEEP at F.1.a.15.15 thence along road to the T of WEEDON POST and the prolongation of this road to the grid line between X.25. and F.1., thence due East along this grid line.

5. Objectives are shown on the attached map:

    First Objective ... the GREEN LINE.
    Second Objective ... the RED LINE.
    Line of exploitation the BLUE LINE.

There will be a pause of about an hour on the GREEN LINE, after which 37th Infantry Brigade will pass through 35th and 36th Infantry Brigades and will attack and capture the RED LINE.
Protective barrage will remain in front of this line for half an hour, after which 37th Infantry Brigade will exploit success as far as the BLUE LINE, the object being to secure the RED LINE and such positions in front of it as will give observation and assist our further advance.

6. Barrage for 35th and 36th Infantry Brigades is shown in yellow on the map.
Assembly positions will be selected by Brigades behind the barrage start lines.
In order that the barrage for 36th Infantry Brigade may catch up the barrage of 35th Infantry Brigade, the first four lifts of the latter will be at the rate of 100 yards in five minutes; remainder of the barrage will move at the rate of 100 yards in 4 minutes.
Barrage for 37th Infantry Brigade will be issued later.

7. Four tanks will be available. Two tanks each are allotted to 35th and 36th Infantry Brigades, but they will not go East of the line MALASSISE FARM - trench in F.2.c. - F.1.b. - X.25.c. and X.25.a.

/8. ....

(2).

8. Two Sections, 12th Battalion, Machine Gun Corps will be under the orders of each of 35th and 36th Infantry Brigades and one Company 12th Bn. M.G.C. under the orders of 37th Infantry Brigade, the remainder being under the orders of O.C., 12th Bn. M.G.C., who will keep one Company in Divisional Reserve.

9. Some machine guns and trench mortars of the 58th Division will be available to assist in the attack from their present positions.

10. It is to be remembered that the trench systems included in the zone of attack are well known to the enemy, whose guns are probably in positions from which they are already registered. It will, therefore, be preferable to dig a new defence line rather than to occupy existing trench systems.

11. The importance of secrecy must be impressed on all ranks.
Many old buried cables exist in the area, which make it easy for the enemy to pick up telephone conversations by means of listening sets which are, no doubt, already installed in the HINDENBURG LINE.
Officers and men must not expose themselves when reconnoitring.
After troops are in position telephone will not be used for communication within the Division previous to the attack, except in cases of urgent necessity.

12. The Division will go into position for the attack on Y Day.

13. Further orders will be issued later.

14. A C K N O W L E D G E.

J. B. Bedgrave
Lieut.Colonel,
General Staff,
12th Division.

Issued at 6 a.m.

Copies to :-

1. G.O.C.
2. G.S.O.1.
3. C.R.A.
4. C.R.E.
5. 35th Infantry Brigade.
6. 36th Infantry Brigade.
7. 37th Infantry Brigade.
8. 12th Bn. M.G. Corps.
9. 5th Northamptonshire Regt.
10. 12th Signal Coy. R.E.
11. A.D.M.S.
12. A.P.M.
13. "Q".
14. III Corps.
15. 18th Division.
16. 21st Division.
17. 58th Division.
18. Division, V Corps.
19. 35th Sqdn. R.A.F.
20. Tank Battn.
21 & 22. War Diary.
23 - 28. G.S. and Records.

Maps issued to Infantry Brigades only.

G.O.C.

SECRET.

Copy No. 4

12th DIVISION ORDER No. 283.

18th September, 1918.

1. 12th Division Order No. 282 is cancelled.

2. At Zero hour on 'Z' day, 12th Division will take part in an attack which is being made on a wide front.

3. 18th Division is attacking on the right of 12th Division; 58th Division will be on the left of 12th Division as far as the GREEN Line; forward of the GREEN Line 21st Division will be on the left of the 12th Division.

4. The attack on the GREEN Line will be carried out by 36th Infantry Brigade (less one battalion) on the right; 35th Infantry Brigade on the left.

The main attack of the 35th Infantry Brigade will be in a North-Easterly direction from the approx. line E.12.d.8.7. to E.12.a.6.7.

The 35th Infantry Brigade is detailing two companies to advance on the right of 58th Division to deal with FISHERS KEEP and WEEDON POST.

36th Infantry Brigade (less one battalion) will detail sufficient troops to move on the right of 35th Infantry Brigade to clear the area as far East as railway line in F.7.a., b. and c. and F.1.d.

The Brigade will be formed up on the line of the railway ready to advance on the GREEN LINE at Zero plus 90 minutes.

35th Infantry Brigade and 36th Infantry Brigade will report their exact forming up positions by noon 17th September.

One battalion, 36th Infantry Brigade will be under the orders of G.O.C., 37th Infantry Brigade.

Brigade Commanders concerned will arrange its march to the forward area and the time the command will pass.

37th Infantry Brigade will move forward in rear of 35th and 36th Infantry Brigades. It will be formed up close to the barrage ready to advance on the RED Line at Zero plus 190 mins.

Alternative routes for assembly positions must be reconnoitred so that, in the event of the route chosen being blocked by fighting or by shell fire the alternative route will be taken without further orders.

The main objective of the attack of this Brigade is the LITTLE PRIEL FARM spur including the Farm itself, and the KILDARE POST spur.

The Brigade will capture and consolidate the RED Line and exploit to the BLUE Line.

5. Boundary lines of the Zone of Attack of the 12th Division are shown in BLUE on the attached map.

Boundary line between 36th and 35th Infantry Brigades is shown by dotted GREEN Line.

6. Objectives are shown on attached map; first objective the GREEN Line; second objective the RED Line; Line of Exploitation BLUE Line.

/The GREEN and RED Lines

The GREEN Line and the RED Line will be consolidated in depth.
The following posts on the RED Line System will be constructed by the R.E. and 5th Northamptonshire Regt. under orders of the C.R.E. :-

    (i) about F.4.d.5.9.   (iii) about KILDARE POST.
    (ii) about LITTLE PRIEL FM.   (iv) about HORSE POST
    (v) about X.27.b.2.5.

These posts will be garrisoned in the first instance by a suitable proportion of the troops who have dug them.

The Brigade Commander, 37th Infantry Brigade, will arrange for the relief of the R.E. and Pioneers by Infantry as soon as the tactical situation is clear. Royal Engineers and Pioneers are not to be retained longer than necessary.

Reconnoitring Patrols will be pushed forward from the BLUE line to Canal and through VENDHUILLE Village to ascertain if the enemy is still west of the canal and if there are any means of crossing it.

7.   Barrage for 35th Infantry Brigade is shown in YELLOW and those for 36th and 37th Infantry Brigades in BROWN on the attached map.

Barrage start line for 35th Infantry Brigade is marked "S - S"; for 36th Infantry Brigade "K - K"; and for 37th Infantry Brigade "F - F".

Barrage for 35th Infantry Brigade will move at 100 yards in 4 minutes for the first 3 lifts; it will then move at 100 yds. in 5 minutes for 6 lifts; after which it will move at 100 yds. in 4 minutes until it reaches the protector.

Barrage for 36th Infantry Brigade will move at 100 yds. in 3 minutes; for 37th Infantry Brigade at 100 yds. in 4 minutes.

The Protective barrage for the GREEN Line will remain until Zero plus 190 minutes, and will then move forward at the rate of 100 yards in 4 minutes. It will thicken up three minutes before the advance to warn the troops of the lift.

8.   112th Field Artillery Brigade will be in close support of 37th Infantry Brigade, and under the orders of G.O.C., 37th Infantry Brigade.

9.   After capturing the RED Line, 37th Infantry Brigade will exploit towards the BLUE Line, making a special effort to secure THE QUARRIES in X.29.d.

10.   Present dispositions of the enemy opposite the 12th Divisional front are believed to be—from RANSOY to PETZIERES—Alpine Corps with Body infantry Regt. 1st Jaeger Regt. and 2nd Jaeger Regt.

11.   Two Tanks are available. They will start with 35th Infantry Brigade and will mop up the village of EPEHY: they will then move to DEELISH POST, keeping on the Southern side of the ridge which runs from EPEHY towards LEMPIRE. After mopping up the trenches in the neighbourhood of DEELISH POST, they will return via valley in F.7.d. and 13. a., mopping up on the way.

All ranks of the infantry will be warned that it is their duty to protect the tanks from Anti-tank guns, and to engage these guns with rifle and Lewis gun fire. Tanks themselves, on account of their limited field of view, are incapable of engaging Anti-tank guns rapidly.

In order to protect the tanks, smoke shell will be used in the barrage, and C.R.A. will detail special Howitzer batteries to make a smoke screen on the trenches between DEELISH POST and NORTH Lane.

13.   2 Sections, 12th Bn. M.G.C.

13.   Two sections, 12th Battalion, Machine Gun Corps will be under orders of each of the 35th and 36th Infantry Brigades, and one company, 12th Battalion Machine Gun Corps under the orders of 37th Infantry Brigade.

O.C., 12th Battalion Machine Gun Corps will arrange in consultation with Brigade Commanders the approximate ultimate positions for defence of these guns.

Headquarters and 2 companies, 100th Battalion Machine Gun Corps are allotted to 12th Division. These companies, together with the remainder of the 12th Battn. be under the orders of O.C., 12th Bn. M.G.Corps will one of his own companies in Divisional reserve.

14.   Stokes Mortars must be pushed well forward to deal with Machine Gun Nests.

15.   Liaison posts on the flanks of the Division are shown by GREEN spots on map. Special parties will be told off to get into touch at these points. Every unit will pay special attention to the defence of its flanks.

A special detachment, of not less than 1 Platoon will be detailed by 37th Infantry Brigade at the junction of KILDARE AVENUE and the Cross Roads (X.22.c.4.3.) and at Southern end of BRAETON POST (F.5.c.3.5.), to form a combined post with 21st Division, V Corps on the left, and with 18th Division on the right, to ensure possession of the high ground.

16.   Tracings showing Machine Gun barrages will be issued shortly.

17.   One troop 1/1st Northumberland Hussars, has been placed at the disposal of 12th Division. Two mounted men will be attached to each of 35th and 36th Infantry Brigades and not less than 4 to 37th Infantry Brigade.

18.   35th Infantry Brigade will move to LIBRAMONT on the morning of the 17th. 35th and 36th Infantry Brigades will move, under cover of darkness, on the evening of the 17th, to positions about F.11.d. and s. respectively. 37th Infantry Brigade will move to a position near SAULCOURT, which will be notified as soon as possible.

19.   The necessity for secrecy must be impressed on all ranks.

Officers and other ranks must be careful not to expose themselves when reconnoitring.

After troops are in position on the 17th, there will be no telephone communication within the Division, except in case of urgent necessity.

20.   In the event of the capture of hostile guns, information will immediately be sent to the nearest Infantry Brigade Headquarters for transmission to the Artillery, giving exact location of guns, nature of guns, and whether ammunition is at hand. This information will be passed on to the C.R.A., who will arrange to send up personnel to mann the guns. On no account will spare parts, sights, etc., be removed as souvenirs from captured guns.

21. C.R.E. will detail one section Field Coy. R.E. to be under orders of each Infantry Brigade; 1 section Field Coy. R.E. to be under orders of C.R.A. and 1 section under orders of O.C., 18th Battn. M.G. Corps, to assist guns and machine guns to advance rapidly.

C.R.E. will detail pioneers to clear the road from SAULCOURT via HAINTON (W.17.c.), and EPEHY to LEMPIRE.

He will also detail special parties of R.E. to reconnoitre for water and install pumps, reporting all details as soon as possible to C.E., III Corps.

22. Contact aeroplanes will fly over the Corps front at the following hours :- Zero plus 2 hours 15 minutes: Zero plus 5 hours: Zero plus 7 hours.

Troops will be specially warned to keep a look out for these planes, and to indicate their location by means of RED flares, discs, rifles in rows, and waving of helmets.

Brigade and Battalion Headquarters will display their ground signal sheets and strips.

Dropping Station will be established close to Divisional Headquarters.

23. 35th Brigade, R.A.F. are supplying aeroplanes for machine-gunning and bombing hostile batteries, and also columns of troops and transport on roads in rear of BLUE Line.

24. Aeroplanes will be sent up on 'Y' / 'Z' night at hours to be notified later to drown the noise of tanks.

25. A Counter-attack plane will be up continuously from daylight with the sole mission of detecting enemy counter-attacks. The plane will fly in the direction of the enemy troops and drop a white parachute flare as near to the counter-attack troops as possible.

The 3rd and Australian Corps S.O.S. Signal will be :- rifle grenade bursting into 3 stars RED over RED over RED.

The 5th Corps S.O.S. will be :- rifle grenade bursting into three stars, GREEN over RED over GREEN.

26. Watches will be synchronized at present 36th Brigade H.Q. at V.28.c.3.1. at 7 p.m., 17th.

27. At Zero hour Command Posts of Brigades will be as follows :-
35th Infantry Brigade   -   approx. E.3.d.2.7.
36th Infantry Brigade   -   approx. E.3.c.0.7.
37th Infantry Brigade   -   approx. E.3.c.2.7.

Brigade Commander, 37th Infantry Brigade, will arrange, in consultation with his Artillery Brigade Commander and the O.C. Divl. Signal Coy. the approximate position to which he will move when he moves forward and will report same to Divisional Headquarters.

O.C. Divl. Signal Coy. will arrange to lay lines as far forward as possible towards the present front line.

Divisional Headquarters will be at D.15.d.8.8.

28. ACKNOWLEDGE.

Lieut-Colonel,
General Staff,
18th Division.

Issued at 6 a.m.

5/Distribution.

Distribution - 12th Division Order No. 283.

1. G.O.C.
2. G.S.O.1.
3. C.R.A.
4. C.R.E.
5. 35th Infantry Brigade.
6. 36th Infantry Brigade.
7. 37th Infantry Brigade.
8. 12th Bn. M.G.Corps.
9. 5th Northamptonshire Regt.
10. 12th Div. Signal Coy., R.E.
11. A.D.M.S.
12. A.P.M.
13. "Q".
14. III Corps.
15. 18th Division.
16. 21st Division.
17. 58th Division.
18. 35th Squad., R.A.F.
19. Tank Battn.
20 & 21. War Diary.
22 - 27. G.S. and Records.

SECRET.

12th Division No. G.O. 132.

15th September, 1918.

Reference 12th Division Order No. 283.

"Z" day will be 18th September, 1918. Zero hour will be notified to Brigades during the afternoon of "Y" day.

Lieut-Colonel,
General Staff,
12th Division.

Addsd. all recipients of 12th Division Order No. 283.

SECRET.

Addendum to 12th Division Order No. 283 -
Divisional O.P. Arrangements.

1. On 17th instant a Divisional O.P. will be established at North end of CHAFFEURS WOOD at E.10.a.
This O.P. will be manned till Zero plus 90.

2. As soon as leading troops advance from GREEN LINE on Z Day, an O.P. will be established in ROOM TRENCH at approx. X.26.central.

3. Units will give the observers all possible facilities for the transmission of information to Divisional Headquarters. N.C.O. i/c Observers will repeat all such information to the nearest Infantry H.Q.

for Lieut.Colonel,
General Staff,
12th Division.

17th September, 1918.

Copies to :-

    C.R.A.
    35th Infantry Brigade.
    36th Infantry Brigade.
    37th Infantry Brigade.
    12th Bn. M.G. Corps.
    18th Division.
    N.C.O. i/c Observers.

Guide   4 a 6 7 to take them to E & 6 65
where forming Kishas Keep & Weedon Post
down rly.

12 c 50 goes with right of Norfolks
Roche S. to rly. then to 36.

SECRET.

Copy No. 2.

Addition to 12th Division Order No. 283.

1. 12th Division will move into concentration area on the night 17th/18th as follows :-

    35th Brigade - In the Valley about E.11.d. and E.18.a.

    36th Brigade - About square: E.10.

    37th Brigade - Squares E.2.c. and d., E.3.c. and d., E.8. and E.9.

2. No movement East of the NURLU - PERONNE Road will take place before 7 p.m.

    Area allotted to 12th Division is shown on the attached tracing. These boundaries come into operation at 10 p.m. 17th.

    In moving up to concentration area troops will keep to this area as far as possible.

3. Following times are allotted to Brigades to pass the NURLU - PERONNE Road :-

    35th Brigade -- 7 p.m. to 7.30 p.m.

    36th Brigade -- 7.30 p.m. to 8.0 p.m.

    37th Brigade -- 8.0 p.m. onwards.

4. A C K N O W L E D G E.

    Lieut.Colonel,
    General Staff,
    12th Division.

Issued at

Copies to :-

    1. G.O.C.
    2. G.S.O.1.
    3. C.R.A.
    4. C.R.E.
    5. 35th Infantry Brigade.
    6. 36th Infantry Brigade.
    7. 37th Infantry Brigade.
    8. 12th Bn. M.G. Corps.
    9. 5th Northamptonshire Regt. (Pioneers).
    10. 12th Div. Signal Coy. R.E.
    11. A.D.M.S.
    12. D.A.D.V.S.
    13. A.P.M.
    14. "Q".
    15. 58th Division.
    16. 38th Division.
    17. 2nd Tank Battalion.
    18 & 19. War Diary.
    20 - 25. G.S. and Records.

SECRET.

Copy No. _____

Addition No. 2 to 12th Division Order No. 283.

1. As soon as Brigades are in positions of assembly ready to advance, they will send to Divisional Headquarters the code word "PLUM".

2. As soon as it is known that 37th Infantry Brigade have established themselves on the RED LINE, 35th Infantry Brigade will take over the whole of the defence of the GREEN LINE from the Divisional Boundary at F.9.c.5.9 to X.26.e.9.9.

   On relief, 36th Infantry Brigade (less 1 Battalion) will be withdrawn into Divisional Reserve South and West of LEFHY about squares E.6. and 12.

   Headquarters for 35th and 36th Infantry Brigades will be established close to each other about E.5.d., E.11.? or E.12.

3. The protective barrage on the RED LINE will remain for 20 minutes and will then stop.

   60 pounders will fire on the QUARRIES till Zero plus 300 and will then fire on OSSUS WOOD for 6 minutes, and will then stop.

   Patrols will be sent out as soon as the protective barrage lifts.

   If the BLUE LINE is found to be held the advance from the RED LINE will begin at Zero plus 420 minutes.

   Special arrangements will be made by 37th Infantry Brigade for obtaining information as to whether our patrols have been able to make good the BLUE LINE.

   This information will be sent back by runner and visual to 37th Infantry Brigade Command Post, and will also be sent by pigeon.

   It is very important that the message should reach the Brigade as early as possible to enable them to inform the Artillery regarding the barrage.

   The barrage will be ordered by G.O.C. 37th Infantry Brigade and arrangements made by him with Colonel QUERIPEL.

   It has been arranged that Colonel QUERIPEL will be in touch with and will have a call on all five Field Artillery Brigades for this operation.

4. At Zero Hour on Z Day the following troops will be in Divisional Reserve :-

   1 Troop, Northumberland Hussars at Divisional Headquarters.

   5th Northamptonshire Regt. (Pioneers) -- D.11.d.

   69th and 87th Field Coys. R.E. (less 3 Sections) - in E.14.c.

   D. Coy. 12th Bn. M.G. Corps. -- E.9.a.6.6.

   B. Coy. 100th Bn. M.G. Corps. Do.

/5.

(2).

5. The following success signal will be fired as soon as troops have established themselves on the GREEN and RED LINES:

Rifle Grenade bursting into 3 stars - WHITE over WHITE over WHITE.

6. The following signals between Tanks and Infantry must be impressed on all ranks :-

Tanks to Infantry.

Green and White flag   -   Come on, all clear.

Red and Yellow flag   -   I am broken down: go on.

Red, White and Blue   -   Tank is coming back to refill.
Tricolour.

Infantry to Tanks.

Steel helmet raised on muzzle of rifle - Tank wanted here (or in direction rifle is pointed.)

7. If an enfilade barrage is likely to be arranged for the BLUE LINE, troops must be reminded that they cannot get as close to an enfilade barrage as they can to an overhead barrage.

[signature]

Lieut.Colonel,
General Staff,
12th Division.

Issued at

Copies to :-

1. G.O.C.
2. G.S.O.1.
3. C.R.A.
4. C.R.E.
5. 35th Infantry Brigade.
6. 36th Infantry Brigade.
7. 37th Infantry Brigade.
8. 12th Bn. M.G. Corps.
9. 5th Northamptonshire Regt. (Pioneers).
10. 12th Div. Signal Coy. R.E.
11. A.D.M.S.
12. D.A.D.V.S.
13. A.P.M.
14. "Q".
15. Troop, Northumberland Hussars.
16. 58th Division.
17. 18th Division.
18. 2nd Tank Battalion.
19 & 20. War Diary.
21 - 26. G.S. and Records.

"A" Form
MESSAGES AND SIGNALS.

Army Form C. 2121
(In pads of 100.)

No. of Message......

Prefix..........Code..........m.	Words	Charge	This message is on a/c of:	Recd. at......m.
Office of Origin and Service Instructions		Sent		Date............
		At	Copy	
TR 15		To	..................Service.	From ....
		By	(Signature of "Franking Officer")	By..........

TO { *Tpr Gun*

Sender's Number.	Day of Month	In reply to Number.	AAA
9823	16		

(*illegible*)			

From
Place
Time

The above may be forwarded as now corrected.   (Z)

....
Censor,   Signature of Addressor or person authorised to telegraph in his name
* This line should be erased if not required.

Order No. 1625   Wt. W3253/   P 511   27/2   H. & K., Ltd. (E. 2634)

"A" Form
MESSAGES AND SIGNALS.

Army Form C. 2121
(In pads of 100.)

No. of Message............

Prefix........Code........m.	Words	Charge	This message is on a/c of:	Recd. at......m.
Office of Origin and Service Instructions	Sent		....................Service.	Date............

FO   VAQA   VAWU   LOJO   GOLU   "Q"
REVU   A.D.M.S.   3rd Corps   18th Divn.
21st Divn.   58th Divn.

TO   G.164   18

The line will be consolidated and held tonight at all costs by 36th Inf. Bde. on right
and 35th Inf. Bde. on left AAA Boundary
between Bdes. Rly. at F.2.a.0.8. - trench
at F.2.a.0.0. - trench at F.3.b.0.5. - AAA
37th Inf. Bde. will be withdrawn into reserve
and reorganized ready to attack tomorrow
morning AAA 37th Inf. Bde. will attack
tomorrow on right passing through 36th Inf.
Bde. - 35th Inf. Bde. will attack on left
AAA Objective line BRAETON POST - BIRD TRENCH
- MULE TRENCH - X.28.a.0.0. - OCKENDEN TRENCH
- ROOM TRENCH AAA Dividing line as above
AAA Barrage will open at 11.0 a.m. and will
move forward at 11.20 a.m. at the rate of
100 yards in 4 minutes AAA It will pause for
20 minutes after it has moved about 900 yds.
and will then move forward to a line 300 yds.
clear of the objective where it will form a
protective barrage for half an hour to cover
consolidation AAA Start line will be issued
later AAA The objective line will be consolidated in depth and held as a Main Line of
Resistance AAA Acknowledge AAA Addsd. Divl.
Units.reptd. Corps & Flank Divns.
12th Division.
11.55 p.m.

From
Place   G.S.
Time

The above may be forwarded as now corrected.   (Z)

....
Censor.   Signature of Addresser or person authorised to telegraph in his name
* This line should be erased if not required.

Order No. 1625.   Wt. W3253/   P 511.   27/2.   H. & K., Ltd. (E. 2820)

MESSAGES AND SIGNALS.

Prefix... Code... m.	Words	Charge.	This message is on a/c of:	Recd. at......m.
Office of origin and Service Instructions		Sent		Date..........
....	At	6 m.	..........Service.	From ....
....	To			
....	By	(Signature of "Franking Officer")		By..........

TO: VAPO VAQA VAWU LOJO GOLU REVU 3rd Corps.
18th Divn. 21st Divn. 58th Divn. 33rd Div.
Tpl/1st North'd Hssrs.

Sender's Number.	Day of Month.	In reply to Number.	AAA
G. 181	19		

As soon as 37th Inf. Bde. have passed through
the 36th Inf. Bde. 36th will withdraw one
Bn. and concentrate it in the vicinity of
W.30.a. ready to advance this afternoon from
line of SUNKEN ROAD in X.20.d. and X.26.a.
with the object of capturing LARK SPUR and
KILDARE POST AAA The right of the 21st. Divn.
will be secured by establishing posts along the
line of KILDARE AVENUE from LIMERICK POST
(exclusive) to the SUNKEN ROAD at X.26.b.8.3.
(inclusive) AAA Touch will be maintained with
the 21st Divn. at LIMERICK POST and with the
58th Divn. in POPLAR TRENCH and liaison posts
established AAA 21st Divn. will be advancing
simultaneously on the left with the object of
capturing LIMERICK TRENCH AAA As soon as
KILDARE POST has been captured troops will be
pushed along the SUNKEN ROAD to gain touch with
37th Inf. Bde. about X.28.central where a
combined post will be established AAA 2
sections D Coy. 12th Bn. M.G.C. are placed
under the orders of 36th Inf. Bde., four of

From	
Place	..1..
Time	

The above may be forwarded as now corrected. (Z)

....
Censor. Signature of Addressor or person authorised to telegraph in his name
* This line should be erased if not required.

Order No. 1625. Wt. W3253/ P 511 27/2 H. & K., Ltd. (E. 2634).

"A" Form
MESSAGES AND SIGNALS.

Army Form C. 2121
(In pads of 100.)

Prefix......Code...... Words	Charge.	This message is on a/c of :	Recd. at......m.
Office of Origin and Service Instructions	Sent		
	At......m.	......Service.	Date..........
	To		From ....
	By	(Signature of "Franking Officer")	By..........

TO	.. 2 ..		

Sender's Number.	Day of Month.	In reply to Number.	AAA
G.181 (cont.)			

which are already in position at X.26.a.
8.1. AAA In addition M.Guns will be
placed in positions to bring fire on to
CATELET VALLEY AAA B.G.C. 36th Inf.
Bde. will consult with B.G.C. Right Bde.
21st Divn. (110th Inf. Bde.) H.Q. at
W.18.d.2.3. and arrange details regarding
points of junction etc. AAA

In conjunction with the attack the 37th
Inf. Bde. will attack and capture LITTLE
PRIEL Fm. and gain touch with the 36th Inf.
Bde. at about X.28.central where a combined
post will be established AAA 37th Inf.
Bde. will detail troops to clear CATELET
VALLEY AAA Details of barrage will be
notified later AAA Acknowledge AAA Added.
Divl. Units. Corps Flank Divs. North'd
Hsrs.

U.O.P.

From   12th Division.
Place
Time   11.50 a.m.

"A" Form
MESSAGES AND SIGNALS.

Prefix. Code. Words Charge.	This message is on a/c of	Recd. at m.
Office of Origin and Service Instructions Sent. At m. To By	Service (Signature of "Franking Officer")	Date From By

TO	56th Inf. Bde.	S.R.E.	A.D.V.S.
	37th Inf. Bde.	T.G.B? Div Sup	J.C. Corps

Sender's Number.	Day of Month.	In reply to Number.	AAA
GLLO	20		

18: Div are attacking tomorrow from the general line QUENCHETTES WOOD — X COPSE — YAK POST (excl) with objective the BLUE line including THE KNOLL ~~...~~ ... are attacking from the general line of MEATH LANE with objective which includes the RED line as far as south as CATELET COPSE aaa 12th Div will attack at the same zero hour ~~...~~ will 37th Inf Bde on right and 56th Inf Bde on left aaa Southern Div boundary ~~through...joining~~ F.?... to F.?... aaa northern div boundary east and west line through X 28 d 08 aaa boundary between Bdes BIRD LANE BIRD TRENCH ~~and~~ both inclusive

From		
Place		
Time		

The above may be forwarded as now corrected. (Z)

Censor. Signature of Addressor or person authorised to telegraph in his name
* This line should be erased if not required.

Order No. 1625 Wt. W3253/ P 511 27/2 H. & K. Ltd. (E. 2634)

"A" Form — Army Form C. 2121
MESSAGES AND SIGNALS. (In pads of 100.)

Prefix....Code....m.	Words	Charge	This message is on a/c of:	Recd. at....m.
Office of Origin and Service Instructions	Sent At....m. To By		....................Service. (Signature of "Franking Officer")	Date.... From.... By....

TO —

Sender's Number. | Day of Month. | In reply to Number. | AAA

to 37th Blo Have to N.W corner of MAY COPSE as objective
to touch up then form F0060 - HEYTHORP POST - HEYTHORP LANE - MULE TRENCH (if not already taken) as 36th Inf will close up then objective will be consolidated and defences organized in depth as in addition 36th Inf will close up LITTLE PRIEL FARM and trenches to the south as the the divisional boundary and touch will be gained with 17th Div at touchers and of trench at FH269 and with 58th Div by touch in out of CATELET ...

From
Place
Time

The above may be forwarded as now corrected. (Z)

Censor. Signature of Addressor or person authorised to telegraph in his name
* This line should be erased if not required.
Order No. 1625 Wt. W3253/ P 511 27/2. H. & K., Ltd. (E. 2634)

"A" Form
MESSAGES AND SIGNALS.

Army Form C. 2121
(In pads of 100.)

No. of Message............

Prefix......Code......m.	Words	Charge.	This message is on a/c of :	Recd. at......m.
Office of Origin and Service Instructions	Sent			Date............
....	At ......m.		......Service.	From ....
....	To			
....	By		(Signature of "Franking Officer")	By............

TO {

}

| Sender's Number. | Day of Month. | In reply to Number. | A A A |

details will be issued later. ooo 35" Bde
Bde will hold their present line and
will assist 36" Bde as much as possible
with trench mortar and m.g. fire ooo
30" Bde will relieve R. BERKS tonight
and will order them to a forward
assembly with 36" Bde where they will be
under orders ooo 36" Bde ooo
contact planes will fly over the corps
front at 1½ and 3 hours after zero
ooo troops will be specially warned to
indicate their positions by flares and
there are platoon commander will carry flares
ooo acknowledge ooo addd Bdes H.Q.
M.G. Bn. copied all concerned

From 12 Div
Place
Time 3.15 p.m.

```
"Q"      35th Inf. Bde.    12th Bn. M.G.C.   5th Northants. Regt.
C.R.A.   36th Inf. Bde.    58th Division.
C.R.E.   37th Inf. Bde.    12th Division.
```

G 250   21/9/18.

WARNING ORDER.

Dispositions for defence after objective is gained :-

(1) **RIGHT BRIGADE** :-

37th Inf. Bde. From front line within present Bde. boundaries as far West as HIDER RESERVE inclusive.

LEFT BRIGADE.

36th Inf. Bde. From front line within present Bde. boundaries as far West as ROOM TRENCH inclusive.

(2)   In Divisional Reserve :-

(A) :-

35th Inf. Bde. One battalion on the line DEVLISH POST - PRINCE RESERVE with posts approximately at the following points F.9.c.5.2 - F.9.c.2.9 - F.8.b.7.3 - F.8.b.2.8 - F.2.c.5.3 - F.1.b.9.1 - F.2.a.0.8 - X.26.c.3.6.

This Battn. will form the permanent garrison of this line and will not move without orders from Division.

The remaining two Battalions will be concentrated in F.7. and F.13. and will be ready to counter-attack when ordered.

(B)   5th Northamptonshire Regt. (Pioneers).

(C)   69th Field Coy. R.E.
          70th Field Coy. R.E.
          87th Field Coy. R.E.

(3)   In the event of the enemy counter-attacking and penetrating our outpost system, he will be immediately counter-attacked by the troops in Brigade Reserve.

The troops in Divisional Reserve will counter-attack under orders of Division.

The most probable direction of attack will be from about RIDGE RESERVE SOUTH in a North Easterly direction, so as to strike the enemy's left flank as he advances.

(4)   12th Battn. M.G.C.   One Coy. in each Brigade front on and in front of the general line YAK POST - HORSE POST - OGIENDEN X.27.c.0.8.

1 Coy. on general line ENFER WOOD - OLD COPSE - ROOM TRENCH.

1 Coy. on general line MAY COPSE - MALASSISE FARM - CHESTNUT AVENUE, two Sections of this Coy. will be under orders of Brigade Commander Reserve Brigade for counter-attack.

1 Coy. disposed for the defence of EPEHY.

1 Coy. concentrated in reserve about squares E.5. & 11.

(5)   A C K N O W L E D G E   B Y   W I R E.

12th Division.

1. 45 p.m.

Lieut.Colonel,
General Staff.

12th Division No. G.O. 233.

22nd September, 1918.

12th Divnl. Artillery.
35th Inf. Bde.
36th Inf. Bde.
37th Inf. Bde.
12th Bn. M.G. Corps
"Q".

1. The 175th Brigade are attacking KILDARE POST tonight under a barrage which lifts off KILDARE POST at 9.50 p.m.

2. For this operation the 58th Division require to move troops through the Northern portion of our area and arrangements to facilitate this will be made by 35th and 36th Brigades with 175th Brigade.

3. 12th Bn. M.G. Corps will assist the operation by fire from 16 guns. Details will be arranged direct with 58th Bn. M.G. Corps.

4. 36th Inf. Bde. will send out patrols on the conclusion of the operation to gain touch with the 175th Brigade at CATELET COPSE.

5. A C K N O W L E D G E.

Lieut.Colonel,
General Staff,
12th Division.

Copies to :- 58th Division.
18th Division.

SEEN BY :-
G.O.C.
G.S.O.I
G.S.O.II
G.S.O.III

SEEN BY:-
G.O.C..........
G.S.O.I.........
G.S.O.II........
G.S.O.III.......

SECRET.

Copy No:

12th DIVISION ORDER No. 284.

Ref. St. EMILIE Sheet, 1/20,000.   22nd September, 1918.

1. (a) The front of the Division will be re-adjusted tomorrow night 23rd/24th instant and will be in accordance with boundaries shown on the attached trace.

   (b) All arrangements for the relief will be made by Brigadiers concerned, the 36th Infantry Brigade relieving the 175th Infantry Brigade, 58th Division, in the portion taken over North of the present Divisional Northern boundary.

   (c) On night 24th/25th a further slight adjustment will be made in the Divisional Southern boundary, which will be notified later.

2. O.C. 12th Battn. M.G. Corps will arrange for the Machine Gun defence of the new area.

3. Command of the Sector taken over from 58th Division will pass to 35th Infantry Brigade on completion of the Infantry relief in the front line, at which time G.O.C. 12th Division will also take over command from G.O.C. 58th Division.

4. A C K N O W L E D G E.

        Lieut. Colonel,
        General Staff,
        12th Division.

Issued at 11 p.m.

Copies to :-
1. G.O.C.
2. G.S.O.1.
3. C.R.A.
4. C.R.E.
5. 35th Infantry Brigade.
6. 36th Infantry Brigade.
7. 37th Infantry Brigade.
8. 12th Bn. M.G. Corps.
9. 5th Northamptonshire Regt. (Pioneers).
10. 12th Div. Signal Coy. R.E.
11. "Q".
12. A.D.M.S.
13. 12th Div. Train.
14. A.P.M.
15. III Corps.
16. 18th Division.
17. 58th Division.
18. 33rd Division.
19 & 20. War Diary.
21 - 26. G.S. and Records.

"A" Form
MESSAGES AND SIGNALS.

Army Form C. 2121
(In pads of 100.)

Prefix....Code....m.	Words	Charge	This message is on of...	Recd. at ...m.
	Sent			Date
Office of Origin and Service Instructions	At ....m.		Service	From
Priority	To			By
	By	(Signature of "Franking Officer")		

TO— 36 Bde
58 Div CRE

Sender's Number	Day of Month	In reply to Number	
G 313	23		AAA

58 Div refused capture of SPRINT DADOS LOOP DADOS LANE HOLT TR KILDARE POST KILDARE LANE aaa these trenches will be taken over by 36th Inf Bde in accordance with 12th Div order No 284 aaa 5th Northants Pioneers are placed at disposal of GOC 36th Inf Bde from receipt of this message aaa acknowledge aaa added 36th Bde and Pioneers 1/5th 58th Div & CRE

SEEN BY:—
G.O.C.
G.S.O.I
G.S.O.II ✓
G.S.O.III ✓

Priority

38
EaD 5am
11-5am

Lt Col.

From 12th Div
Place
Time 10 am

J Belgrave Lt Col
GS

S	X
A	F

Div'l Boundary

36 Bde.

Inter Bde. Boundary

35 Bde.

Div'l Artillery Boundary

Identification Trace for use with Artillery Maps.
Superimpose on
St. Emilie Map ½0000.

W	X
E	F

"A" Form
MESSAGES AND SIGNALS.

Army Form C. 2121
(In pads of 100.)

No. of Message............

Prefix........Code.........m.	Words	Charge	This message is on a/c of :	Recd. at......m.
Office of Origin and Service Instructions	Sent			Date............
....	At ....m.		...............Service.	From ....
....	To			
....	By	(Signature of "Franking Officer")	By............

TO:
35th Inf.Bde.   C.R.A.   5th Northants.   "Q".
36th Inf.Bde.   C.R.E.   A.D.M.S.   3rd Corps.
?th Inf.Bde. 12th Bn.M.G.C.   27th Am.Div.

| Sender's Number. | Day of Month. | In reply to Number. | 18th Div. |
| G 432 | 26 | | 33rd Div. 35th Sq. R.A.F. |

At Zero Hour tomorrow 27th American Div.
is attacking the line QUENNEMONT FARM -
GILLEMONT FARM - THE KNOLL AAA 12th Div.
will co-operate with a view to protecting
the left flank of 27th American Division AAA
In addition to the creeping barrage which
will extend as far North as an East and
West line just North of BIRD POST
C.R.A. and O.C. M.G. Bn. will arrange to
bring concentrated Artillery Trench Mortar
and Machine Gun fire on to trenches in
X.29.d. 30.c.   F.5. and 6 and A.1.
during the attack and while consolidation
is in progress AAA   They will also make
every possible preparation for the immediate
opening of this fire in case of subsequent
counter-attack or the threat of a counter-
attack AAA 35th Inf. Bde. will establish
posts in F.5.d. and 6.c. with Lewis Guns
to cover TOMBOIS VALLEY and the Western
slopes of the spur running North from the
KNOLL AAA Within their own boundaries
35th and 36th Inf.Bdes. will also send
strong reconnoitring patrols along BIRD LANE

From .... /CATELET
Place
Time
The above may be forwarded as now corrected. (Z)
....
Censor.   Signature of Addresser or person authorised to telegraph in his name
* This line should be erased if not required.

Order No. 1625. Wt. W3253/ P 511. 27/2. H. & K., Ltd. (E. 2634).

"A" Form
MESSAGES AND SIGNALS.

Army Form C. 2121 (In pads of 100.)

Sender's Number.	Day of Month.	In reply to Number.	
G 43P	26		AAA

CATELET TRENCH and STONE LANE with the object of finding out the enemy's dispositions opening a way to the occupation of any of the enemy's present trench system which he may have vacated and establishing such advanced posts as will assist the subsequent advance whether for occupation permanently or by night only AAA 36th Inf. Bde. will attack and capture DADOS LOOP DADOS LANE and KILDARE AVENUE as far East as about X.22.d.5.8 AAA This operation will be carried out simultaneously with the above AAA Further details later AAA ACKNOWLEDGE AAA Addsd. all concerned.

From 12th Div.
Place
Time 1.45 p.m.

Lt.Col. G.S.

"A" Form
MESSAGES AND SIGNALS.

Army Form C. 2121
(In pads of 100.)

No. of Message............

Prefix.........Code............m.	Words	Charge.	This message is on a/c of:	Recd. at......m.
Office of Origin and Service Instructions	Sent			Date............
....	At ....m.		....................Service.	
....	To			From ....
....	By		(Signature of "Franking Officer")	By............

TO: 35th Bde.   C.R.A.   27th Anzac Div
    36th Bde.   33rd Divn.
    [illegible]

Sender's Number.	Day of Month.	In reply to Number.	AAA
G.450	26		

In continuation of G.433 AAA four 18
pdr batteries and one 4.5 How battery
will be available to support the
operations carried out by 36th Inf Bde
AAA Arrangements will be made by C.O.
36th Inf. Bde. direct with his Bde.
Group Commander AAA Heavy Arty. does
not lift off MEN ROAD or the junction
of [illegible] AVE. with MEN and
[illegible] with CROWN TRENCH till
Z plus 60 minutes so patrols will not
be able to go within 600 yards of these
places till that time AAA The Heavy
Arty. on MEN ROAD is lifting off at
Z plus 60 minutes AAA Medium T.M.s
will fire on the trenches OWL HIGH
OWL, OWL and FROST OWL plus
60 minutes AAA Heavy Arty. lifts off
DEAD OWL at Z plus 60 minutes AAA
[illegible] carrying parties is formed forthwith AAA Patrols sent into the trenches
will take a good supply of red flares
which the leading men will lit and

From			
Place			
Time			

The above may be forwarded as now corrected.   (Z)

....
Censor.   Signature of Addressor or person authorised to telegraph in his name

* This line should be erased if not required.

Order No. 1625. Wt. W3253/   P 511. 27/2.   H. & K. Ltd. (E, 2634)

"A" Form
MESSAGES AND SIGNALS.

Army Form C. 2121
(In pads of 100.)

Prefix......Code......m.	Words	Charge.	This message is on a/c of:	Recd. at......m.
Office of Origin and Service Instructions	Sent		..................Service.	Date............
....	At ......m.			From ....
....	To			
....	By		(Signature of "Franking Officer")	By............

TO (2).

Sender's Number.	Day of Month.	In reply to Number.	AAA
G 436	26		

threw out of trenches to show Artillery
as well as contact aeroplanes where
they are AAA ACKNOWLEDGE AAA
Added. all concerned.

Later.   O.C. M.G. Bn. is synchronising
M.G. barrages as far as possible but
Brigade Commanders will go into the times
of lifts with their M.G. Group Commanders.

From 18th Divn.   (Sgd) J.D. BELGRAVE,
Place   Lt.Col. G.S.
Time 4.55 p.m.

LEGEND

- Objective for Aug. 8th — ××××××××
- 1st Objective for Aug. 9th — ××××××××
- 2nd " " — ooooooo
- Objective for Aug. 10th — ××××××××
- Line on night 8/9th Aug. — (blue line)
- " " " 9/10th " — (red line)
- " " " 10/11th " — (green line)
- Advanced Posts — • • •
- Reserve Line dug 13th–21st Aug. — (black line)

MAP 'A'

Superimpose on 1/20,000 62d NE.

16	17 Meaulte	18
19 Dernancourt		24
25 Ville-sur-Ancre		30
K 1		K
7 Morlancourt		12
13	15	16	17	18

Touch with 129th American Regt.
Touch with 129th American Regt.
Touch with 129th American Regt.
Touch with 58th Div.
Touch with 58th Div.
Touch with 18th Div.

E K
E K

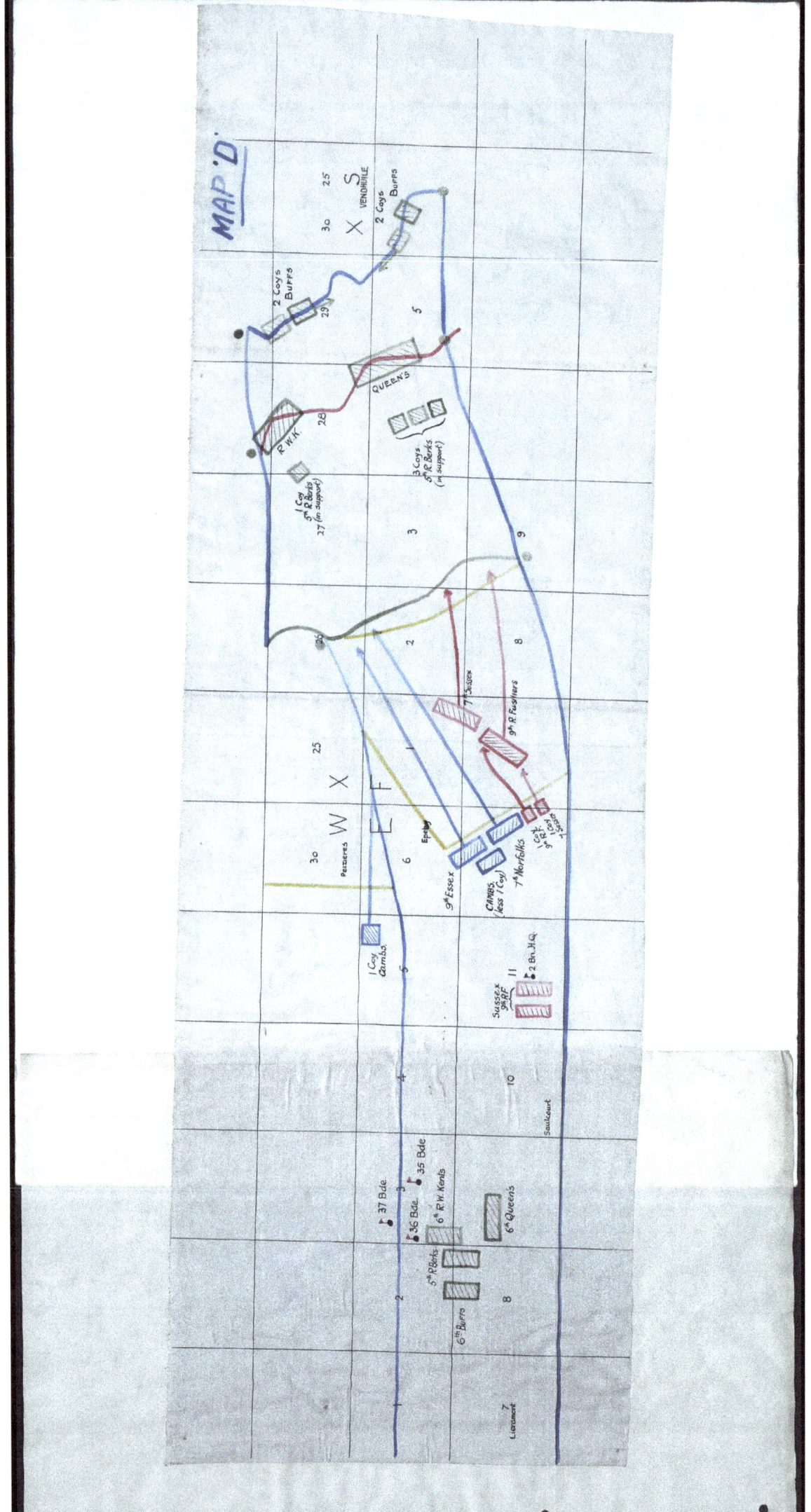

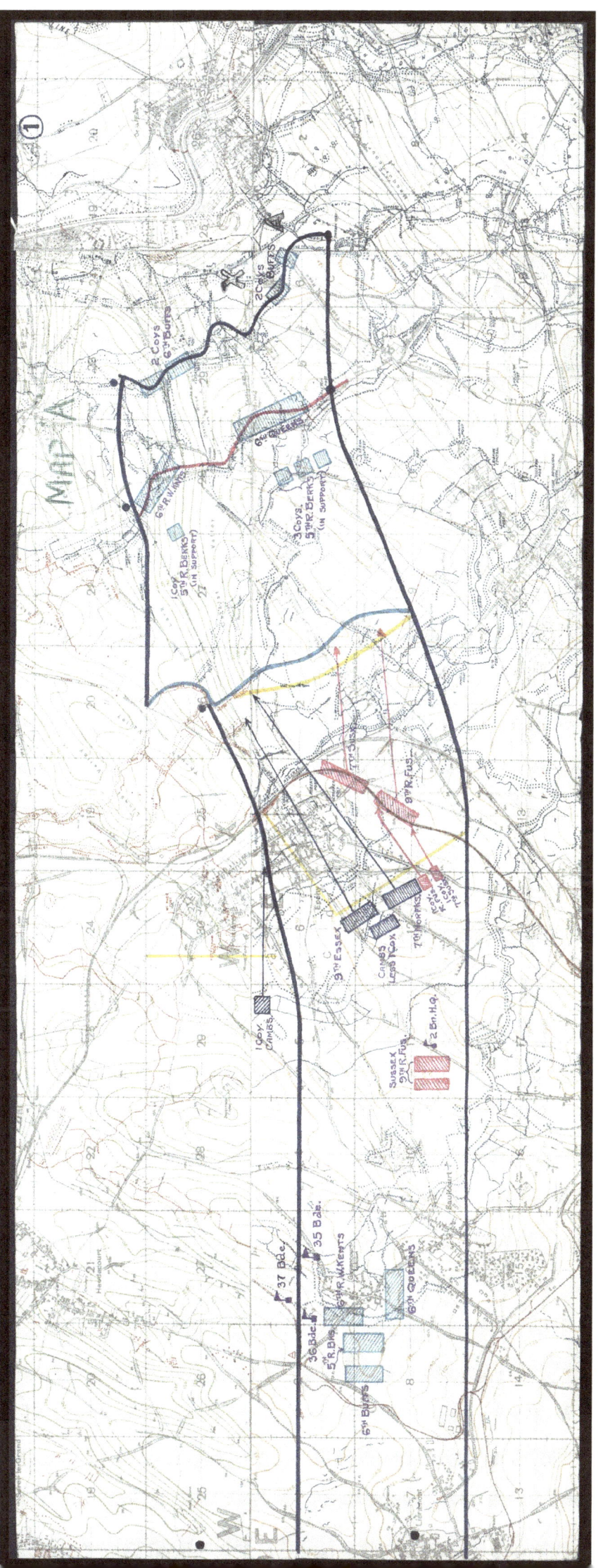

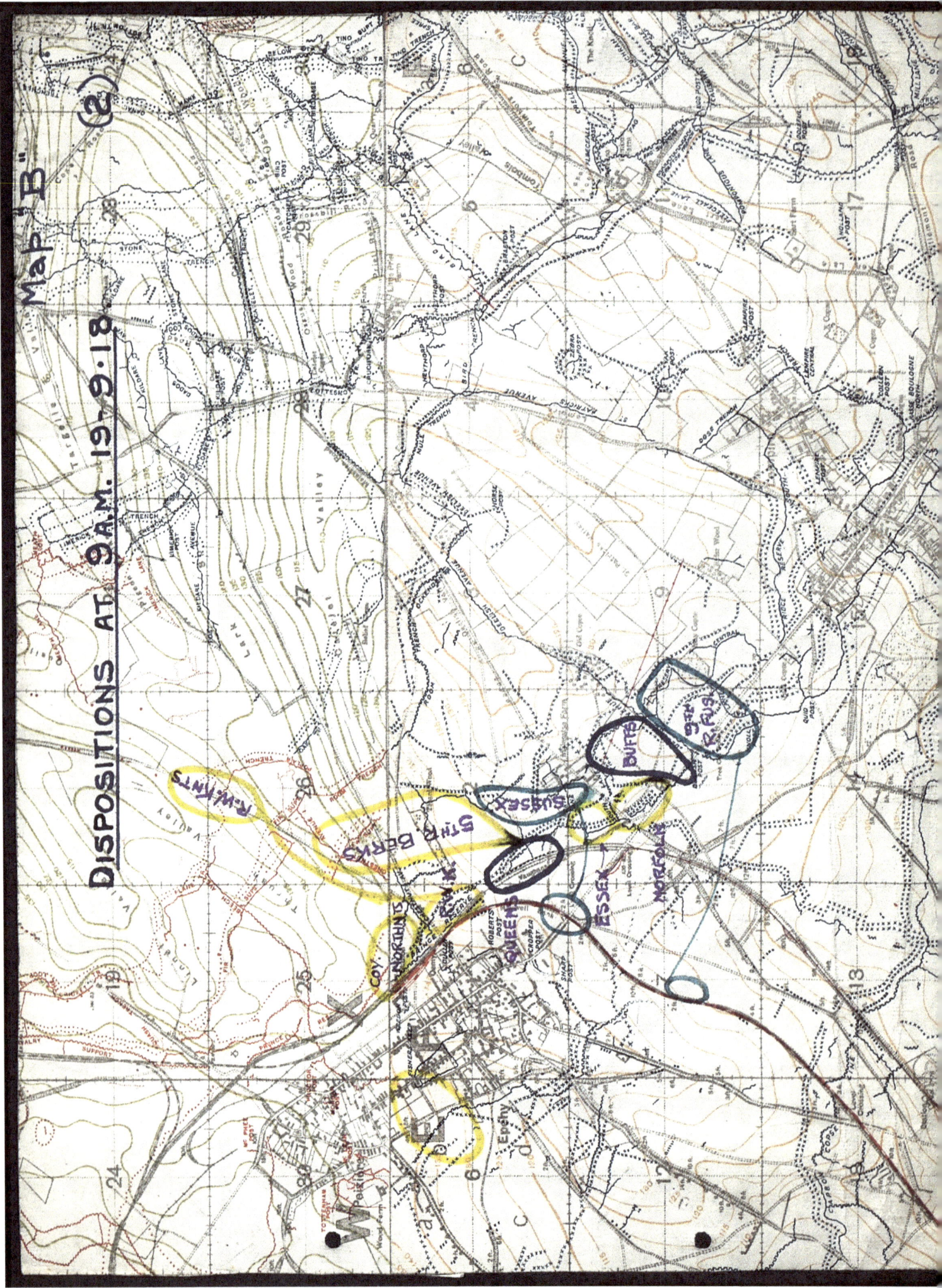

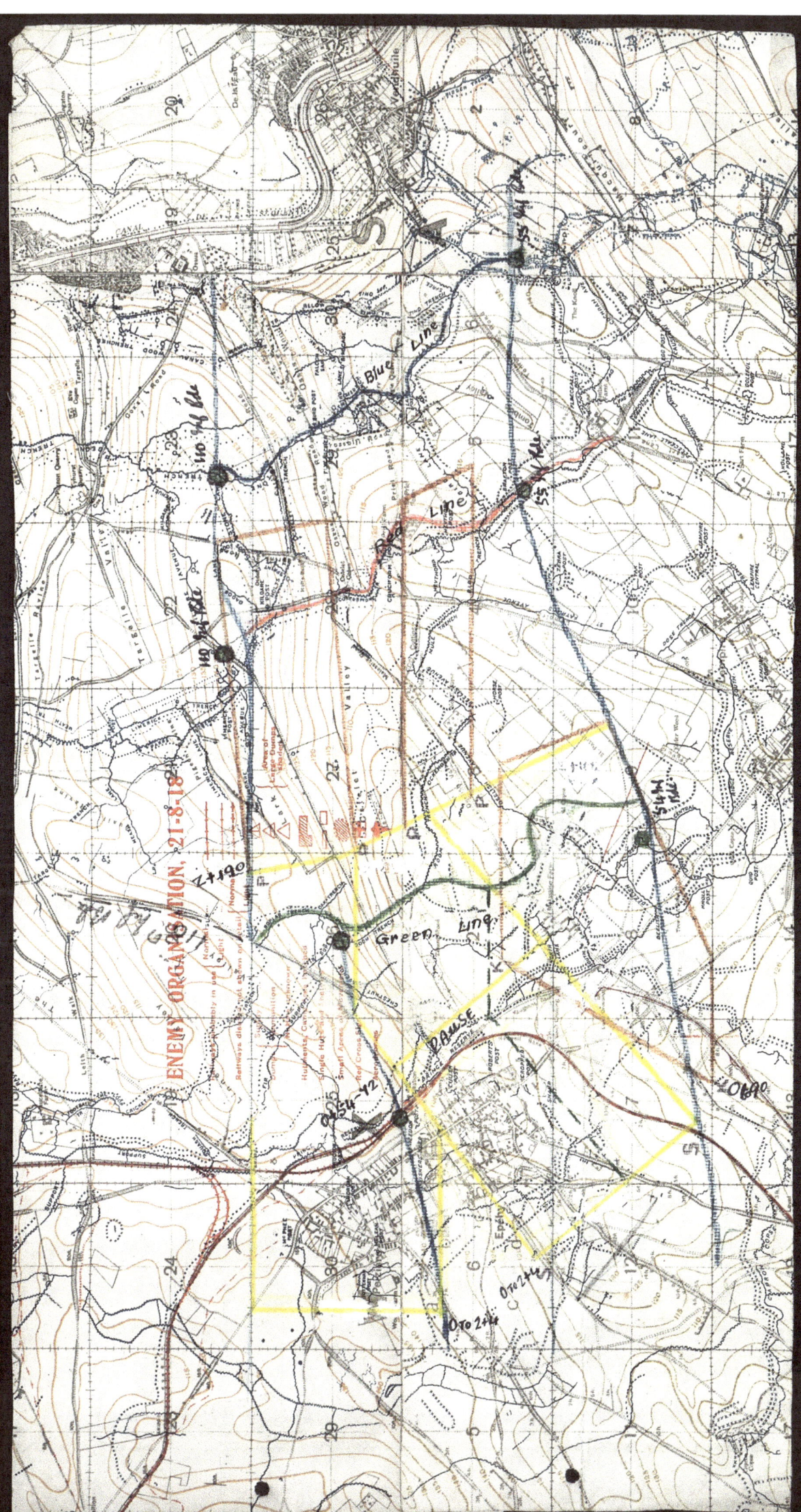

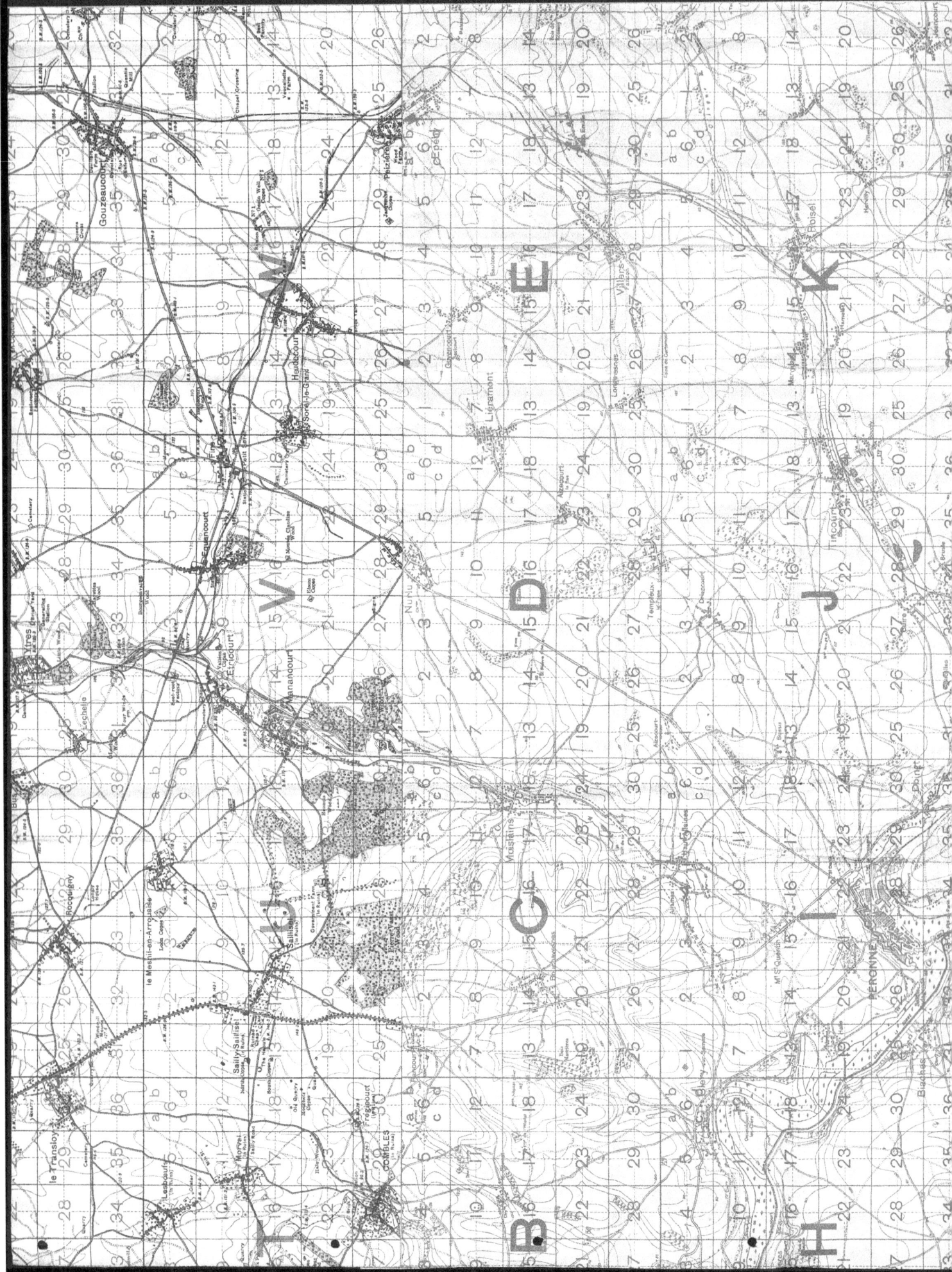

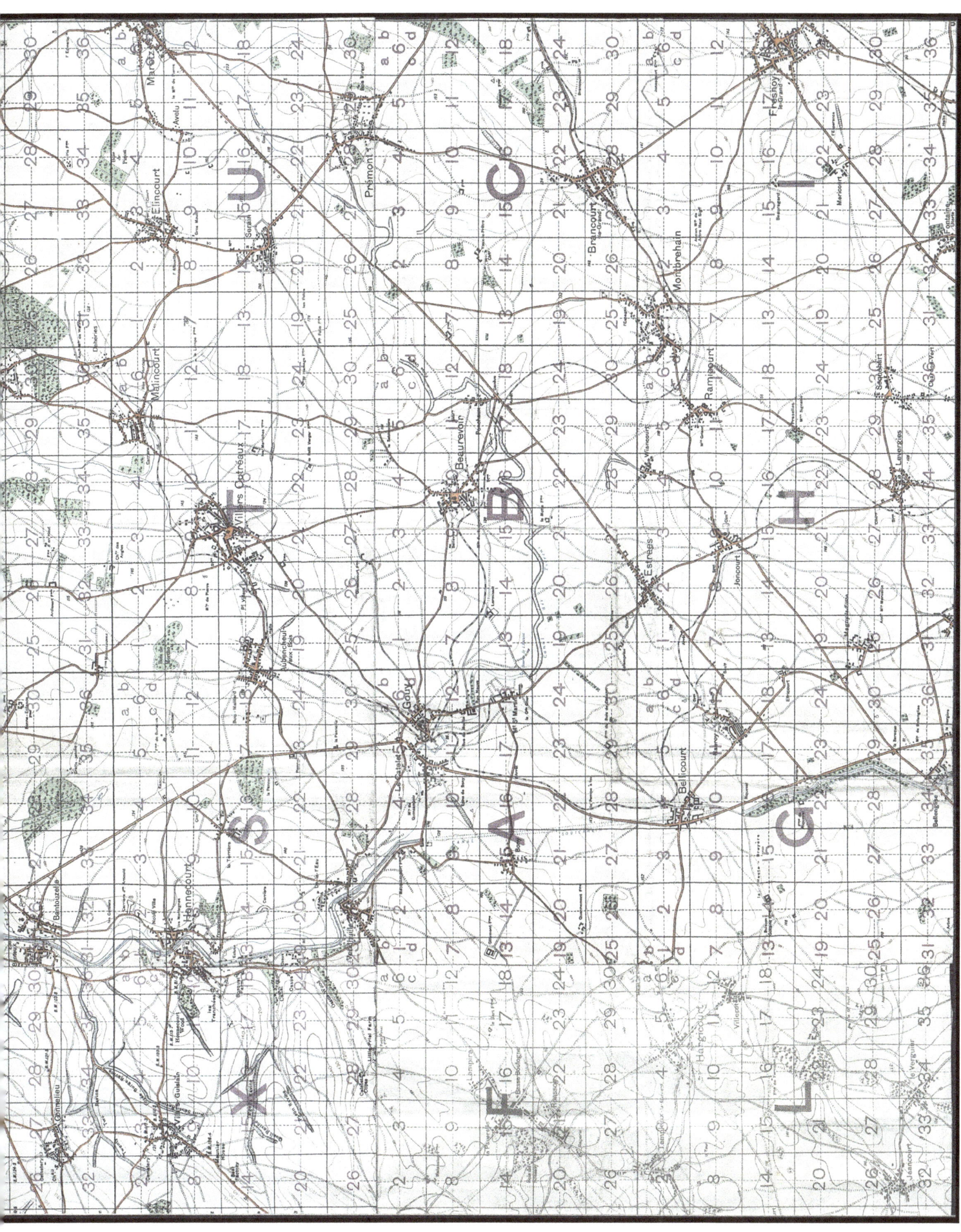

Orphelinat -	Orphanage.
Oseraie - -	Osier-beds.
Ouvrage - -	Fort.
Ouvrages hydrauliques	Water works.
Papeterie -	Paper-mill.
Parc - -	Park, yard.
„ aéronautique-	Aviation ground.
„ à charbon -	Coal yard.
„ à pétrole -	Petrol store.
Passage à niveau P.N.	Level-crossing
Passerelle, Pas[lle] -	Foot-bridge.
Pépinière - -	Nursery-garden.
Peuplier - -	Poplar tree.
Phare - -	Light-house.
Pilier, Pil[r] -	Post.
Plaine d'exercice-	Drill ground.
Pompe - -	Pump.
Ponceau - -	Culvert.
Pont - -	Bridge.
„ levis - -	Drawbridge.
Poste } de garde- côte Station }	Coast-guard station.
Poteau P[au] -	Post.
Poterie -	Pottery.
Poudrière, Poud[re] } Magasin à poudre }	Powder magazine.
Prise d'eau	Water supply.
Puits	Pit-head, Shaft, Well.
„ artésien	Artesian well.
„ d'aérage } „ ventilateur }	Ventilating shaft.
„ de sondage -	Boring.
Quai - -	Quay, Platform.
„ aux bestiaux -	Cattle platform.
„ aux } marchan- „ des } dises	Goods platform.
Raccordement -	Junction.
Raffinerie - -	Refinery.
„ de sucre	Sugar refinery
Râperie - -	Beet-root factory.

Réservoir, Rés[r] -	[illegible]
Route cavalière -	Bridle road.
Rubanerie - -	Ribbon Factory
Ruine } Ruines } En ruine } Ruiné - e } -	Ruin.
Sablière - -	Sand-pit.
Sablonnière, Sablon[re]	„
Sapin - -	Fir tree.
Saule - -	Willow tree.
Saunerie - -	Salt-works.
Scierie, Sc[ie] -	Saw-mill.
Sondage - -	Boring.
Source - -	Spring.
Sucrerie, Suc[ie] -	Sugar factory.
Tannerie - -	Tannery.
Tir à la cible -	Rifle range.
Tissage - -	Weaving mill
Tôlerie - -	Rolling mill
Tombeau - -	Tomb.
Tour - -	Tower.
Tourbière -	Peat-bog, Peat-bed.
Tourelle - -	Small tower.
Tuilerie -	Tile works.
Usine à gaz - -	Gas works.
„ électrique } „ d'électricité }	Electricity works.
„ métallurgique	Metal works.
„ à agglomérés -	Briquette factory.
Verrerie, Verr[ie] -	Glass works.
Viaduc - -	Viaduct
Vivier -	Fish Pond.
Voie de chargement - } „ „ déchargement } „ „ d'évitement - } „ „ formation - } „ „ manœuvre - }	Siding.
Zinguerie - -	Zinc works.

0 1 2 3 4 5 6 7 8 9

INSTRUCTIONS AS TO THE USE OF THE SQUARES.

1. The large rectangles on the map, lettered A, B, C, etc., are divided into squares of 1,000 yards side, which are numbered 1, 2, 3, etc. Each of these squares is sub-divided into four minor squares of 500 yards side. These minor squares are considered as lettered a, b, c, d. (See Square No. 6 in each rectangle.)

A point may thus be described as lying within Square B.6, M.5.b, etc.

2. To locate a point within a small square, consider the sides divided into tenths, and define the point by taking so many tenths from W. to E. along Southern side, and so many from S. to N. along Western side: the S.W. corner always being taken as origin, and the distance along the Southern side being always given by the first figure. Thus the point Z would be 63, i.e., 6 divisions East and 3 divisions North from origin.

3. When more accurate definition is wanted (on the 1 : 20,000 or 1 : 10,000 scales) use exactly the same method, but divide sides into 100 parts and use four figures instead of two. Thus 0847 denotes 08 parts East and 47 parts North of origin (see point X). Point Y is 6503.

4. Use 0 not not 10; use either two or four figures; do not use fractions (6½, 4¼, etc.).

On squared maps all bearings should be given with reference to the vertical grid lines, which are parallel to the East and West edges of the sheet. Bearings should always be reckoned clockwise from 0° to 360°.

Grid bearings are less than compass bearings, the difference being called the deviation of the compass. To find out what this deviation is, take a compass bearing to a distant point, and measure on the map the grid bearing to that point. The difference between the two bearings is the deviation of that compass from Grid North. To obtain the grid bearing of any point this deviation must be subtracted from the compass bearing (adding 360° to the latter if necessary).

On this sheet the mean deviation of a normal compass is 12° 17'; but to obtain accurate results the exact deviation of each compass should be tested as described above, and this test should be repeated in each locality.

TABLE FOR CONVERTING METRES TO FEET.

Mtrs.	0	1	2	3	4	5	6	7	8	9
0	0	3·3	6·6	9·8	13·1	16·4	19·7	23·0	26·2	29·5
10	32·8	36·1	39·4	42·6	45·9	49·2	52·5	55·8	59·0	62·3
20	65·6	68·9	72·2	75·4	78·7	82·0	85·3	88·6	91·8	95·1
30	98·4	101·7	105·0	108·2	111·5	114·8	118·1	121·4	124·6	127·9
40	131·2	134·5	137·8	141·0	144·3	147·6	150·9	154·1	157·4	160·7
50	164·0	167·3	170·6	173·8	177·1	180·4	183·7	187·0	190·2	193·5
60	196·8	200·1	203·4	206·6	209·9	213·2	216·5	219·8	223·0	226·3
70	229·6	232·9	236·2	239·4	242·7	246·0	249·3	252·6	255·8	259·1
80	262·4	265·7	269·0	272·2	275·5	278·8	282·1	285·4	288·6	291·9
90	295·2	298·5	301·8	305·0	308·3	311·6	314·9	318·1	321·4	324·7
100	328·0	331·3	334·6	337·8	341·1	344·4	347·7	351·0	354·2	357·5

FRAN

SHEET

EDITION

INDEX TO ADJOININ

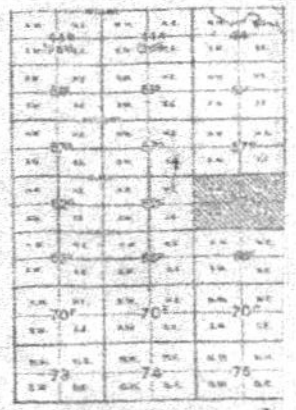

SCALE 40,0(

OR

12th Division No. G.C. 1344.

19th February, 1919.

VIII Corps.

I forward copies of list of officers recommended for the Staff College in accordance with para. 721 of King's Regulations, with recommendations on A.F. W.3723 attached. These names are in addition to those forwarded with reference to your No. G.b.127/1 (2 May 1918) (Lt.Col. A.T.SHAKESPEAR, D.S.O., M.C., and Major H.W.L.WALLER, D.S.O., M.C.), and come after these two officers in priority of recommendation.

H. W. Higginson

Major-General,
Commanding 12th Division.

List of Officers recommended for the Staff College
in accordance with para. 721 K.R.

1st March 1919

Name	Unit	Age	Remarks
Captain (Temp.Lt.Col.) R.H.J. NICOLLS, D.S.O., M.C.	East Surrey Regt. (Commanding 5th Bn. Royal Berkshire Regiment).	32½	
Captain (Temp.Lt.Col.) W.G.A. COLDWELL	Northamptonshire Regiment. (Commanding 12th Bn. M.G.Corps).	26	
Captain (Temp. Major) C.F.M.N. RYAN, D.S.O., M.C.	R.E. (Special Reserve) G.S.O.2 12th Division.	27	
Capt. (Temp. Major) C. MACDONALD, M.C.	Gordon Highlanders D.A.A.G. 12th Division.	23/24	

Forwarded to VIII Corps
under GC. 1344 - 19.2.19.

GENERAL STAFF,

12th DIVISION,

OCTOBER 1918.

Army Form C. 2118.

WAR DIARY
12th DIVISION – October, 1918.
INTELLIGENCE SUMMARY.

(Erase heading not required.)

Instructions regarding War Diaries and Intelligence Summaries are contained in F. S. Regs., Part II. and the Staff Manual respectively. Title pages will be prepared in manuscript.

Place	Date	Hour	Summary of Events and Information	Remarks and references to Appendices
			Ref. Sheets – 1/40,000. 44.A. 44. 45.	
Bois de l'EPINETTE	1st		Divisional Headquarters moved to VILLERS CHATEL. Brigades commenced entraining for SAVY, ACQ and AUBIGNY.	
VILLERS CHATEL.	2nd		Brigades moving to new area.	
,,	3rd		12th Division Order No. 287 issued relative to relief of 20th Division in Centre Divisional Sector of VIII Corps Front.	App. 1.
,,	4th		Units resting. Officers reconnoitring new front. Divisional Order No. 288 issued re relief of 20th D.A. by 50th D.A.	App. 2.
,,	5th		Relief of 20th Division commenced. One battalion from 35th Inf. Bde. and one battalion from 37th Inf. Bde. relieved one battalion of 61st Inf. Bde. and 60th Inf. Bde. respectively in the BROWN LINE, i.e., Support Line running along East side of VIMY RIDGE.	
,,	6th		On night 5th/6th, 36th Inf. Bde. relieved 60th Inf. Bde; M.G. relief was also carried out. Divisional H.Q. opened at 18.00 hrs. at CHATEAU de la HAIE.	
CHATEAU de la HAIE.	7th		On night 6th/7th, the 35th and 37th Inf. Bdes, each less one battalion already in BROWN LINE, took over their respective Sections. On completion of relief, the Division was disposed as follows :- Right Section (ARLEUX) 35th Inf. Bde. Centre Section (MERICOURT) 36th Inf. Bde. Left Section (AVION) 37th Inf. Bde. As the 20th Division had found that the enemy was holding his line with outposts only, and had apparently moved his guns back, they sent over reconnoitring patrols. Several of these established themselves in the enemy's Front Line. Vigorous patrolling was therefore ordered	

Army Form C. 2118.

WAR DIARY
12th DIVISION or October, 1918.
INTELLIGENCE SUMMARY.
(Erase heading not required.)

Instructions regarding War Diaries and Intelligence Summaries are contained in F. S. Regs., Part II and the Staff Manual respectively. Title pages will be prepared in manuscript.

Place	Date	Hour	Summary of Events and Information	Remarks and references to Appendices
CHATEAU de la HAIE.	8th		Our patrols occupied the greater part of the enemy's front system, including ACHEVILLE SUPPORT TRENCH and the village of MERICOURT. 12th Divisional Order No. G. 591 issued - Brigades to push out patrols to maintain touch with the enemy. In the event of it being found that the enemy had withdrawn, patrols to be strongly supported, and the advance continued by bounds.	App. 3.
"	9th		12th Division Order No. 289 issued relative to relief of 50th D.A. by 12th D.A. This relief to take place on nights 11th/12th and 12th/13th October. the portion of the FRESNES-ROUVROY Line between U.27.a.4.1. and U.21.c.5.1. was occupied by our troops. Also a platoon post was established in CHEZ BONTEMPS. On the left, a line of posts was taken up between N.36.d.8.6. and N.36.a.4.8.	App. 4.
"	10th		At dawn posts were established at BOIS BERNARD and later on ST JOHNS ROAD in U.15 and 16.c. was occupied. Patrols made good the line MABEL COPONS, exclusive, East of MERICOURT; west of ROUVROY and from North of NOYELLES to N.29. A few enemy still remained in NOYELLES; steps were being taken to clear these up. village. 12th Division Order No. G. 643 issued relative to action to be taken by Brigades to eject enemy from his present positions. During the afternoon the enemy evacuated ROUVROY and our troops took up a line East of the village. NOYELLES was also cleared.	App. 5.
"	11th		12th Division Order No. 290 issued relative to reorganization of the Divisional Front. 36th Inf. Bde. to relieve 37th Bde. as far north as new Divisional Boundary (northern), and 175th Inf. Bde., 58th Division to relieve 37th Bde. as far south as new Divisional Northern Boundary. The reorganization to take place during the period 11th/13th October, and on completion of same, 37th Bde. to come into Divisional Reserve. In consequence of the above order, a general advance was made on the whole Divisional Front at dawn, and notwithstanding considerable hostile M.G. fire, the whole of the DROCOURT-QUEANT Line and its first and second lines were occupied by our troops. The villages of FOUQUIERES BILLY MONTIGNY and HENIN LIETARD were occupied, and by midnight the line ran just East of the latter village.	App. 6.
LIEVIN.	12th		Orders issued that all three Bdes. would, if possible, push on at 06.00 hrs. to the HAUTE de DEULE CANAL, patrols to be sent out from there to the line of the railway from Q.27.d. to P.5.d.	

(A7092) Wt. W12339/M1293. 75,000. 1/17. D.D. & L., Ltd. Forms/C.2118/14.

Army Form C. 2118.

WAR DIARY

12th DIVISION or OCTOBER, 1918.

INTELLIGENCE SUMMARY.

(Erase heading not required.)

Instructions regarding War Diaries and Intelligence Summaries are contained in F. S. Regs., Part II. and the Staff Manual respectively. Title pages will be prepared in manuscript.

Place	Date	Hour	Summary of Events and Information	Remarks and references to Appendices
LIEVIN	12th Ctd.—		35th and 36th Bdes. met with considerable opposition from enemy M.Gs, particularly from DOURGES, CITE BRUNO and AUBY. NOYELLE-GODAULT and part of COURCELLES were occupied by our troops. There was a good deal of street fighting in COURCELLES. On the left, the 37th Inf. Bde. were able to advance to within about 1,000 yards south and east of COURRIERES. Some opposition was encountered at JERUSALEM in P.7.a. where a party of Germans held out, but these were subsequently forced to retire. This they did across the open, towards COURRIERES. Fire was opened on them by the 6th R.W. Kent Regt, who inflicted casualties. Attempts made the same day to capture COURRIERES were unsuccessful. Divisional Headquarters moved to L'ABBATH. CITE M. L'ABBATTOIR, S.E. of LIEVIN.	
,,	13th		Reliefs detailed in Order No. 290 completed. 37th Inf. Bde. in Divisional Reserve in BILLY MONTIGNY area. Our positions on CANAL improved. 36th Inf. Bde. on left attacked western side of the CANAL de HAUTE DEULE. CITE BRUNO and DOURGES were cleared but the line of the CANAL could not be reached. 35th Bde. on right still held up by vigorous enemy opposition in AUBY. The small enemy rearguard which had at first held the western outskirts of the village had, by this time been augmented by more troops who infiltrated into the houses. On the left of this Bde, however, the 9th Essex Regt, reached the CANAL in P.23.a. and b.	
,,	14th		Enemy Artillery active on DOURGES, NOYELLE GODAULT and on FOSSE 4 and 7. 1/1st Cambridgeshire Regt. (35th Inf. Bde.) attacked AUBY, but were unable to capture the whole of the village owing to the extremely strong enemy opposition. 1 Officer and 39 O.R. of the enemy were captured, and in addition 19 wounded Germans were taken who could not be evacuated. On the left the 36th Bde. made some progress, as shown on the attached map.	
,,	15th		Situation unchanged. Two attempts were made by 35th Inf. Bde. to establish post at P.30.b. 8.7. on the western bank of the CANAL. The post was established but was found to be untenable owing to hostile M.G., T.M. and Artillery fire. During the afternoon, the 36th Bde. were able to establish a Joint Post with the 58th Division on the east bank of the CANAL at PONT A SAULT, P.15.b.	
VENIN LIETARD	16th		During the night 15th/16th, 36th Inf. Bde. succeeded in moving two companies across the CANAL at PONT A SAULT. The northern end of AUBY was found by the 35th Bde. to be still strongly held by M.Gs, Snipers and T.Ms. There was a good deal of scattered shelling during the	

(A7032) Wt.W12599/M1293. 75,000. 1/17. D.D. & L., Ltd. Forms/C.2118/14.

Army Form C. 2118.

WAR DIARY
INTELLIGENCE SUMMARY.

12th DIVISION ..... OCTOBER, 1918.

(Erase heading not required.)

Instructions regarding War Diaries and Intelligence Summaries are contained in F. S. Regs., Part II. and the Staff Manual respectively. Title pages will be prepared in manuscript.

Place	Date	Hour	Summary of Events and Information	Remarks and references to Appendices
HENIN LIETARD.	16th		night, but notwithstanding this a pontoon bridge was constructed over the CANAL, 100 yards south of PONT A SAULT. Divisional Headquarters opened at HENIN LIETARD at 11.00 hrs.	
"	17th		During the night 16th/17th the enemy evacuated his positions East of the CANAL, and in AUBY. Our patrols followed him closely and the advance was continued from East and West of HAUTE de DEULE CANAL to eastern outskirts of LE FOREST. The enemy, apparently, pivoted his retirement on our front on AUBY, as his rearguard there just managed to get away before they could be cut off. Later in the day the advance was resumed as far as the line RAIMBEAUCOURT-ROOST-WARENDIN (exclusive) to W.4. About 600 civilians were liberated in CORDELA and RAIMBEAUCOURT.	
"	18th		The advance was continued at 8.30 a.m. on this day. On the right, the 37th Bde. passed through a portion of the left Bde., 8th Division, and part of the 35th Bde., who sidestepped and passed through 36th Inf. Bde., who thereupon came into Divisional reserve. Touch was early obtained with an enemy patrol and 2 M.Gs at R.14.c.8.8.; it was driven off across the COUTICHE STREAM. An infantry patrol was encountered by 7th Norfolk Regt. at R.14.c.9.2. and 4 prisoners and one M.G. captured. North of LA PLACETTE another Cavalry patrol attempted to charge a patrol of the 6th R.W. Kent Regt. but was driven off with loss. An infantry patrol was also encountered; three of this patrol were killed and three taken prisoner. After some fighting, FLINES and FLINES WOOD were cleared of the enemy. About 3,500 civilians were liberated in FLINES and 600 in BOUJON. The enemy shelled FLINES heavily during the day notwithstanding its being encountered village occupied by civilians.	
RAIMBEAU-COURT	19th		The advance was continued by 35th and 37th Inf. Bdes., each on a one battalion front, with a section of cyclists. Our patrols established themselves on the line shown on attached map. 5 prisoners were taken in COUTICHES. Divisional Headquarters opened at RAIMBEAUCOURT during the morning.	
"	20th		Advance was continued with little opposition to SAMEON. All the villages contained civilians. The total advance of the day was 6,000 yards. A large timber dump of the enemy's was found at LANDAS. Ten prisoners were captured by 1/1st Cambridgeshire Regt. just west of SAMEON. Hostile artillery was quiet during the night.	
"	21st		Owing to the difficulty of supply only a short advance was ordered for the 21st. Touch	

Army Form C. 2118.

WAR DIARY

12th DIVISION or OCTOBER 1918.

INTELLIGENCE SUMMARY.

(Erase heading not required.)

Instructions regarding War Diaries and Intelligence Summaries are contained in F. S. Regs., Part II. and the Staff Manual respectively. Title pages will be prepared in manuscript.

Place	Date	Hour	Summary of Events and Information	Remarks and references to Appendices
RAIMBEAU- COURT.	21st		was obtained with the enemy East of LECELLES. Our advance on the left was held up from the CENSEE DE CHOQUES I.18.a. 36th and 37th Bdes continued advance at midnight 21st/22nd with the object of crossing the SCARPE at NIVELLE and the ZINC WORKS (J.16.), and making bridge-heads at these two places. Considerable opposition was met with East of the River ELNON. The following approximate line was however reached P.4.a., J.34.a., J.28.d., thence J.20.d. and b., J.14.d., c., and a., J.13.b.	
ORCHIES	22nd		All the bridges over the SCARPE Canal were found to be destroyed. Attempts to cross the Canal were unsuccessful as the enemy held the Eastern side in strength. 57th Inf. Bde. succeeded in moving 1 Coy across SCARPE at ST.AMAND, and up to J.34.b. The left of the 36th Bde. was definitely held up from FORT DE MAULDE and MONT DE LA JUSTICE. Enemy's artillery and M.Gs were very active. Divisional Headquarters opened at ORCHIES during the forenoon.	
SAMEON	23rd		During the morning the enemy re-entered some houses at P.5.central, where we had established a post the previous night. They were, however, soon ejected. The villages of THUN, HAUTE RIVE and FLAGNIES were occupied by our troops and a post established in BURIDON. Divisional Headquarters moved to SAMEON. During the afternoon the enemy evacuated MAIRIE DE NIVELLE, J.34. The houses there were occupied by our troops and a footbridge was constructed across the canal.	
"	24th		The advance was continued by the 6th Buffs, 37th Inf. Bde. and the villages of BRUILLE and BUHOT were captured. These villages were strongly held, especially the village of BRUILLE, and in addition a strong belt of wire ran round the W. side of the village. A large number of the enemy fled on seeing our men approach. They were pursued through the village, the Buffs shooting them down as they ran. While doing so the enemy barrage came down on their own retreating infantry, inflicting many casualties. 1 Officer and 16 O.R. were captured and many German wounded were left, as they could not be evacuated.	
"	25th		Our troops succeeded in entering southern outskirts of CHATEAU L'ABBAYE, FME LOCRON and MOTTE de MIN were also occupied. Elements of the enemy still held northern half of CHATEAU L'ABBAYE.	M/2

Army Form C. 2118.

WAR DIARY
12th DIVISION or OCTOBER 1918
INTELLIGENCE SUMMARY.
(Erase heading not required.)

Instructions regarding War Diaries and Intelligence Summaries are contained in F. S. Regs., Part II. and the Staff Manual respectively. Title pages will be prepared in manuscript.

Place	Date	Hour	Summary of Events and Information	Remarks and references to Appendices
SAMEON	26th		Enemy still holding the northern half of the village of CHATEAU L'ABBAYE. MONT de la JUSTICE and ZING WORKS in J.16.c. evacuated by enemy and occupied by our troops.	Appendix to
,,	27th		During the night 26th/27th, the 7th Royal Sussex Regt., 36th Inf. Bde. attacked part of CHATEAU L'ABBAYE with Artillery bombardment and succeeded in capturing it, forcing the enemy to take up positions on East side of ESCAUT. The ground between CHATEAU L'ABBAYE and the ESCAUT was found to be greatly inundated. SLAG HEAP in J.10.c. was occupied by 36th Inf. Bde. 36th Inf. Bde. took over the whole Divisional front.	
,,	28th		Quiet day. Some gas shelling of BRUILLE. At 22.00 hrs the 36th Inf. Bde. endeavoured to establish a Bridgehead over the ESCAUT at J.28.a.5.7. in conjunction with 8th Division, who were attempting to establish a Bridgehead further South. Heavy opposition was met with from enemy M.Gs, and the operation was not a complete success. A cork bridge, however, was constructed across the River at the above point and a post established on the East bank.	
,,	29th		Relief of 36th Inf. Bde. who were holding the whole Divisional front by 156th Inf. Bde., 52nd Division, completed. Command passed at 10.00 hrs to G.O.C. 52nd Division. Divisional Headquarters moved to PLINES. Quiet day.	
FLINES	30th		Division resting and preparing for training periods.	
,,	31st		Division resting and preparing for training periods. Divisional area visited by the Army Commander who addressed the troops. H.R.H. The Prince of Wales, who came later on in the day, visited two Brigades.	

CASUALTIES 7th - 28th OCTOBER.

Officers - Killed 7; Wounded 36; Missing 2.
O.R. - ,, 110; ,, 513; ,, 42.

H.S. Higgins.

Major General,
Commanding 12th Division.

12th DIVISION.

REPORT ON OPERATIONS OF OCTOBER, 1918

WITH VIII CORPS.

Oct. 5th.　　On the night of the 5th/6th October, the 36th Inf. Bde. relieved the 60th Inf. Bde., 20th Division, in the centre sub-sector.　　At this time it was thought that there was a possibility of the enemy withdrawing, and orders were given for patrolling to be carried out actively, and constant touch to be maintained with the enemy.

Divisional Headquarters was at VILLERS CHATEL.

Oct. 6th.　　On the 6th inst., an attempt was made by the left Bde. of the 20th Division to enter MERICOURT, but the village was found to be strongly held.

On the night of the 6th/7th Oct., the relief of the 20th Division was continued, and by midnight was completed, the 35th Bde. holding the right (ARLEUX) sector, 36th Bde. holding the centre (MERICOURT) and the 37th holding the left AVION) sector

The line taken over from the 20th Division is shown on the attached map.

Oct. 7th.　　During the night 6th/7th inst., patrols had no difficulty in entering the enemy front and support lines, but any further advance was met with heavy machine gun fire.　　The enemy was also holding the western edges of MERICOURT.

At 11.00 hrs, in conjunction with an operation by the 24th Bde., 8th Division on our right, the 1/1st Cambridgeshire Regt. 35th Inf. Bde. pushed out fighting patrols, under a barrage to the line CONNIE TRENCH - VILLAGE TRENCH, C.1.d. and b., J.25.d but found this strongly held occupied by the Germans.

Divisional Headquarters moved in the morning from VILLERS CHATEL to CHATEAU de la HAIE.

Oct. 8th.　　On the night 7th/8th, patrols found the enemy occupying his reserve line as usual throughout the whole Divisional Front but, during the day, the 8th Division reported the enemy to be withdrawing opposite their front.

All three Bdes. pushed out patrols, which met with little
Oct. 9th. opposition, and by 09.00 hrs. on the 9th inst., they had reached the general line shown on the attached map.

The advance was continued during the day, but was held up in the centre by enemy M.G. fire from ROUVROY and trenches N.W of the village, and on the left by a small party of the enemy in the centre of NOYELLES.

There was little change in the situation during the night, but patrols pushed forward at dawn on the 10th instant.

Oct.10th.　　The 7th Norfolk Regt (left Bn. of the 35th Bde.) succeeded in reaching the IZEL-LES-EQUERCHIN road, but on their right the 1/1st Cambridgeshire Regt was unable to gain complete possession of the line of this road until dark, owing to M.G. fire from the QUEANT-DROCOURT Line, which was strongly held by the enemy.

On the left of the 35th Bde. the 5th Royal Berks Regt. and 9th Royal Fusiliers, 36th Bde., were unable to make progress during the morning owing to M.G. fire from the western edge of ROUVROY.　　A hostile counter attack was also attempted on them in U.8.a., from the village, but this failed, and the 9th Royal Fusiliers made further progress up BERNARD TRENCH.

During the afternoon the enemy withdrew from ROUVROY, and our patrols established themselves East of the village.

The 5th Royal Berks Regt. also moved forward and gained touch with the left of the 35th Bde.

On the left Bde. front, progress was made during the day and NOYELLES was completely cleared of the enemy.

Oct.11th.　　The night of the 10th/11th passed without incident, and at dawn on the 11th, the advance was resumed.

/On the

2.

On the left, opposition was met with at first by M.Gs and T.Ms from the QUARRY in O.19.a., but this was soon overcome and the 6th "Queens" continued the advance, capturing FOUQUERIES.

Progress North of the SOUCHEZ River, however, was slower and the left flank of the 6th "Queens" had to be thrown back considerably to keep touch with the 58th Division.

In the morning, the 6th R.W. Kent Regt. captured LONDON COPSE and made good progress towards BILLY TRENCH, west of which they were temporarily held up. About midday, however, they went forward again, and cleared the whole of BILLY MONTIGNY, gaining touch with the 6th "Queens" on their left.

Meanwhile, the 35th and 36th Bdes. had both captured the DROCOURT-QUEANT Line within their Brigade boundaries with very little opposition, and patrols were pushed forward to DROCOURT SUPPORT SECOND and DROCOURT SUPPORT THIRD.

In the meantime the 9th Essex Regt., with one 18 pdr. battery attached, exploited this success, and moved through BILLY MONTIGNY and HENIN LIETARD, and established themselves before midnight on the line shown on the attached map.

Oct.12th.
The advance was resumed by all three Bdes. at 06.00 hrs. and little opposition was met with at first.

On the right, rearguards of the enemy were found at FOSSE 5 and FOSSE 4, but they withdrew hastily on the commencement of an enveloping move by our troops.

Considerable fighting took place in COURCELLES, practically all of which was in our hands by dusk, but the enemy prevented all attempts to debouch from the Eastern exits of the by heavy M.G. fire at NOYELLE GODAULT, but eventually withdrew. Before this, however, the enemy had delayed our advance for some time He also held AUBY strongly, and the 35th Bde. did not succeed in entering that village at all on this day. During the evening it was shelled by our artillery and at 22.00 hrs. patrols attempted to enter the village, but the enemy was still holding it, and they did not make progress.

In the centre, the 36th Bde. met with no resistance until they came within range of CITE BRUNO and DOURGES, both of which the enemy held, and continued to hold all day. During the afternoon and evening these villages were shelled by our Artillery.

On the left, the 37th Bde. reached the line shown on the map, at the end of the day. Opposition was very slight except at JERUSALEM in P.7.a., where a small party of Germans held out for some time but eventually withdrew across the open, towards COURRIERES, and were heavily fired on, casualties being caused, by the 6th R.W. Kent Regt. Subsequently attempts to capture COURRIERES proved unsuccessful.

Divisional Headquarters moved in the morning from CHATEAU de la HAIE to LIEVIN.

Oct.13th.
During the night 12th/13th, the 58th Division had relieved the 37th Bde. on the left, and the latter had concentrated in the BILLY MONTIGNY area, in Divisional reserve.

The advance was resumed on the 13th inst., but met with considerably more resistance on the part of the enemy.

On the right, in conjunction with the 8th Division, an attack was made on AUBY, but though the western portion of the village was reached, our troops were compelled to withdraw to the line shown on the map.

On the left of the 35th Bde. however, the 9th Bn. Essex Regt. made considerable progress, after stiff fighting, in the outskirts of COURCELLES, and reached the CANAL in P.23.a. and b.

/The 36th Bde.-

The 36th Bde. cleared CITE BRUNO and DOURGES, but were unable to gain the line of the HAUTE DEULE CANAL.

During the day the enemy's artillery fire was unusually heavy and also his trench mortar fire, on areas just west of the HAUTE DEULE CANAL. Owing to the bad weather it was not possible to carry out counterbattery work and the infantry suffered a good deal in consequence.

Oct.14th. On this day there was no material change on the front of the 36th Bde. Attempts by patrols were made continuously to reach the CANAL on their left battalion front, and to cross it in P.17.c and P.23.a. on their right battalion front, but all these attempts were stopped by the enemy. A certain amount of progress was made as shown on the map.

At 15.15 hrs. however, in conjunction with the left Bde. 8th Division, the 35th Bde. attacked AUBY, under a barrage. They captured the village within their boundaries and advanced to the CANAL east of it. On their right, however, the attack was not successful, and their right flank was very exposed. In addition, they came under very heavy artillery, T.M. and M.G. fire all along the eastern edges of AUBY and the ground between it and the CANAL. The enemy also trickled across the bridge in P.33.a. to reinforce his men who were still holding out in the eastern portion of the village, and succeeded in delivering a counter attack which drove our troops back to the line shown on the attached map, where it was maintained.

Oct.15th. During the night of the 14th/15th inst., the 36th Bde. Bde. made attempts to cross the Canal in P.17.c. and P.23.a. but owing to heavy trench mortar fire, the attempt was not successful the enemy still holding the eastern bank strongly.

In the afternoon, however, the 5th Royal Berks Regt. manage to establish a joint post with the 174th Bde., 58th Division, on the East side of the Canal, at PONT A SAULT.

Oct.16th. During the night 15th/16th, the 5th Royal Berks Regt. succeeded in getting two companies across the Canal at PONT A SAULT. Movement East of the Canal by day, however, was impossible, and it was not possible to extend the bridgehead. On the 35th Bde. front there was no change. Attempts to push out a post to the Canal bank in P.30.b. proved unsuccessful.

Divisional Headquarters moved in the morning from LIEVIN to HENIN LIETARD.

Oct.17th. On night 16th/17th inst., a pontoon bridge was completed 100 yards south of PONT A SAULT.

At 04.00 hrs. on morning of 17th, the enemy was still holding his usual position both opposite PONT A SAULT and also at AUBY.

At daylight, however, he commenced to retire and was closely followed up by our troops who crossed the CANAL at PONT A SAULT in P.23.a. and by a raft E. of AUBY, where a pontoon bridge was completed before dusk.

The retirement of the enemy was very rapid and touch was lost during the day.

By dusk the line was as shown in attached map, and the enemy was shelling LA COUCHETTE, Q.21.a.

About 600 civilians were liberated in CORDELA and RAIMBEAUCOURT, but no reliable information was gained about the enemy.

In the afternoon, the 37th Bde. moved forward to the COURCELLES-AUBY front, preparatory to advancing on the next day.

/Oct. 18th.

Oct.18th.   The advance was resumed at dawn.
On the right, 37th Bde. passed through a portion of the left Bde., 8th Division, and a part of the 35th Bde. the latter side stepping and passing through the 36th Bde. who came into Divisional reserve.

No opposition was met with until LA PLACETTE, R.21.c. was reached, where the 6th R.W. Kent Regt. had an encounter with a cavalry patrol of the enemy, inflicting casualties and taking a prisoner.

The 35th Bde. also advanced and met with little opposition except from a few isolated patrols, particularly at MT COUVE, N.14.c. and LA PIETERIE, R.4.a. and b. where prisoners were captured, and by dusk the line was as shown on attached map.

During the day the enemy shelled WARENDIN, RACHES and FLINES rather heavily from 17.00 to 20.00 hrs.

About 3,000 civilians were liberated in FLINES, and 500 in BOUJON.

Touch with the enemy was obtained west of COUTICHES and S.W. of MOLINEL.

Oct.19th.   The advance was continued by 35th and 37th Bdes. at 07.30 hrs. each on a one battalion front, with a section of cyclists.

Slight opposition was met with - a German patrol held on for a little time at LES FOSSES FARM, M.4.c. but by the end of the day the line reached was as shown on attached map.

During the day, the enemy shelled ORCHIES and BEUVRY heavily from 15.00 to 17.00 hrs.

About 6,000 civilians were found in ORCHIES and 2,000 in COUTICHES.

Much difficulty and inconvenience was caused to our advance by the craters that had been blown at nearly every cross road or road junction, and particularly by the blowing up of the bridge S.W. of COUTICHES in M.8.a., but on no occasion during the whole advance did ammunition and rations fail to reach the troops.

Divisional Headquarters moved in the morning from HENIN LIETARD to RAIMBEAUCOURT.

Oct. 20th.   The advance was continued again, and no opposition was met with until the troops approached the western outskirts of SAMEON, when the enemy ran out of the village and manned some short disconnected lengths of trenches on the western side.   They were attacked by the 1/1st Cambridgeshire Regt. and driven back, about 10 prisoners being captured.

The hostile artillery was fairly quiet throughout the day, and patrols at night were not in touch with the enemy.

Oct. 21st.   During the night 20th/21st inst., our patrols pushed well ahead of the line shown on the map for 21.00 hrs, 20th inst., without obtaining touch with the enemy, and on the 21st inst. owing to the increasing difficulties of supply, and also to conform to the plans of the flanking divisions, only a short advance was ordered.

This was carried out without much difficulty to the line shown on the map.

Slight trouble was met with for a time from a party of the enemy at the CENSE de WABEMPRE, and they also continued to hold the CENSE DE CHOQUES for the whole day.

In the afternoon, touch was obtained with the enemy at RUE LASSON - RUE BOUCHARD, and along the eastern banks of the stream running E. of LECELLES, over which all the bridges were blown up.

/A squadron.-

A squadron of 4th Hussars ~~were~~ [was] employed this day by the leading Brigades for the first time during the advance.

During the day the enemy shelled RUMEGIES and LECELLES with all calibres of shells, including Heavies. No civilians were found in the latter village.

In the morning, plans were laid for a night advance on the night of the 21st/22nd, with a view to reaching the SCARPE CANAL at dawn, surprising the enemy, and seizing the bridges before the latter had time to destroy them. It was hoped that this would be possible as the enemy, by this time, had become accustomed to our advances each day.

A further reason to hope for the success of the operation was that there was a bright moon after midnight, which made progress easier than it would otherwise have been.

For this purpose, the 36th Bde. who had moved forward daily in Divisional reserve, sent two battalions to SAMEON in the afternoon, preparatory to moving through the 35th Bde., shortly after midnight on the night 21st/22nd., the 37th Bde. conforming on their right.

Oct.22nd. The 9th Royal Fusiliers, 36th Bde. passed through LECELLES at 01.00 hrs.

The enemy was shelling the village at intervals, and also the RUMEGIES-LECELLES Road.

Progress was made without opposition by the 37th Bde. on the right, and the right of the 36th Bde., but the left of the 36th Bde. was held up as it reached the ST AMAND -MAULDE Road, and at 09.00 the line was as shown on attached map.

37th Bde. had sent a patrol of cyclists to the Canal in J.29.c. and they reported that the bridges were all blown up as were the bridges over the DESCOURS river.

During the day attempts were made to send an infantry patrol across the canal at MAIRIE DE NIVELLE but these were prevented by machine gun fire from the western bank.

About midday patrols of the 37th Bde. crossed the river at ST AMAND and by the evening had occupied CUBRAY.

Meanwhile on the left the 36th Bde. were definitely held up by the enemy from FLAGNIES, FORT de MAULDE and MONT de la JUSTICE, and at 21.00 hrs. the line was as shown on the attached map.

Divisional Headquarters moved in the morning from RAIMBEAUCOURT to ORCHIES.

Oct.23rd. During the night of 22nd/23rd inst., the 6th "Buffs" 37th Bde. and a company of the 6th R.W. Kent Regt. crossed the SCARPE at ST AMAND, and moved northwards up the Eastern bank.

At 04.30 hrs. the latter attacked the bridge in J.29.c. meeting with considerable machine gun fire.

During the morning the "Buffs" had hard fighting N. of CUBRAY and towards HAUTE RIVE, in which village they succeeded in establishing themselves by dusk.

Meantime, efforts were made during the morning to establish a footbridge for infantry across the CANAL in J.29.c. but they were not successful and the R.E. Officer of the 87th Field Coy. in charge of the work was killed.

The enemy was still holding the houses at the MAIRIE de NIVELLE, and his snipers and machine guns were very active from them.

During the afternoon, however, he withdrew from this point, the footbridge was erected, and the houses occupied by us.

/On the left.-

On the left, the 36th Bde. occupied FLAGNIES, but made little further progress - the enemy continued to hold FORT de MAULDE and MONT de la JUSTICE strongly.

At 21.00 hrs. the line was as shown on the attached map.

Divisional Headquarters moved in the morning from ORCHIES to SAMEON.

Oct.24th.
At 07.45 hrs. under cover of an artillery bombardment the 6th "Buffs" of 37th Bde. advanced on BURIDON. The enemy was holding the village strongly with machine guns, and was protected by a continuous double belt of low barbed wire entanglement.

Considerable fighting took place before the 37th Bde. were able to capture BURIDON, and many Germans were killed, in addition 1 Officer and 14 O.R. being taken prisoners.

As soon as BURIDON was captured, however, the enemy retired in disorder and left BRUILLE and LE LONG BUHOT without attempting to defend them. By mid-day both these villages were in our possession.

In the afternoon, the enemy shelled both of them and also HAUTE RIVE and BURIDON, very heavily with all calibres up to 8 inch.

On the left, the right Bn. of the 36th Bde. made progress capturing MOTTE du MIN, LOCRON FARM, and the southern half of CHATEAU L'ABBAYE without much difficulty. Attempts to enter the northern half of the village latter village were unsuccessful however, the enemy were holding it strongly with machine guns and the approaches were rendered difficult by the fact that the area in between the two halves of the village was flooded to a depth of about a foot.

West of the SCARPE CANAL patrols had entered THUN on the night 23rd/24th and found it empty, but otherwise no further progress was made though a heavy bombardment of the MONT de la JUSTICE was carried out during the morning by a battery of 6 inch Hows. that had been got into action.

Oct.25th.
There was practically no change on the whole Divisional Front.

Patrols were pushed out with a view to getting across the ESCAUT and JARD CANALS, but found all the bridges blown up, the ESCAUT deep and unfordable, and enemy machine guns very active from the eastern banks.

The 36th Bde. made an attempt to clear the Germans out of CHATEAU L'ABBAYE, but they were not successful.

During the day, the enemy's shelling was not so severe as on the 24th. Many explosions were seen in J.9. and J.10, and also at the FORT de MAULDE.

Oct.26th.
On the 26th October there was no change on the front of the 37th Bde., but on the west of the SCARPE CANAL patrols advancing at dawn found that the enemy had withdrawn, and our line was soon established along the Canal bank. All the bridges were destroyed.

The enemy was still holding the northern half of CHATEAU L'ABBAYE.

Oct.27th.
During the night 26th/27th the 7th Bn. Royal Sussex Regt. attacked the portion of CHATEAU L'ABBAYE held by the enemy, after a short hurricane artillery bombardment, and succeeded in capturing it. Two prisoners were taken, and more would have been captured but for the fact that a party of our own troops, who had reached the western end of the village, mistook a party of about 20 Germans for some more of our troops who were known to be advancing from the east end of the village. When challenged they broke and fled to the north through J.17.b.

/Patrols were.-

Patrols were pushed out during the day and found the enemy still holding the CHATEAU de MORTAGNE.

During the night 27th/28th, a raft footbridge (with petrol cans for floats) was completed across the ESCAUT opposite BRUILLE, in spite of heavy enemy machine gun fire.

Oct.28th. There was no change in the situation. During the night 27th/28th, the 36th Bde. took over the whole Divisional Front, relieving the 37th Bde. in the right sub-sector.

Oct.29th. 155th Bde., 52nd Division relieved the 36th Bde. during night 28th/29th, and command of the sector passed to them at 10.00 hrs. on 29th October.

There had been no further change in the situation - the enemy was still holding CHATEAU de MORTAGNE and the east bank of the JARD.

During the whole of the above operations the work carried out by the 69th, 70th and 87th Field Companies R.E. and also by the 5th Northamptonshire Regt. (Pioneers), was exceptionally heavy, and entailed long hours of duty frequently followed at once by a long march to catch up the remainder of the Division.

These units responded cheerfully to every call upon them and a special Appendix is attached giving some details of their work for the period under review.

Attached are 4 Appendices, as follows :-

Appendix "A"..............The work of the 12th Divisional R.E. and 5th Northamptonshire Regt. (Pioneers) during the Operations 7/10/18 to 11/11/18 East of VIMY Sector.
Appendix "B"..............Prisoners and Material captured.
Appendix "C"..............Casualties.
Appendix "D"..............Lessons Learnt during the Operations.

28.11.18. Major-General,
Commanding, 12th Division.

Appendix "A"

THE WORK OF THE 12th DIVISIONAL R.E. AND 5th NORTHAMPTONSHIRE REGT. (PIONEERS) DURING THE OPERATIONS 7/10/18 to 11/11/18 EAST OF VIMY SECTOR.

On arrival in this sector preparations were made for following up the expected retreat of the enemy – roads were carried forward and a little screening was done, but the extent of the area occupied and the backward condition of the roads caused a bad start to be made. The existing scheme was to make 4 roads forward :-

       (a). LENS - HENIN LIETARD.
       (b). AVION - DROCOURT.
       (c). VIMY - ACHEVILLE.
       (d). THELUS - BOIS BERNARD.

It was obvious from the start that this was impossible; (a) is a good pave road and only craters has to be made good, (b) was fair to AVION and possible afterwards, (c) and (d) were hopeless. This caused considerable trouble as RAILHEADS etc. were being arranged on the South flank and the roads had to go along the Northern flank. By dint of great exertions on the part of all ranks including a whole Brigade of Infantry working on (b) road for 3 days and on (a) road for 2 days the Division was able to feed itself up to the HAUTE DEULE CANAL. During this period the inactivity of Light Railways in this Sector was most marked and trebled the difficulties of the advance. About 40 Mine Craters and over 1,000 Booby Traps were dealt with during this period and 26 wells were repaired with improvised buckets and winches.

On night 15th/16th October, the enemy retired from PONT A SAULT and the 70th Field Coy. R.E. had a pontoon bridge over by 6 a.m. on the 16th followed up by a H.T. Trestle Bridge completed on the 18th, the Pontoons being picked up. The 87th Field Coy. R.E. had a cork bridge across at COURCELLES by 6 a.m. on 16th. The 69th Field Coy. R.E. got a Pontoon Bridge over at AUBY on the 17th by 4.30 p.m. and the 87th Field Coy. R.E. got a bridge of 80 feet span to carry M.T. across at COURCELLES by 8 a.m. on the 17th, an extremely creditable job done in 16 hours, mostly at night. The bridge at AUBY was replaced before evening 18th by a H.T. Trestle Bridge.

The above bridges carried a great deal of the transport of the Divisions on both flanks and the COURCELLES bridge for 48 hours was carrying practically all the M.T. of the Corps and even some from 5th Army. The 2 Flank Bridges were made for H.T. only owing to the shortness of heavy timber and urgency of work.

During this time the Pioneers assisted with approaches to the Bridges and mending craters on both sides of the Canal.

The next bound was to ORCHIES and the Field Coys. R.E. and Pioneers followed up the work; these units worked all day and often far into the night.

28 Craters were filled, the debris of 2 heavy Steel Bridges was removed from the roadway and a heavy culvert 12 ft. span to carry Tanks was made near COUTICHES. On this latter the 70th Field Coy. R.E. had to use Poplars, as no other material was available and were assisted by a party of male and female civilians. This Company marched 12 miles and after about 4 hours rest did 36 hours continuous work on this bridge.

By 22nd inst. all the Companies R.E. and Pioneers were moving forward again, and got up to the SAMEON - RUMEGIES - NIVELLE areas.

On the 23rd the 87th Field Coy. R.E. had a H.T. Bridge across the DECOURS thus allowing infantry transport to get up to the SCARPE.

A machine driven Saw Bench from LENS Junction was installed at SAMEON on this day to cut equal Road Bearers and decking for prospective bridges. This was found to be very useful.

The main work was then concentrated on making good the road Craters and destroyed Culverts between ORCHIES and the SCARPE. About 75 Craters were repaired in this area. As this area is very low lying, in 25% of the cases Culverts had to be made to carry lorries. The 5th Northampton- -shire Regt. (Pioneers) made several of these Culverts up to 10 ft. span very successfully out of local materials.

P. T. O.

By the 25th, the 87th Field Coy. R.E. had a pontoon Bridge across the ~~TRAITORE~~ SCARPE near NIVELLE and a H.T. Trestle Bridge across the TRAITORE. The approaches to these Bridges were extremely awkward but this could not be avoided. This work was of a very difficult nature, the enemy had not retired far from the Eastern bank and when the first foot bridge was put over an enemy M.G. was in a house about 100 yards away. Whilst the H.T. Bridges were being made the party were being shelled continuously and two 8 inch shells fell within a few feet of the bridgehead, partly burying an Officer and some men. All the stores had to come through NIVELLE which was also being heavily shelled during the 36 hours the work was in progress.

By the 29th these bridges at NIVELLE had been replaced by a lorry bridge with over 100 yards of Plank Road approach.

On the 27th the 69th Field Coy. R.E. had a cork bridge across the ESCAUT near PONT DE LA VERNETTE and had 120 ft of Petrol Tin Bridge ready at BRUILLE to bridge the JARD CANAL. As the enemy was still holding the ground between the JARD and ESCAUT and the cork bridge had not been crossed by anyone except the working party, the Petrol Tin Bridge was not needed at the moment.

On the 29th, the R.E. and Pioneers of this Division were relieved and the area was left clear for lorry traffic up to the ESCAUT with the Cork Bridge across the River.

For some days the Companies rested and carried out a few jobs on improving bridges and craters in the ORCHIES-BOUVIGNIES area. Considerable work was done by the transport on several consecutive nights getting stores up for a plank road at HERGNIES.

On the 9th November, the 3 Field Companies, R.E. and the Pioneers were employed making the Plank Road 1,000 yards long at HERGNIES. This was finished by 10.0 a.m. on the 10th and a certain amount of assistance was given to the 52nd Divisional R.E. in making the bridges there.

Until the Armistice was signed, work with Infantry assistance was continued on Roads and Bridges forward, 7 heavy Canal Bridges being completed up to 21st inst., including one of three 30 foot spans.

                            Sgd/ A.T. SHAKESPEAR.
12th Division H.Q.   Lt. Col. R.E.
24th November 1918.   C.R.E. 12th Division.

APPENDIX "B".

PRISONERS OF WAR.

Officers.................... 1.
Other Ranks................. 108.

MATERIAL CAPTURED.

Machine Guns................ 22.
Light T.M. Batteries........ 2.

APPENDIX "C".

CASUALTIES.

Since Division came into VIII Corps to
29/10/1918.

UNIT.	Killed.		Wounded.		Missing.	
	Offrs.	O.R.	Offrs.	O.R.	Offrs.	O.R.
35th Inf. Bde.	3.	53.	15.	202.	2.	27.
36th Inf. Bde.	2.	35.	10.	152.	—	4.
37th Inf. Bde.	1.	15.	11.	106.	—	10.
5th Northants (Pns).	—	—	—	—	—	—
12th Bn.M.G.C.	—	—	—	17.	—	1.
12th Div.Artillery.	—	5.	—	21.	—	—
Royal Engineers.	1.	—	—	9.	—	—
Other Units.	—	—	—	6.	—	—
Total	7.	108	36.	513.	2.	42.

APPENDIX "D".

LESSONS LEARNT DURING

THE OPERATIONS.

1. " Few new lessons were learnt during this period, but nearly all those learnt during the SOMME fighting were emphasised, particularly -
   (a). The value of the Brigade group as the fighting unit.
   (b). The importance of liason units with flanking formations meeting at certain points during the day's advance - such points to be arranged by Divisions and notified by them to Brigades.
   (c). Insufficient training of all units in open warfare involving self protection, with especial reference to the flanks, and of many Officers and N.C.Os in the use of the compass and in map reading.
   (d). The value of some artillery, usually an 18 p dr. battery, and machine guns - usually a section - being under the direct orders of the leading Bn. commander, though in some cases the latter were not always sufficiently experienced to make proper use of them. Commanders of such batteries or M.G. sections should be at the headquarters of the Bn. they are working under.

2. The following points were also brought out in the course of the advance -

INFANTRY.
   (a). 1 N.C.O. and 6 O.R. is a satisfactory number for a section, but it is a minimum number. When the strength of a section falls below it, the section is unable to work efficiently as an L.G. section (a minimum of 12 drums being required) nor is it able to find a double sentry post. For these reasons, therefore, a supply of reserves should be available at, or near, battalion Headquarters, to fill up casualties below a strength of 1 N.C.O. and 6 O.R. per section.
   (b). For proper relief and for the best tactical handling in action it is considered that the organization of a Bde. on the 4 Bn. basis should be reverted to.
   (c). The superiority of the German L.T.M. over our own Stokes Mortar was very marked, chiefly due to the longer range of the former. If leading battalions had with them a section of German L.T.M's or a similar weapon, the delay from isolated machine guns left behind by the enemy would have been much decreased.

COMMUNICATIONS.
   (a). Difficulty in lateral communication was considerable throughout. Brigades were unable to lay lines to flank Brigades, and it was often impossible for Divisions to do so. Liason Officers did not altogether overcome the difficulty because during this kind of warfare plans are made or altered at such short notice that the Liason Officer was often away with one message which it subsequently became necessary to modify considerably. Wherever possible, Divisions should be connected up by a lateral line, as they are then able to arrange details for the next operations by telephone and notify the arrangements to their own Brigades sufficiently early to allow the necessary orders to be issued in good time to units.
   (b). In order to maintain efficient communication in open warfare it is considered essential that a proportion of mounted troops and cyclists should be attached to a Division. On the occasions when such troops were attached during recent operations, they were invaluable.

ARTILLERY.
   (a). As regards the Artillery, the Heavy Artillery, until placed

/under Div.-

under Divisional Control, was inclined to push ahead too fast, before the roads were ready for them. In one or two cases blocks and delays were caused in consequence. Heavy Artillery attached to a Division should be retained under the direct orders of the Division, but should have a liason Officer with the leading Brigade.

(b). During moving warfare of this nature, the M.T. ammunition echelon should be in direct touch with the D.A.C. The system of supply for stationary warfare did not seem satisfactory for moving warfare, though no real test of it actually took place during this advance.

(c). The plan of attaching 2 Army F.A. Brigades to the Divisional Artillery (making 4 Artillery Brigades in all) worked well. Reliefs were carried out easily, and Artillery Brigades got thoroughly to know the Infantry Brigades they were working with.

The following points were brought out in connection with the work of the R.E.-

ROYAL ENGINEERS.

(a). The work to be done in moving warfare by Field Coys.R.E. is of a far more permanent character than was ever anticipated before this war. For this reason the equipment of Field Coys. needs drastic revision, and also the method of carrying this equipment, viz:- by H.T. or its partial replacement by M.T. Reference was made to this in a report sent in on lessons learnt in the SOMME fighting with regard to water supply, and during October the experience was repeated, this time in connection with heavy bridging.

(b). Field Coys.R.E. must be able to deal with new work. Stocks, Dies, and Acetylene Cutting plant were needed on numerous occasions, and reliance on the provision of these stores from back areas proved hopeless.

(c). For heavy bridging a machine driven saw is essential, particularly for cutting equal road bearers and decking.

(d). It was found unprofitable to carry on heavy bridging throughout the night unless there was a good moon, or means of artificial light provided. The men got overtired and better and quicker work was got by working in daylight only.

(e). Pontoon equipment was frequently used, but it should be altered so as to allow easy and safe conversion to carry lorry traffic. Varnish on chesses should be removed as it appears to be responsible for an excess of dry rot. Shore Bays of Pontoon Bridges should be longer and splayed, as approaches are nearly always bad.

PIONEERS.

As regards the Pioneer Battalion, the suggestion is put forward that the question of forming this into a R.E. Bn. should be considered. The present system is not altogether satisfactory.

MEDICAL.

As regards clearing the wounded, the work was made extremely difficult owing to the efficient destruction of roads and bridges by the enemy. In this connection the small Ford Ambulances were of great value. Owing to their speed and handiness they were very useful in exploring all possible routes between the A.D.S. and R.A.P's. Often, with the aid of infantry, they were got across bad bits of road or minecraters that would have been impossible to the heavy ambulance cars. Once across they could work from R.A.P. to the crater or other obstacle, whence casualties were carried on stretchers to a large car waiting the other side of the crater to carry them to the A.D.S.

28.11.1918.

App 1.

SECRET.

Copy No......

12th DIVISION ORDER NO. 187

Ref : Sheets 44.A. S.W.
51.B. N.W.

3rd October, 1918.

(1).   If the tactical situation permits the 12th Division (less Artillery) will relieve 20th Division (less Artillery) in the centre Sector of the VIII Corps front during the period 5th/7th October, in accordance with attached Movement Table.

(2).   The Divisional and inter-Brigade Boundaries will be as shewn on attached map.

(3).   The Line will be taken over as held.   Details of relief will be arranged between Commanders concerned.

(4).   Relief of Field Companies will be arranged between C.R.Es direct.   One Field Company, R.E. will work in each Brigade Sector and will be affiliated to the Brigade.

(5).   Relief of Medical Units will be arranged between A.Ds.M.S. concerned.

(6).   Movement of relieving troops to forward area with exception of the Pioneer Battalion which will proceed by March Route, will be by Bus.   Bussing arrangements will be issued separately.

(7).   The move to the forward area will be conducted in accordance with S.S. 724 (March Discipline and Traffic Control).

(8).   Relieving Units will take over Maps, Air photos, Defence Schemes etc., relating to their respective Sectors.

(9).   Completion of each serial in the Movement Table will be reported to Divisional H.Q.

(10).   Relief will be completed by 6 a.m. on 7th October. Command of the Sector will pass to G.O.C. 12th Division at 6 p.m. on 6th October.

(11).   Divisional H.Q. will close at VILLERS CHATEL and opened at CHATEAU de LA HAIE at 6 p.m. on the 6th October.

(12).   A C K N O W L E D G E.

Lieut-Colonel.
General Staff.
12th Division.

Issued at : 23.45.

Copies to/..........

	1. G.O.C.
	2. G.S.O. I.
	3. C.R.A. (50th Div.)
ø	4. C.R.E.
ø	5. 35th Inf. Bde.
ø	6. 36th Inf. Bde.
ø	7. 37th Inf. Bde.
	8. 5th Northamptonshire Regt. (Pioneers).
ø	9. 12th Bn. M.G.C.
	10. 12th Signals.
ø	11. A.D.M.S.
	12. D.A.D.V.S.
	13. 12th Div. Train.
	14. S.S.O.
	15. D.A.P.M.
	16. D.A.D.O.S.
	17. 214th Div'l. Emp. Coy.
	18. Div. Reception Camp.
	19. Camp Commandant.
	20. Div. Gas Officer.
	21. "Q"
	22. VIII Corps.
	23. 8th Division.
	24. 20th Division.
	25. 58th Division.
	26 & 27. War Diary.
	28 - 33. G.S. & Records.

ø Map attached.

-- MOVEMENT TABLE ISSUED WITH 4th DIVISION ORDER NO. 237 --

SERIAL NO.	DATE.	UNIT.	FROM.	TO.	RELIEVING.	REMARKS.
1.	5th Oct.	1 Bn. 35th Inf. Bde.	GAMBLAIN L'ABBE Area.	FRONT LINE ARLEUX SECTION.	1 Bn. 61st Inf. Bde.	NOTE - Reliefs will be carried out as only and expeditiously as possible.
2.	do.	1 Bn. 37th Inf. Bde.	CAUCOURT Area.	FRONT LINE AVION SECTION.	1 Bn. 59th Inf. Bde.	
3.	5/6th.	12th Bn. M.G.C.	GOUY SERVINS.	CENTRE SECTOR.	20th Bn. M.G.C.	
4.	do.	36th Inf. Bde. and affiliated Field Coy.R.E.	CHATEAU de LA HAIE Area.	HERICOURT SECTION.	60th Inf. Bde.	
5.	6th Oct.	5th Northants. Regt.	ESTREE CAUCHIE.	CARENCY.	20th Divnl. Pioneer Bn.	
6.	6/7th.	35th Inf. Bde. (less 1 Bn) & affiliated Field Coy.R.E.	GAMBLAIN L'ABBE Area.	ARLEUX SECTION.	61st Inf. Bde. (less 1 Bn.)	
7.	do.	37th Inf. Bde. (less 1 Bn) & affiliated Field Coy.R.E.	CAUCOURT Area.	AVION SECTION.	59th Inf. Bde. (less 1 Bn.)	

S E C R E T.

ADDENDUM NO. 1 to 12th DIVISION ORDER NO. 287

The Machine Gun Battalion relief will now be carried out as follows, and not as stated in Movement Table issued with above Order.

On night 5th/6th, Centre and Reserve Coys will carry out relief.

On night 6th/7th Flank Coys will relieve.

                                            Lieut-Colonel,
                                            General Staff.

4th October, 1918.   12th Division.

Copies to all recipients of 12th Division Order No. 287.

App No 2

SECRET.
Copy No. 2

12th DIVISION ORDER NO. 288

Ref. Sheets 44.a. S.W.
51.b. N.W.   4th October, 1918.

(1)   Reference 12th Division Order No. 287 of 3rd instant.

(2)   50th Divisional Artillery will relieve 20th Divisional Artillery in the line during the period 6th/8th October. One Section per Battery will relieve on the night 6th/7th and remainder on night 7th/8th October.

(3)   Details of relief will be arranged between Cs.R.A. direct.

(4)   Command of the Field Artillery covering the front of 12th Division will pass to C.R.A. 50th Division at 10.00 on 8th instant.

                                    D. Belgrave
                                    Lieut.Colonel,
                                    General Staff,
                                    12th Division.

Issued at 19.45.

Copies to :-

     1. G.O.C.
     2. G.S.O. 1.
     3. C.R.A. (50th Division).
     4. C.R.E.
     5. 35th Inf. Bde.
     6. 36th Inf. Bde.
     7. 37th Inf. Bde.
     8. 5th Northamptonshire Regt. (Pioneers).
     9. 12th Bn. M.G.C.
    10. 12th Div. Signal Coy. R.E.
    11. A.D.M.S.
    12. D.A.D.V.S.
    13. 12th Div. Train.
    14. S.S.O.
    15. D.A.T.M.
    16. D.A.D.O.S.
    17. 214th Div. Employment Coy.
    18. Div. Reception Camp.
    19. Camp Commandant.
    20. Div. Gas Officer.
    21. "Q".
    22. VIII Corps.
    23. 8th Division.
    24. 20th Division.
    25. 58th Division.
    26 - 27. War Diary.
    28 - 33. G.S. and Records.

"A" Form
MESSAGES AND SIGNALS.

Army Form C. 2121
(In pads of 100.)

No. of Message............

Prefix.........Code........m.	Words	Charge.	This message is on a/c of :	Recd. at......h.
Office of Origin and Service Instructions	Sent			Date............
PRIORITY.	At........m.		........Service.	From............
	To........			By............
	By	(Signature of "Franking Officer")		

TO — 35th Inf.Bde. 36th Inf.Bde. 37th Inf.Bde.
C.R.A. C.R.E. A.D.M.S. A.P.M. "Q" 8th Corps.
8th Divn. 58th Divn. 12th Bn. M.G.C.

Sender's Number.	Day of Month.	In reply to Number.	
G 501	8		AAA

In confirmation of verbal instructions
Brigades will push out patrols to maintain
touch with the enemy AAA If patrols are
successful in gaining ground immediate
information will be sent back AAA If it is
found that the enemy has withdrawn patrols
will be strongly supported and the advance
will be made in bounds as follows AAA
First bound general line FOOT HILL - BOIS
VILAN - ACHEVILLE - MERICOURT all
inclusive AAA Second bound FRESNES ROUVROY
LINE as far North as ROUVROY -
FOSSES 5 and 15 in O.25.c. inclusive -
NOYELLES inclusive AAA Third bound TOM
HOUSE - DROCOURT - ROBERT MAZE - DOROTHY
CORONS - BILLY MONTIGNY - FOUQUIERES -
ROLL MAZE in O.13.b. all inclusive AAA
ACKNOWLEDGE AAA Addsd. 35th Inf.Bde.
36th Inf.Bde. 37th Inf.Bde. reptd. C.R.A.
C.R.E. A.D.M.S. A.P.M. "Q" 8th Corps
8th Div. 58th Divn.

From	12th Divn.	(Sgd) J. D. BELGRAVE,
Place		Lt. Col. G.S.
Time	2100	

The above may be forwarded as now corrected. (Z)

....
Censor. Signature of Addressor or person authorised to telegraph in his name
* This line should be erased if not required.

Order No. 1625. Wt. W3253/ P 511. 27/2. H. & K., Ltd. (E. 2634)

SECRET.

Copy No. 1

12th DIVISION ORDER No. 289.

9th October, 1918.

1. 12th Divisional Artillery is detraining at ACQ and AUBIGNY on 10th October, and will be accommodated in the FREVIN CAPELLE Area.

2. 12th Divisional Artillery will relieve 50th Divisional Artillery in the line covering 12th Division on nights 11th/12th and 12th/13th October.

3. On relief, 50th Divisional Artillery will be accommodated in the FREVIN CAPELLE Area, and will entrain on 14th October to join another Army.

4. Details of Artillery reliefs will be arranged between C.R.As. concerned.

5. Orders for entrainment of 50th Divisional Artillery are being issued by VIII Corps "Q".

6. A C K N O W L E D G E.

J B Belgrave

Lieut.Colonel,
General Staff,
12th Division.

Issued at 2359

Copies to :-

1. G.O.C.
2. G.S.O.1.
3. C.R.A., 12th Division.
4. C.R.A., 50th Division.
5. C.R.E.
6. 35th Inf. Bde.
7. 36th Inf. Bde.
8. 37th Inf. Bde.
9. 12th Bn. M.G.C.
10. 12th Div. Signal Coy. R.E.
11. A.D.M.S.
12. D.A.D.V.S.
13. A.P.M.
14. "Q".
15. VIII Corps.
16. 8th Division.
17. 50th Division.
18.- 19 War Diary.
20 - 25. G.S. & Records.
26. S.S.O.
27. 12th Div. Train.

"A" Form.
MESSAGES AND SIGNALS.

Prefix	Code	m.	Words.	Charge.		Recd. at ... m.
Office of Origin and Service Instructions.			Sent		This message is on a/c of:	Date
						From
					Service	
			By.		(Signature of "Franking Officer.")	By

TO. 35th Inf.Bde. 36th Inf.Bde. 37th Inf.Bde. C.R.A. M.G.Bn. 9th Corps. 9th Divn. 58th Divn.

Sender's Number.	Day of Month.	In reply to Number.	
G. 643	10		A A A

Germans appear to hold line of posts along road through U.22.central – ROUVROY VILLAGE (inclusive) – railway cutting N. of ROUVROY thence along ALGOMA CENTRAL to BILEN TRENCH thence to CANAL MAZE with posts still in LOISON and NOYELLES and in the neighbourhood of the COTONS DE MERICOURT SALLAUMINES CEMETERY and FOSSE 4 DE COURRIERES AAA 37th Inf.Bde. will clear up NOYELLES and in conjunction with Bde. on their left push forward strong fighting patrols under a barrage to clear FOSSE 4 DE COURRIERES – SALLAUMINES CEMETERY – SLOPPY TRENCH – SALEY MAZE – FOSSES 3 and 15 in O.25.c. and QUARRY East of NOYELLES G.O.C. 37th Inf. Bde. will arrange with G.O.C. Right Bde. AAA posts will be established on the line FOSSES 3 and 15 – QUARRY + CANAL AAA

From

Place

Time

The above may be forwarded as now corrected. (Z)

Censor. Signature of Addressee or person authorised to telegraph in his name.

*This line, except A A A, should be erased if not required.

"A" Form.
MESSAGES AND SIGNALS.

Army Form C. 2121.
(In pads of 100.)

Sender's Number.	Day of Month.	In reply to Number.	AAA
G*643	10		

50th Divn. regarding co-operation AAA
Artillery of Centre Group will be available
to assist if required AAA The patrols will
be supported by other troops moving forward
in readiness to occupy ground gained AAA machine
guns will also be pushed forward to cover
the advance AAA Centre Bde. will make good
ROUVROY and will keep touch with Left and
Right Bdes. AAA Right Bde. will push forward
machine guns into BOIS FERNARD to assist the
operations of Centre Bde. and will occupy
the IZEL - ROUVROY Road AAA Right Bde. will
work in close co-operation with Bde. on Right
with a view to gaining footing in the DROCOURT
QUEANT LINE AAA ACKNOWLEDGE AAA Addsd. Bdes.
reptd. all concerned.

PRIORITY TO BRIGADES

12th Divn.
1230

B. Belgrave
Lieut.Col., G.S.

MARCH AND RELIEF TABLE - ISSUED WITH 12th DIVISION ORDER No. 292.

DATE.	SERIAL LETTER.	UNIT.	FROM.	TO.	ROUTE.	REMARKS.
OCTOBER.						
27th.	A.	156th Inf.Bde. Group.	COUTICHES area.	LECELLES area.	ORCHIES - LANDAS.	
	B.	157th Inf.Bde. Group.	FLINES area.	LANDAS area.	do.	
28th.	C.	155th Inf.Bde. Group.	do.	do.	do.	No restrictions.
	D.	35th Inf.Bde.	COUTICHES area.	RACHES area.	No restrictions.	Not to move before 155th Inf. Bde. Group have passed through COUTICHES area. Time will be notified later.
	E.	37th Inf. Bde.	SAMEON area.	COUTICHES area.	BEUVRY - BOUVIGNIES.	Not to enter COUTICHES until 35th Inf. Bde. is clear. Time to be notified later.
	F.	157th Inf.Bde. Group.	LANDAS area.	LECELLES area.	SAMEON RUE MORI- METZ - POQUEN.	
	G.	156th Inf. Bde. 1 Coy. 52nd Bn.M.G.C.	LECELLES area.	Line.	No restrictions.	
28th/29th.	H.	36th Inf. Bde. 1 Coy. 12th Bn.M.G.C.	Line.	SAMEON area.	LAVIELLE EGLISE - I.35.d.& c. - I.34.d. & c. - I.33. central.	On completion of relief by Serial G.

attached to
app. no. 19.

S E C R E T.

12th DIVISION NO. G.C. 639

26th October, 1918.

VIII Corps.	37th Inf. Bde.	A.D.M.S.
8th Division.	12th Bn.M.G.C.	D.A.D.V.S.
58th Division.	12th Div. Signal	12th Div.Train.
C.R.A.	Coy. R.E.	S.S.O.
C.R.E.	5th Northants Regt.	D.A.P.M.
35th Inf. Bde.	(Pioneers).	D.A.D.O.S.
36th Inf. Bde.	"Q"	214th Empt Coy.
Camp Commandt.	Div. Gas Officer.	12th Div.M.T.Coy.

-- WARNING ORDER --

(1).   The 12th Division will be relieved in the Left Section of the VIII Corps Front by the 52nd. (Lowland) Division, on the night 28th/29th October.

(2).   On completion of the relief the Division will be disposed in the FLIXES - BACHES - COUTICHES area.

Orders will follow regarding the Artillery.

Lieut-Colonel,
General Staff,
12th Division.

SECRET.

Copy No. _____

12th DIVISION ORDER No. 290.

11th October, 1918.

1. During the period 11th/13th October, the Divisional Front will be reorganised.

2. On completion of reliefs and moves ordered in Paras 4 and 5, the Division will be disposed with two Brigades in Line and one Brigade in Reserve.

3. Boundaries will be as follows :-

Southern Divisional Boundary: As before to V.7.c.0.0 thence to V.7.central - V.8.a.0.0 - V.4.central to HAUTE DEULE CANAL at Q.25.b.7.3.

Inter Brigade Boundary: As before to DRASTIC TRENCH U.4.c. thence c.4.5 - U.4.central (FOSSE 1 De DROCOURT inclusive to Right Brigade).- O.35.c.0.0 - O.30.d.9.0 - P.25.c.0.0 - Railway at P.27.c. 85.50 - P.23.central - thence to Canal at P.23.b.40.25.

Northern Divisional Boundary: As before to N.21.a.85.50 - thence to N.29.A.60.45 - O.26.b.0.5 - O.21.d. 0.0 - O.23.c.0.6 - PONT-a-SAULT.P.15.b.1.9.

4. On night 12th/13th the following reliefs will take place :-

(a) 36th Infantry Brigade will, if necessary, take over from 37th Infantry Brigade as far North as now Divisional Northern Boundary.

(b) 174th Infantry Brigade (58th Division) will take over from 37th Infantry Brigade as far South as new Divisional Northern Boundary.

5. On relief, 37th Infantry Brigade will be in Divisional Reserve, and will be accommodated in
the ACHEVILLE-MERICOURT LINE.

/ 6. ....

(2).

6. Completion of reliefs will be reported to Divisional Headquarters by Code Words "SCREW PICKETS".

7. Command of front north of New Divisional northern boundary will pass from G.O.C. 12th Division to G.O.C. 58th Division at 0600, 13th October.

8. A C K N O W L E D G E.

J.D. Belgrave

Lieut-Colonel,
General Staff,
12th Division.

Issued at *1500*

Copies to :-

1. G.O.C.
2. G.S.O.1.
3. C.R.A.
4. C.R.E.
5. 35th Infantry Brigade.
6. 36th Infantry Brigade.
7. 37th Infantry Brigade.
8. 5th Northamptonshire Regt. (Pioneers).
9. 12th Bn. M.G. Corps.
10. 12th Div. Signal Coy. R.E.
11. A.D.M.S.
12. D.A.D.V.S.
13. 12th Div Train.
14. S.S.O.
15. D.A.I.M.
16. D.A.D.O.S.
17. 214th Div. Emplt. Coy.
18. Div. Reception Camp.
19. Camp Commandant.
20. Div. Gas Officer.
21. "Q".
22. VIII Corps.
23.   do.
24. 8th Division.
25. 58th Division.
26. 15th Squadron R.A.F.
27 & 28. War Diary.
29 - 34. G.S. and Records.

app No 4

SECRET.
Copy No. 21

12th DIVISION ORDER No. 292.

27th October, 1918.

1. 12th Division (less Artillery) will be relieved by 52nd (Lowland) Division (less Artillery) on 28th, and night 28th/29th instant in accordance with Table attached.

    Details of relief will be arranged between Brigade Commanders, C.R.E., O.C. Bns. M.G.C. and A.Ds.M.S. concerned.

2. Orders for the relief of the Artillery will be issued later.

3. Field Companies R.E. and Pioneers will be relieved under orders issued by Chief Engineer, VIII Corps.

4. Nos. 1 of Machine Gun Detachments will be left behind for 24 hours after the relief of the remainder of their Detachments.

5. 12th Division "Q" are arranging for the relief and move of all units not mentioned in Table attached.

6. Divisional Headquarters will close at SAMEON at 10.00 on 29th instant, and open at FLINES at the same hour, when command of Sector passes to G.O.C., 52nd (Lowland) Division.

7. A C K N O W L E D G E.

Issued at 07.45.

J.D. Belgrave
Lieut.Colonel,
General Staff,
12th Division.

Copies to :-

1. G.O.C.
2. G.S.O.1.
3. C.R.A.
4. C.R.E.
5. 35th Inf. Bde.
6. 36th Inf. Bde.
7. 37th Inf. Bde.
8. 5th Northamptonshire Regt. (Pioneers).
9. 12th Bn. M.G.C.
10. 12th Div. Signals.
11. A.D.M.S.
12. D.A.D.V.S.
13. 12th Div. Train.
14. S.S.O.
15. D.A.P.M.
16. D.A.D.O.S.
17. 214th Empl'y. Coy.
18. Div. Reception Camp.
19. Camp Commandant.
20. Div. Gas Officer.
21. "Q"
22 & 23. VIII Corps.
24. 8th Division.
25. 52nd Division.
26. 58th Division.
27 & 28. War Diary.
29 - 34. G.S. and Records.

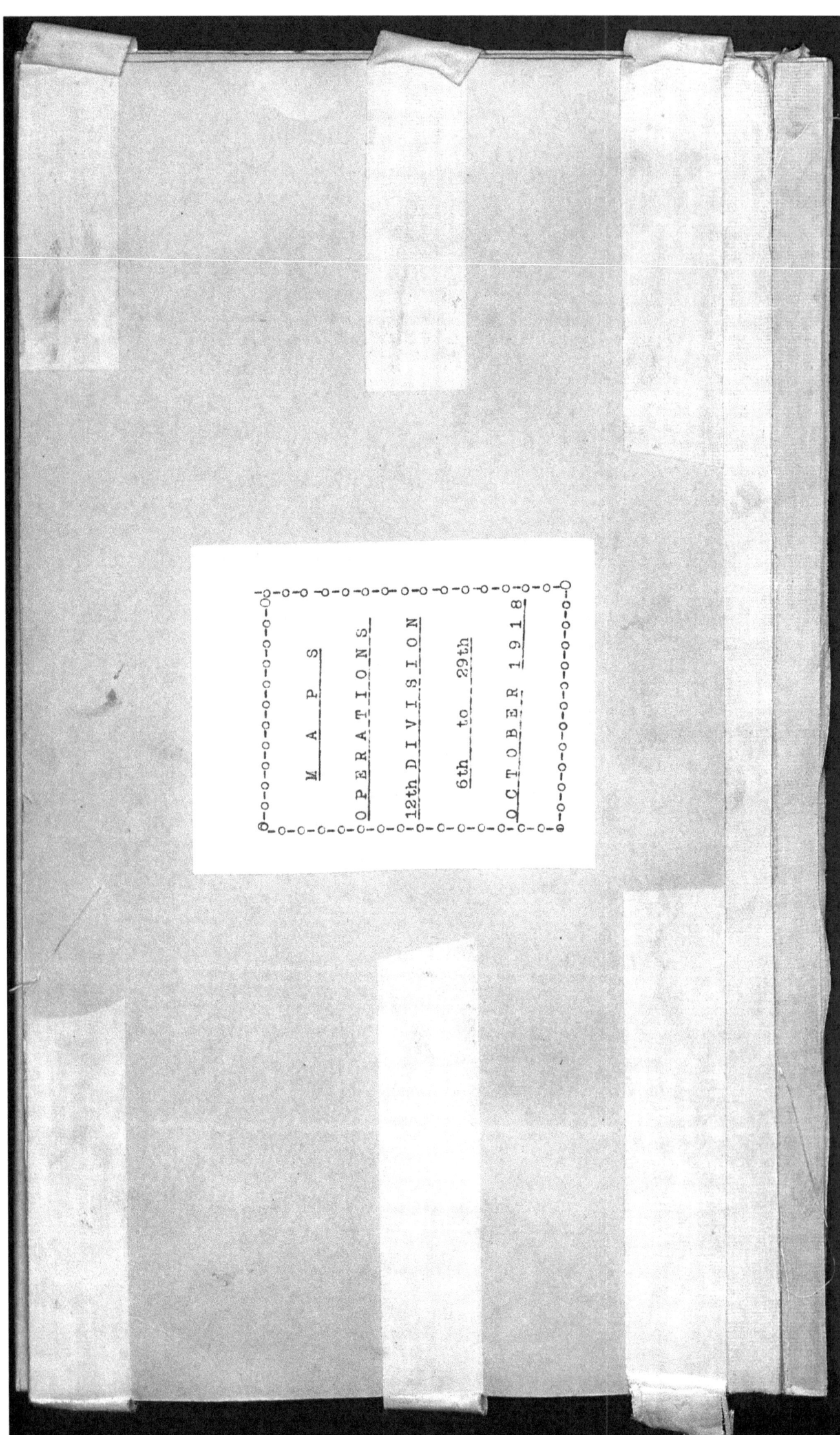

MAPS
OPERATIONS
12th DIVISION
6th to 29th
OCTOBER 1918

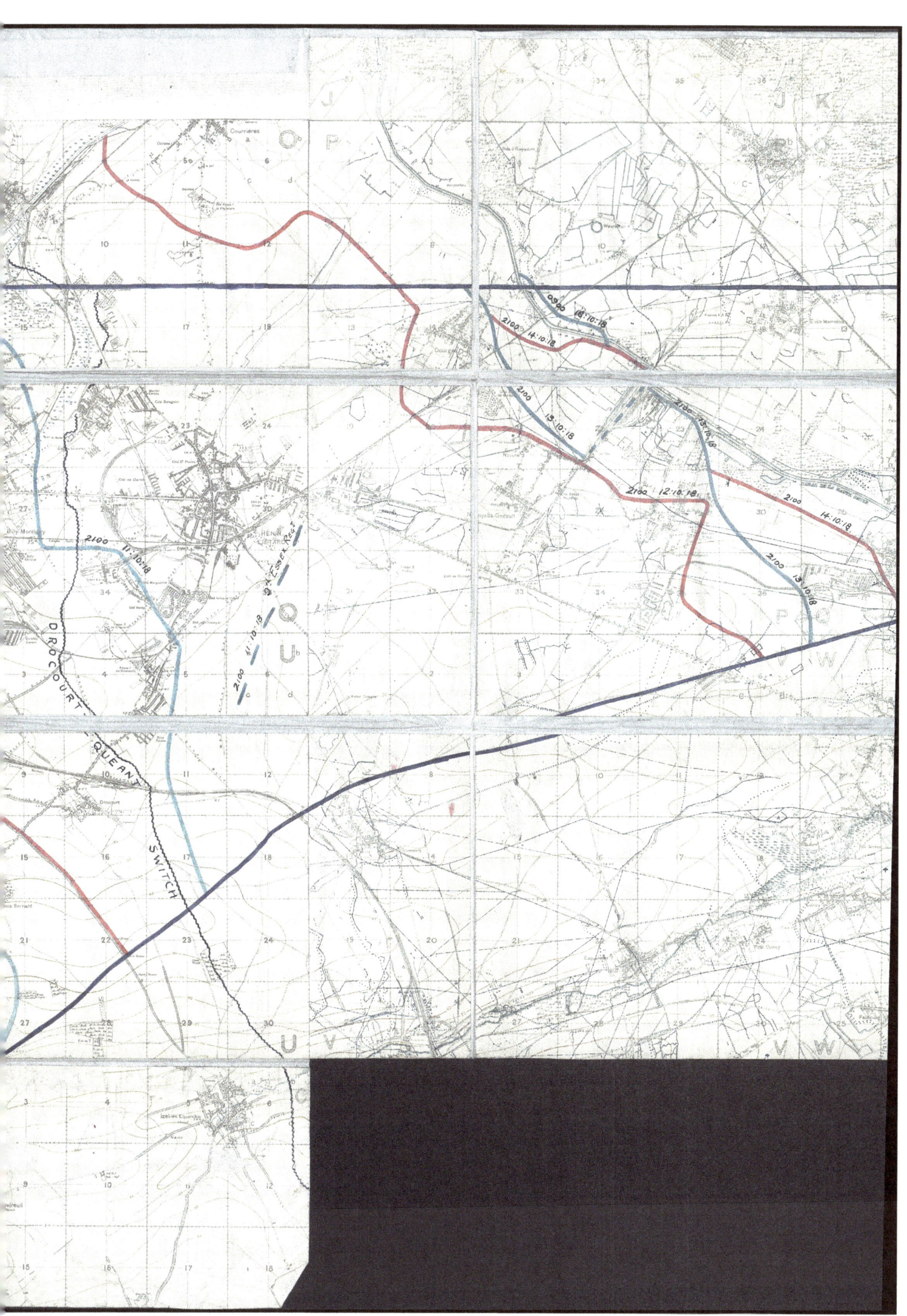

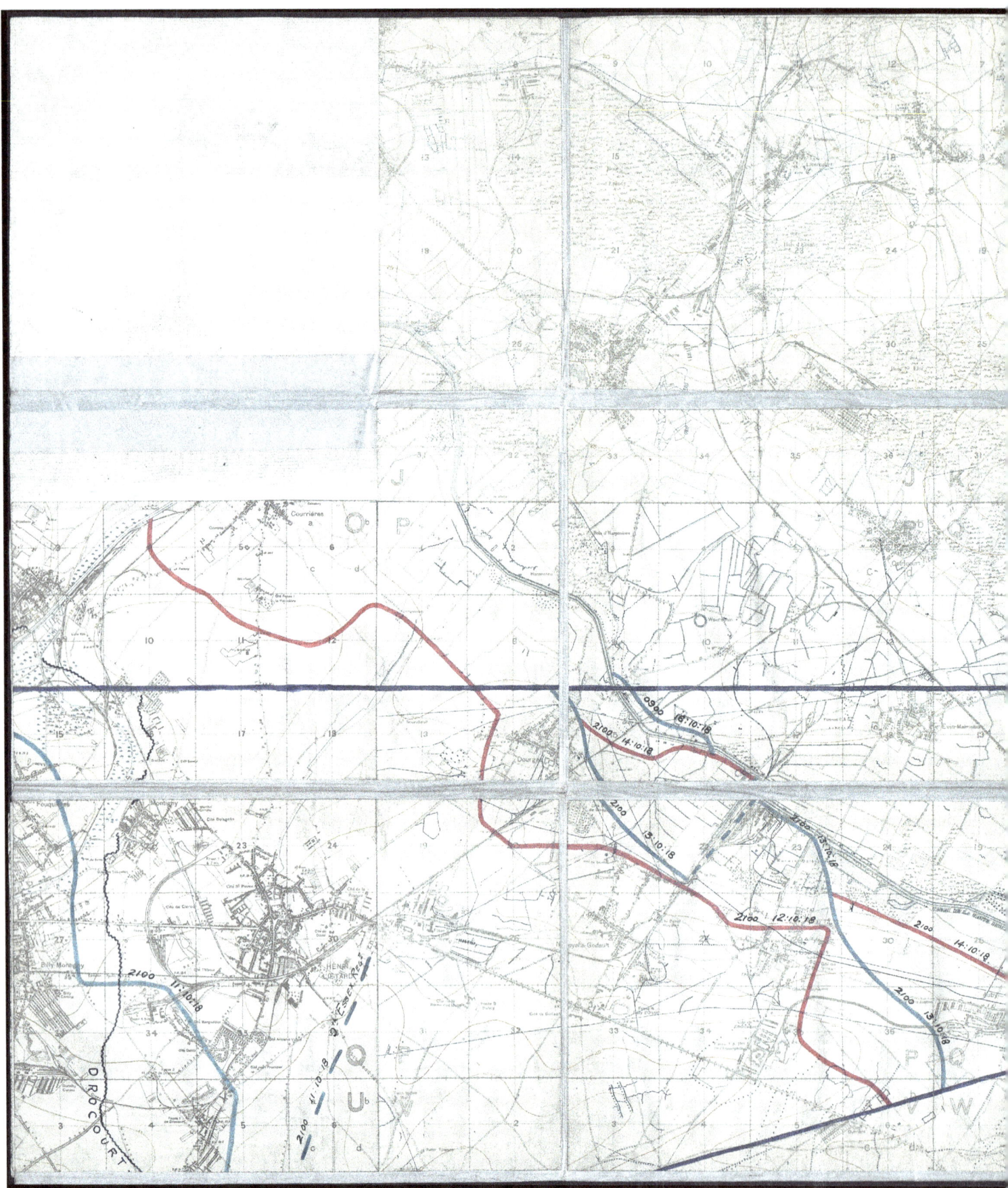

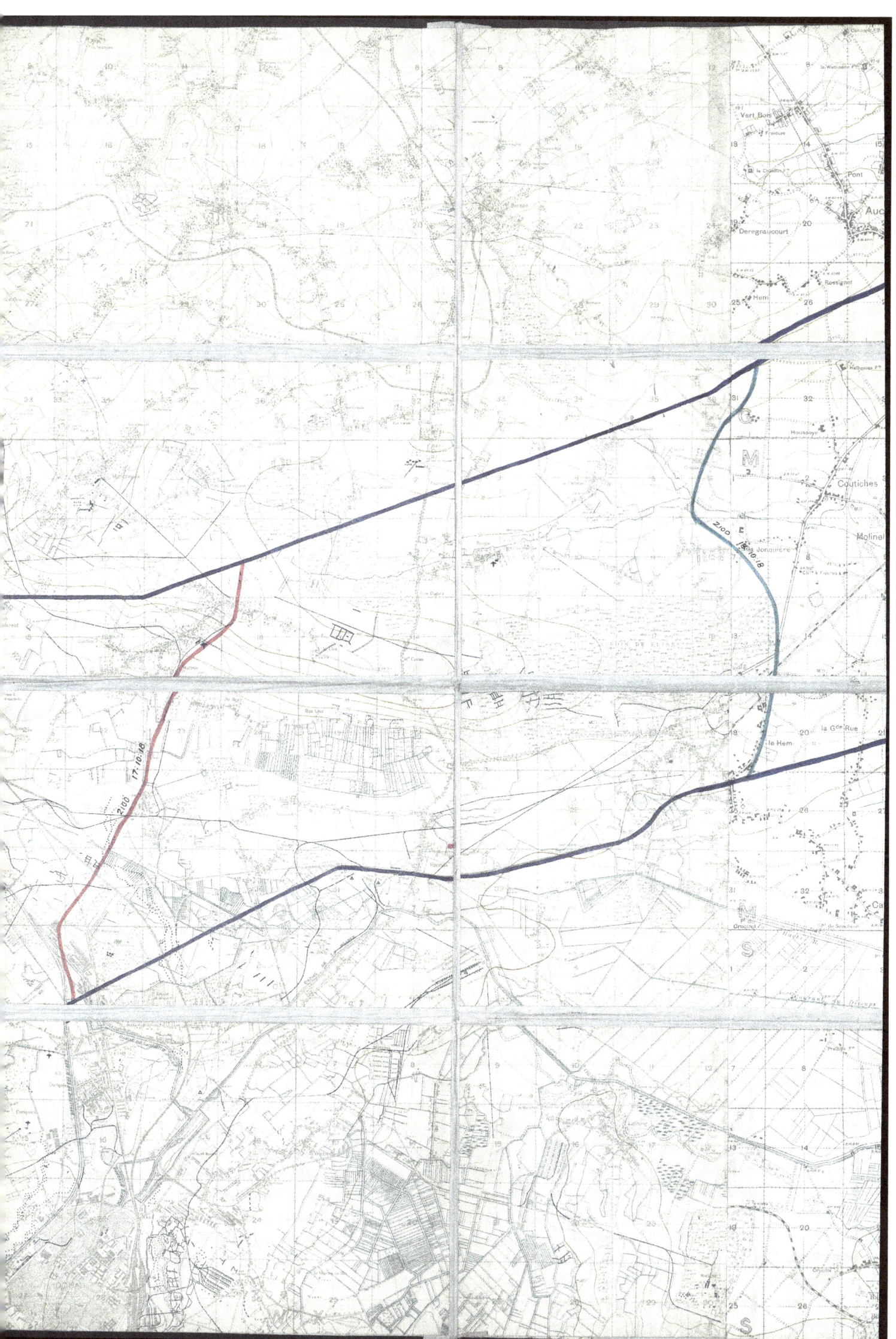

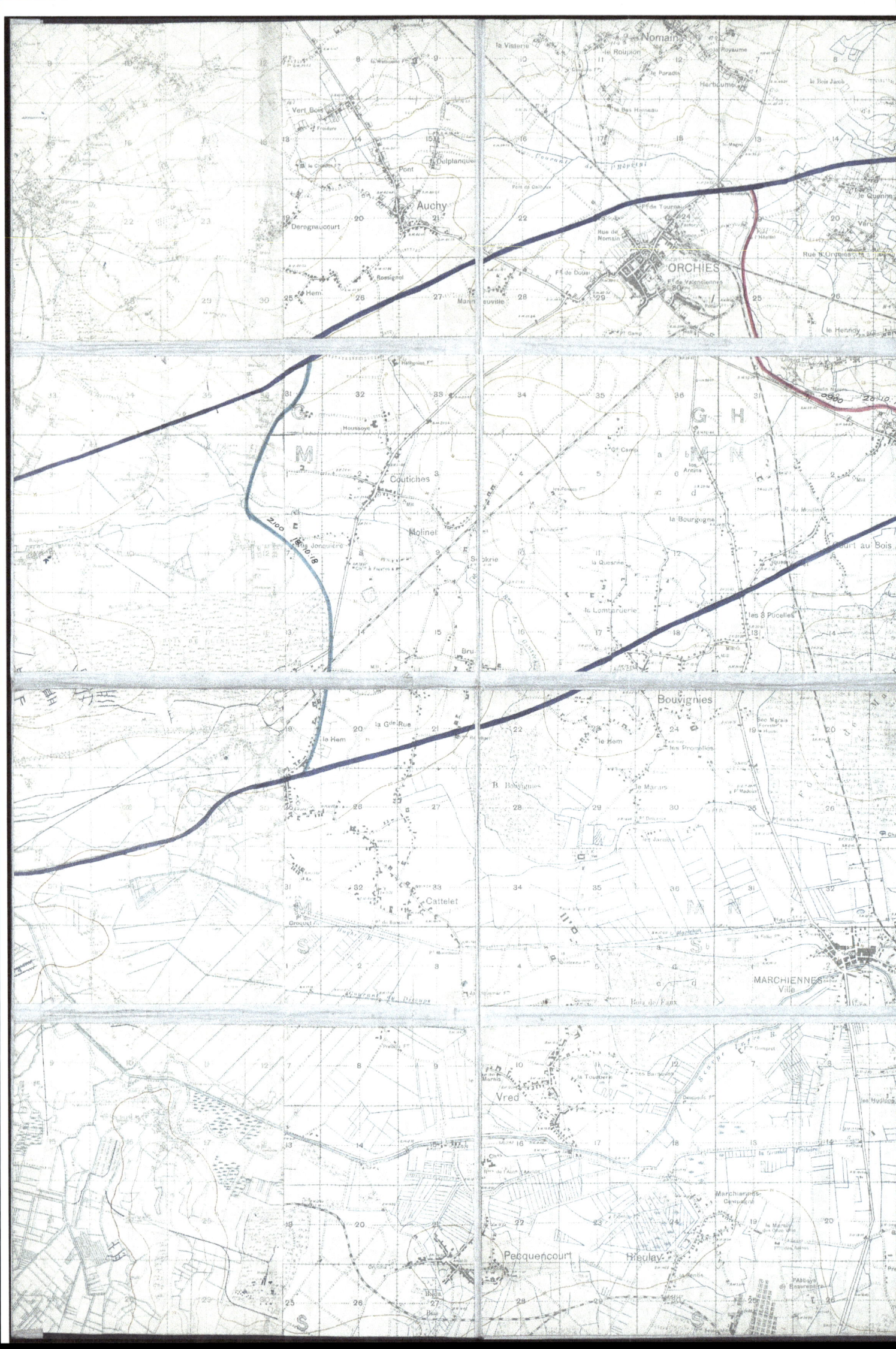

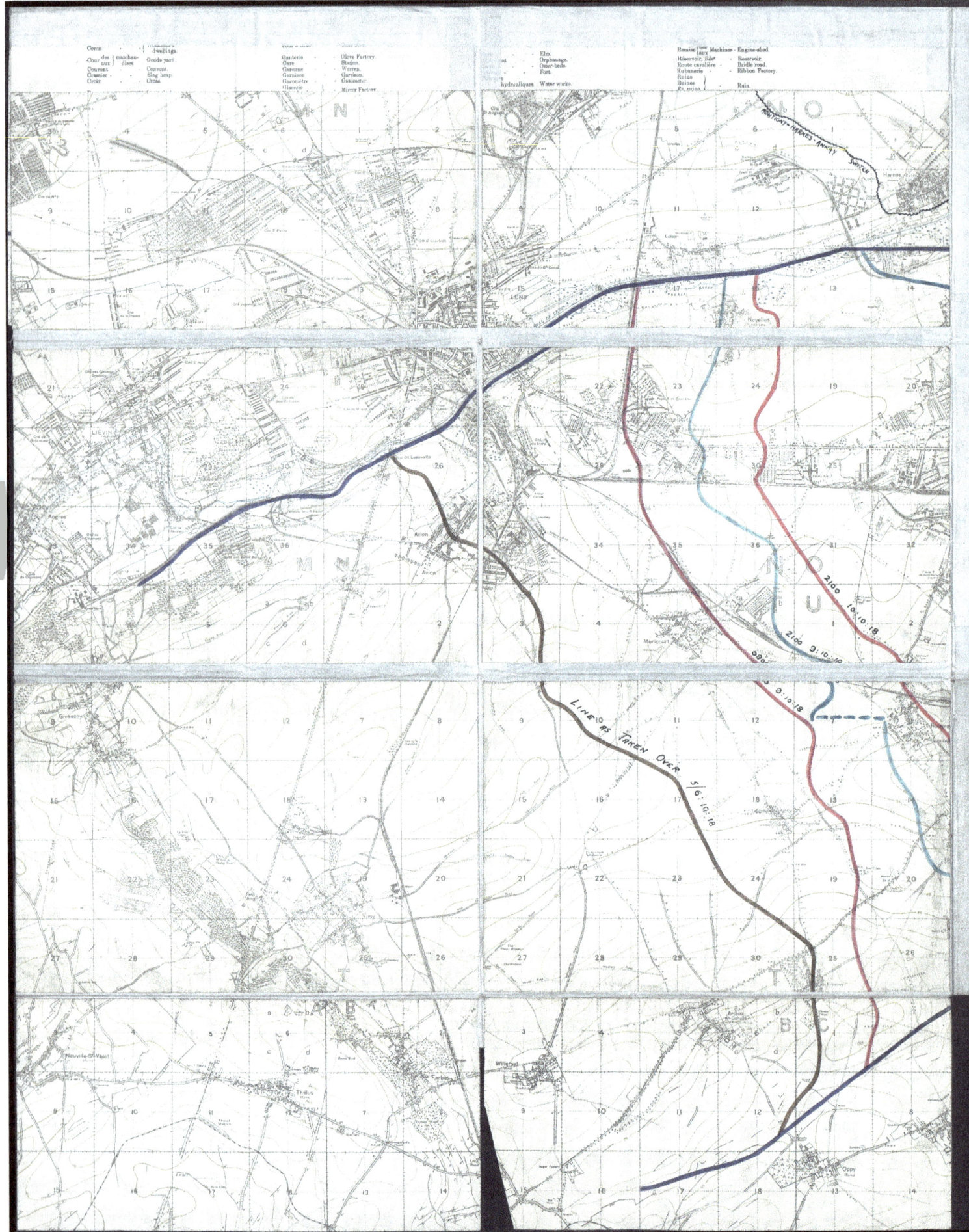

FRANCE.

SHEET 44 S.W.
EDITION 3.

INDEX TO ADJOINING SHEETS

SCALE $\frac{1}{20,000}$

12th Division
Operations
6th – 29th September

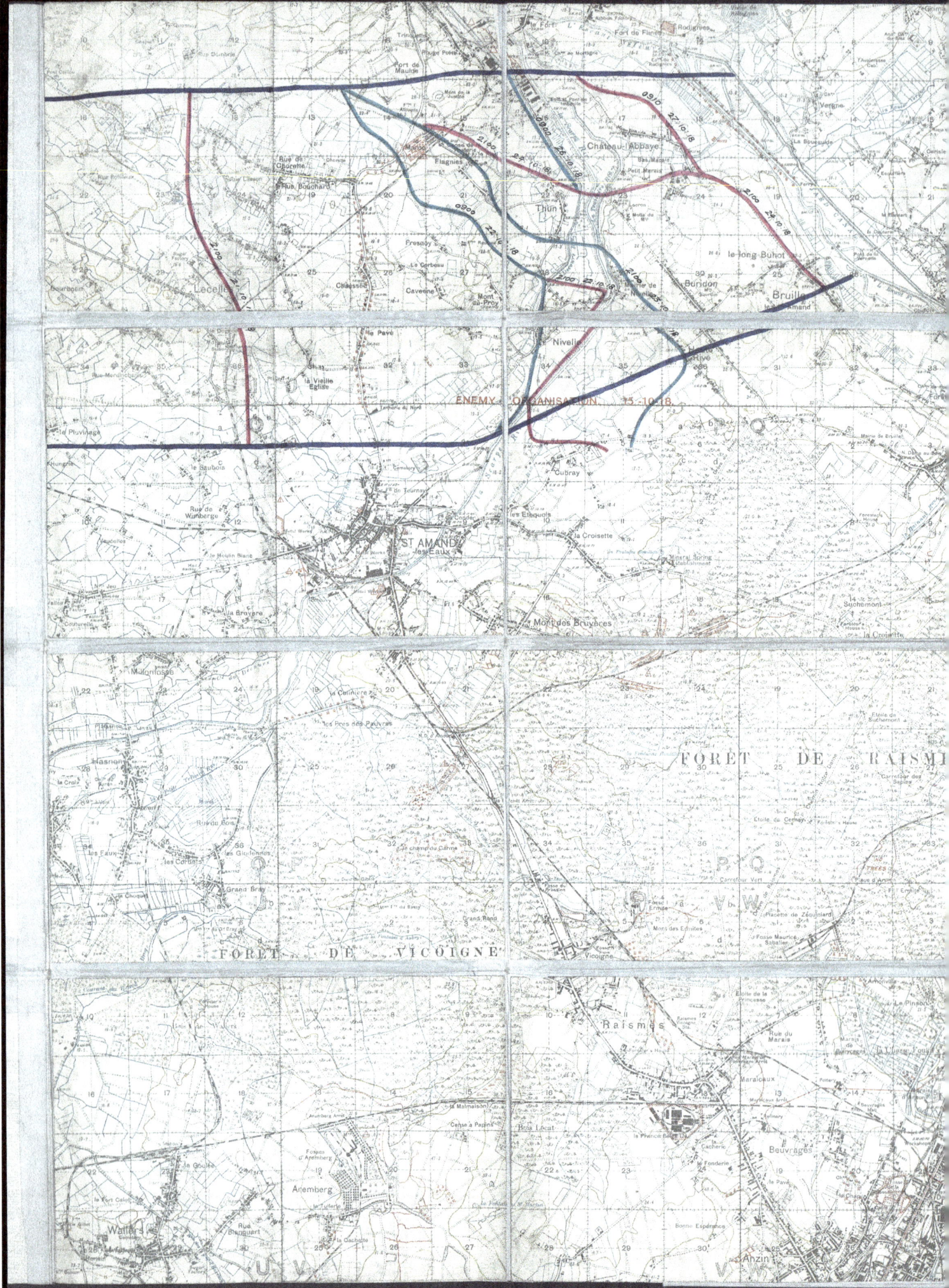

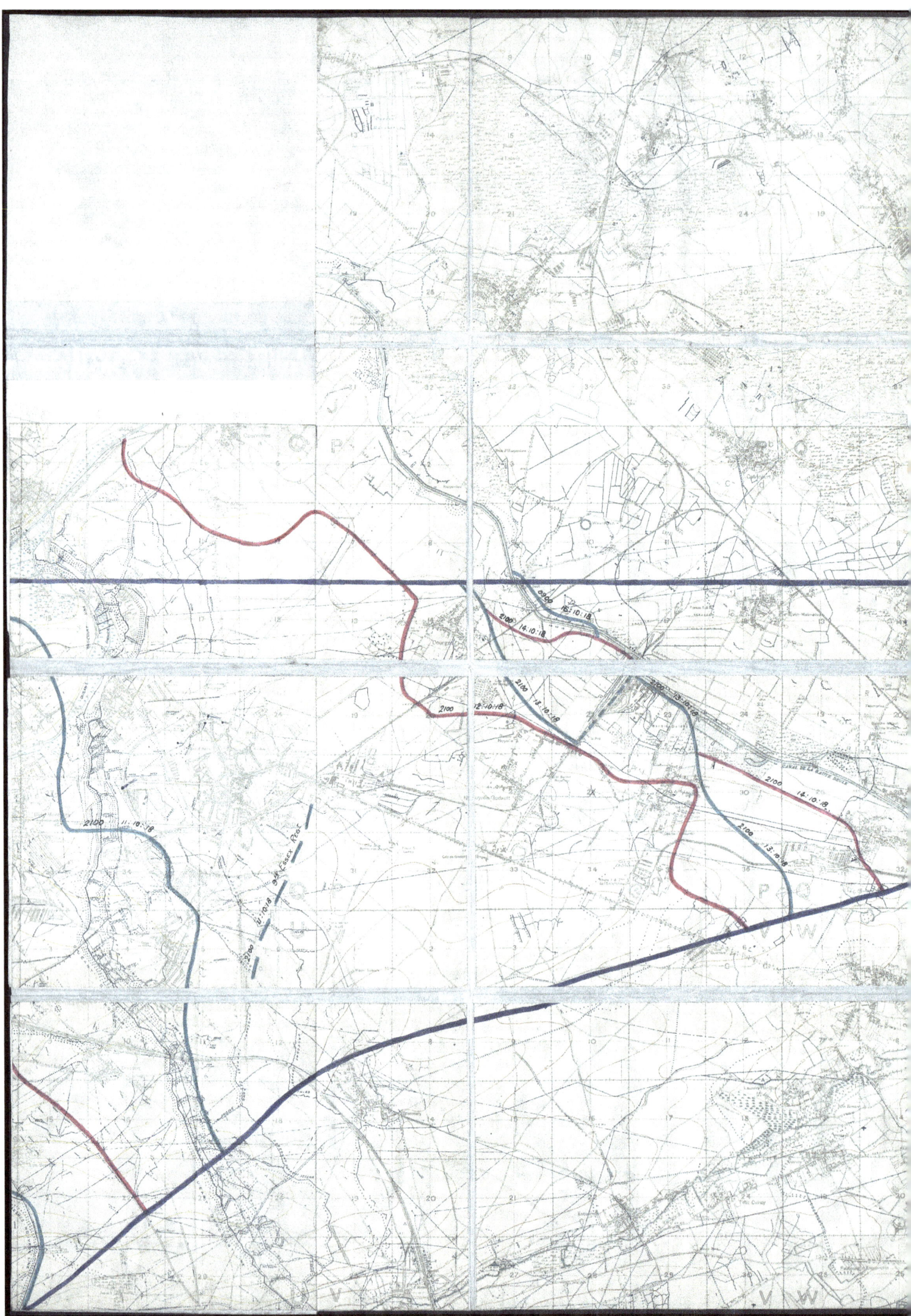

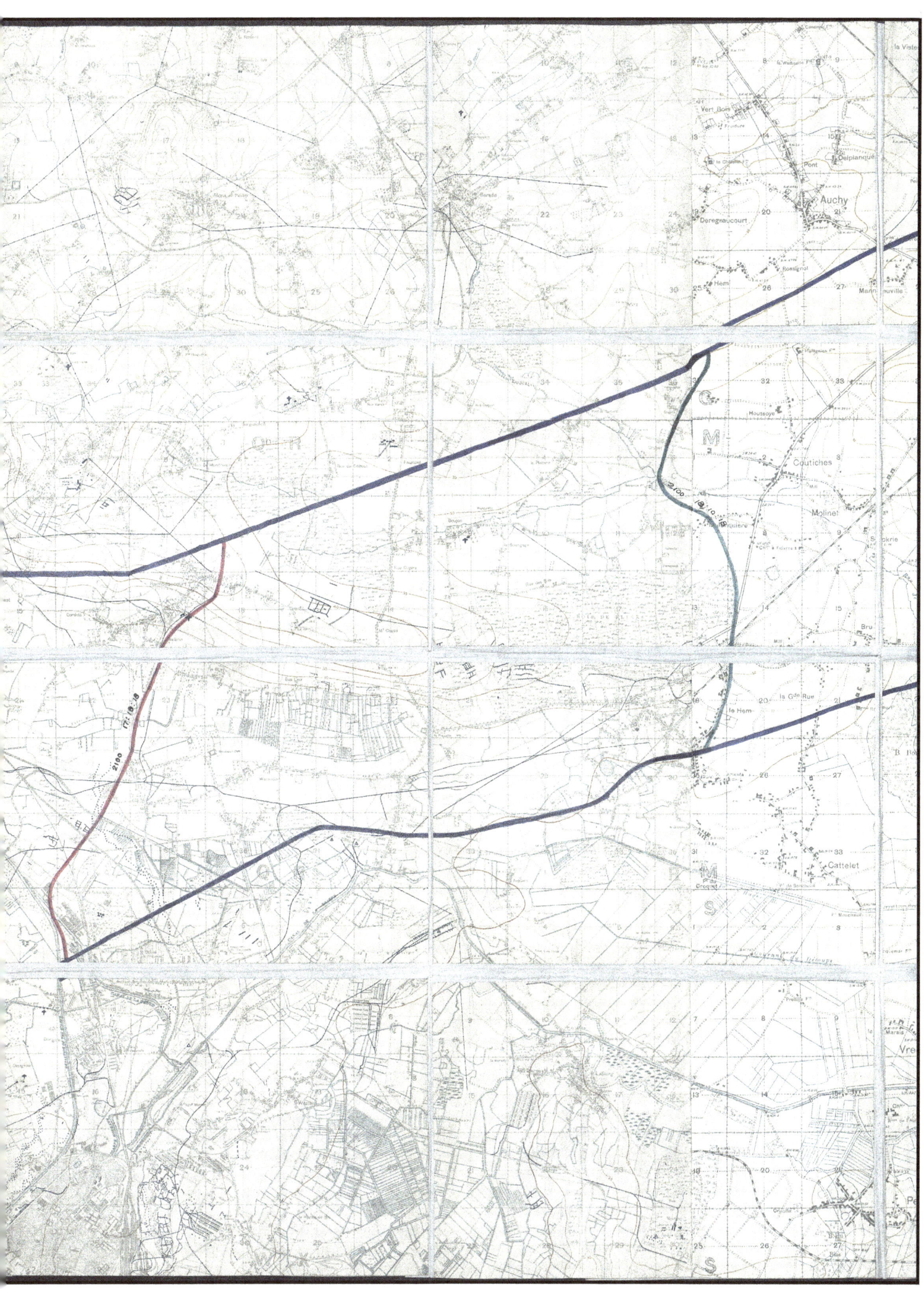

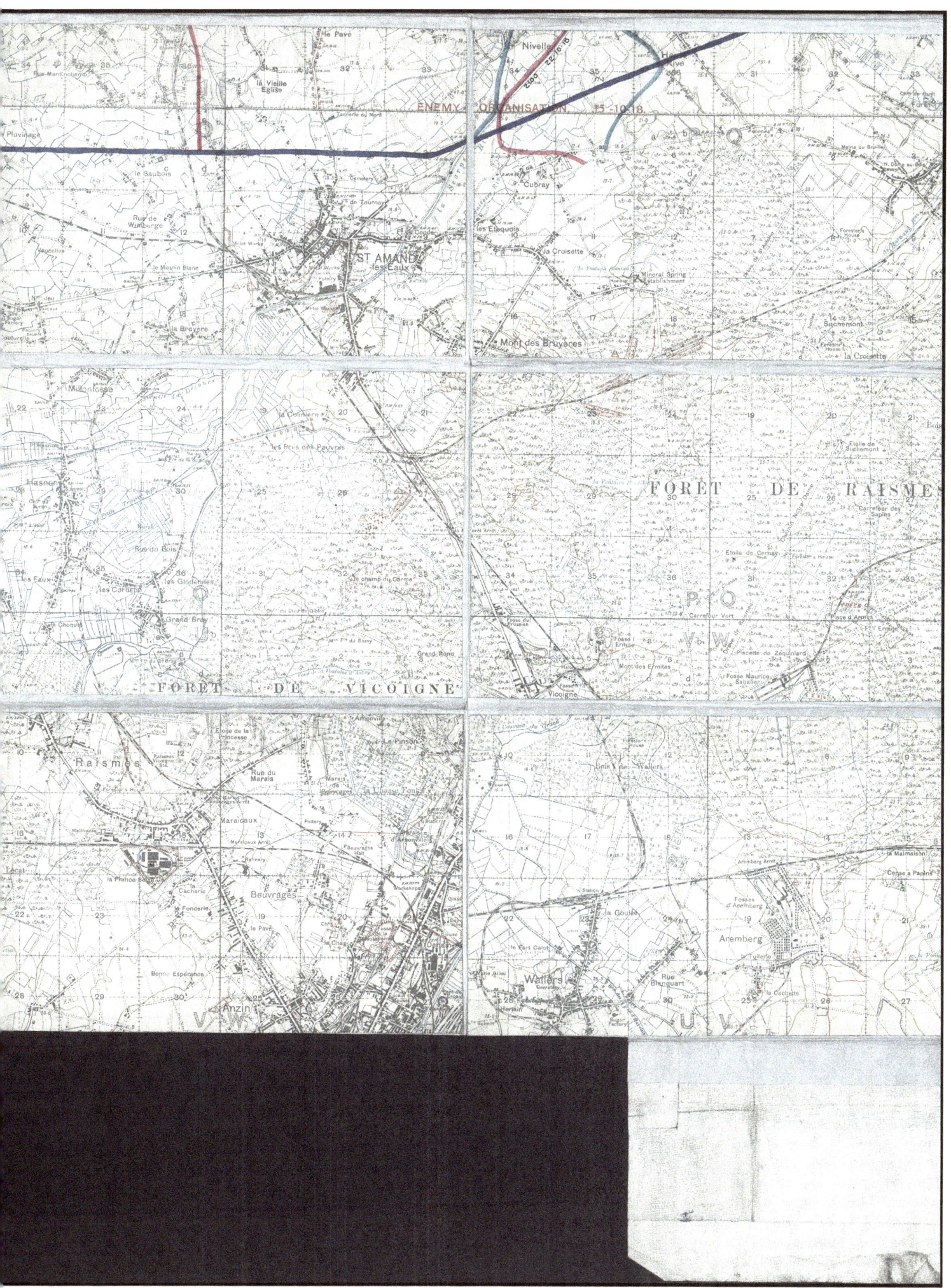

GENERAL STAFF,

12th DIVISION
0-N-0-0-0-0-0-0-0-0-0

NOVEMBER 1918.

Army Form C. 2118.

WAR DIARY
12th DIVISION or NOVEMBER, 1918.
INTELLIGENCE SUMMARY.

(Erase heading not required.)

Instructions regarding War Diaries and Intelligence Summaries are contained in F. S. Regs., Part II. and the Staff Manual respectively. Title pages will be prepared in manuscript.

Place	Date	Hour	Summary of Events and Information	Remarks and references to Appendices
	REF.	VALENCIENNES SHEET 1:100000		
FLINES	1st		(Fine). G.O.C., left for England, on leave. Brigadier General VINCENT, C.M.G. assumed command of the Division. Recreation Committee formed. News received that Armistice between AUSTRIA and ITALY had been signed.	
,,	2nd		(Wet). Ordinary routine training, under cover.	
,,	3rd		(Fine). Meeting of Recreation Committee. Lt. Col. LEVEY, D.S.O., and Major NEILSON, D.S.O., I.G.T. Staff arrived. VIII Corps Order No. 44 received ordering a battalion of 12th Division to move to LANDAS on November 6th. This move was subsequently advanced 24 hours by VIII Corps. A Warning Order was consequently sent to 35th Infantry Brigade.	
,,	4th		(Fine). Major NIELSON, D.S.O., I.G.T. Staff visited 9th Royal Fusiliers and 5th Royal Berkshire Regt. on parade ground, and gave some demonstrations. 12th Division Order relative to move of 35th Inf. Bde. to LANDAS issued.	App. 1.
,,	5th		(Wet). 35th Inf. Bde. moved to LANDAS. Remainder of troops carried on training, under cover.	
,,	6th		(Wet). Route March of 36th and 37th Infantry Brigades under Brigade arrangements.	
,,	7th		(Dull). Demonstration and Conference on training by Brigadier General GUGGISBERG and Lt. Col. LEVEY.	
,,	8th		(Wet). VIII Corps Wire G. 607 received, ordering two battalions of forward brigade to work under orders of C.R.E., 12th Division, in neighbourhood of HERGNIES. Instructions sent to 35th Inf. Bde. by wire.	
,,	9th	15.45	(Fine). Enemy plane very high over FLINES at 10.15 hrs. A.A. guns very active. Instructions received by 'phone: Divisional Headquarters to move to SAMEON, 35th Inf. Bde. to NIVELLE, 36th Inf. Bde. to LANDAS, 37th Inf. Bde. to RUMEGIES. This message was confirmed by order from VIII Corps, by wire; Division to move less Artillery. Divisional Order No. 294 issued.	App. 2.

Army Form C. 2118.

WAR DIARY
12th DIVISION or NOVEMBER, 1918.
INTELLIGENCE SUMMARY.
(Erase heading not required.)

Instructions regarding War Diaries and Intelligence Summaries are contained in F. S. Regs. Part II. and the Staff Manual respectively. Title pages will be prepared in manuscript.

Place	Date	Hour	Summary of Events and Information	Remarks and references to Appendices
FLINES. SAMEON.	10th	10.30 15.00	12th Division Order No. 295 issued relative to move of Divisional Artillery. Divisional Headquarters closed at FLINES, and opened at SAMEON at 15.00 hrs.	App. 3.
"	11th	00.30 07.20 19.00	Wireless message received that Armistice was signed. VIII Corps wire G.682 received - Hostilities to cease at 11.00 hrs. This was repeated to all units by wire - G.197. Orders received that 35th Inf. Bde. would move to BONSECOURS, for work under C.R.E. 12th Division Operation Order No. G.201 was therefore issued.	App. 4. App. 5.
"	12th		(Fine). Thanksgiving Service at RUMEGIES, held by the Rev. P.W. BLACKBURNE, Ass. Chaplain General. Orders received from Corps that Division would find guards for suspected delay action mines; 36th Inf. Bde. detailed to find the party required. Instructions received from VIII Corps re the advance of British Armies to the RHINE. The First Army in which the Division is at present, remaining in present area. Message from H.M. THE KING to his troops received from Corps Headquarters.	
"	13th		(Fine). G.O.C.; G.S.O.1 and D.A.Q.M.G. went to VALENCIENNES to attend Corps Conference. Terms of Armistice received.	
"	14th		(Fine). Brigades engaged in training.	
"	15th		The Army Commander and General HORNE, made an entry into MONS, where he was received by the principal Citizens. There was also a March Past of troops.	
"	16th		Major-General WILKINSON, Inspector of Musketry Training, arrived and visited 36 and 37 Brigades.	
"	17th		Army Commander attended Service at RUMEGIES by Rev. P.W. BLACKBURNE. Short address to the troops by the Army Commander at the close of the Service.	
"	18th		Brigades engaged in training.	
"	19th		Brigades engaged in training. Major Gen. H.W. Higginson returned from leave & assumed Command of the Div.	

Army Form C. 2118.

WAR DIARY
12th DIVISION
or NOVEMBER, 1918
INTELLIGENCE SUMMARY.
(Erase heading not required)

Instructions regarding War Diaries and Intelligence Summaries are contained in F. S. Regs., Part II. and the Staff Manual respectively. Title pages will be prepared in manuscript.

Place	Date	Hour	Summary of Events and Information	Remarks and references to Appendices
SAMEON	20th		Brigades engaged in training.	
,,	21st		Brigades engaged in training.	
,,	22nd		Brigades engaged in training. Orders were received from the Corps that the Division would move to the AUBERCHICOURT area, for salvage purposes.	
,,	23rd		Brigades engaged in training. 12th Division Order No. 296 issued relative to move of Division to AUBERCHICOURT area on 25th, 26th and 27th instant.	App. 6.
,,	24th		Brigades engaged in training.	
,,	25th		36th and 37th Bdes moved to HORNAING-PECQUIN area and AUBERCHICOURT respectively.	
MASNY	26th		Divisional Headquarters opened at the Chateau in MASNY at 11.00 hrs. 35th Inf. Bde. marched from ST. AYAND to SOMAIN.	
,,	27th		Divisional Artillery moved by March Route to LEWARDE.	
,,	28th		Units cleaning up Billets, etc. and carrying out recreational training.	
,,	29th		Units cleaning up Billets, etc. and carrying out recreational training. MR. H. HIGGS, C.B., from the Treasury, gave a lecture at SOMAIN on National Finance. 73: Army Pde RFA moved into Bruinel area and became Corps put Res'vo Arty	App 7.
,,	30th		Cleaning up Billets and recreational training.	

H. W. Higginson
Major-General,
Commanding, 12th Division.

App. No. I

SECRET.
Copy No. 2

12th DIVISION ORDER No. 293.

4th November, 1918.

1. The 35th Infantry Brigade Group, composed as under, will move to the LANDAS area on the 5th instant under orders of B.G.C. 35th Infantry Brigade :-

    35th Infantry Brigade.
    C. Coy., 12th Bn. M.G. Corps.
    37th Field Ambulance.

2. No restrictions as to route, except that no unit of the group will enter LANDAS before 12.00 hours.

3. Administrative instructions are being issued by 12th Division "Q".

4. A C K N O W L E D G E.

C. Ryan
Major for
Lieut.Colonel,
General Staff,
12th Division.

Issued at 13-45.

Copies to :-

1. G.O.C.
2. G.S.O.1.
3. C.R.A.
4. C.R.E.
5. 35th Infantry Brigade.
6. 36th Infantry Brigade.
7. 37th Infantry Brigade.
8. 5th Northamptonshire Regt. (Pioneers).
9. 12th Battn., M.G.C.
10. 12th Div. Signal Coy. R.E.
11. A.D.M.S.
12. D.A.D.V.S.
13. 12th Div. Train.
14. S.S.O.
15. D.A.P.M.
16. D.A.D.O.S.
17. 214th Div. Employment Coy.
18. Div. Reception Camp.
19. Camp Commandant.
20. Div. Gas Officer.
21. "Q".
22 & 23. VIII Corps.
24. 8th Division.
25. 52nd Division.
26 & 27. War Diary.
28 - 33. G.S. and Records.

app No 2

SECRET.
Copy No. 27

12th DIVISION ORDER No. 294.

Ref: Sheets 44 and 44.a.,
1/40,000.

9th November, 1918.

1. The Division (less Divisional Artillery and Engineers) will move tomorrow in accordance with March Table overleaf.

2. (a) Administrative Instructions are being issued by 12th Division "Q".

   (b) Units not mentioned in Table overleaf will move under orders of 12th Division "Q".

3. Divisional Headquarters will close at FLINES at 11.00 and open at RAMION at the same hour.

4. ACKNOWLEDGE.

C.R.Ryan
Major,
General Staff,
12th Division.

Issued at 19.30

Copies to :-

1. G.O.C.
2. G.S.O.1.
3. C.R.A.
4. C.R.E.
5. 35th Inf. Bde.
6. 36th Inf. Bde.
7. 37th Inf. Bde.
8. 5th Northamptonshire Regt. (Pioneers).
9. 12th Bn. M.G.C.
10. 12th Div. Signal Coy. R.E.
11. A.D.M.S.
12. D.A.D.V.S.
13. 12th Div. Train.
14. S.S.O.
15. D.A.P.M.
16. D.A.D.O.S.
17. 214th Div. Employment Coy.
18. Div. Reception Camp.
19. Camp Commandant.
20. Div. Gas Officer.
21. "Q".
22 & 23. VII Corps.
24. 8th Division.
25. 49th Division.
26. 52nd Division.
27 & 28. War Diary.
29 - 34. G.S. and Records.

- 9th November, 1918.

Serial.	Formation or Unit.	From.	To.	Route.	Remarks.
1.	35th Inf. Bde.Group. 35th Inf. Bde. "G" Coy. 12th Bn.M.G.C. 37th Field Ambce.	LANDAS area.	NIVELLE area.	No restriction.	March and billet under orders of B.G.C. 35th Inf. Bde. To clear LANDAS by 13.30 hours.
2.	37th Inf. Bde. Group. 37th Inf. Bde. 38th Field Ambce.	COUTICHES area.	NOMAIN LECELLES areas.	No restriction.	March and billet under orders of B.G.C. 37th Inf. Bde. Bn. at CATTELET can proceed as convenient via BOUVIGNIES and BEUVRY, remainder via ORCHIES head to pass Road Junction H.2.b.9.5. at 10:15 hrs.
3.	Divisional Headquarters.	FLINES	SAMEON.	ORCHIES - LANDAS.	To pass Road and Track Junction H.14.c. 1.5. (N.E. of FLINES) at 10.30 hrs.
4.	12th Bn. M.G.C.	FLINES.	SAMEON.	ORCHIES - LANDAS.	To pass Road and Track Junction H.14.c. 1.5. (N.E. of FLINES) at 1040 hrs.
5.	36 Inf. Bde. Group. 36 Inf. Bde. 36 Field Ambulance.	FLINES.	LANDAS area.	No restriction.	Not to pass Road Junction H.14.c.1.5. before 11.15 hrs. March and billet under orders of B.G.C. 36th Inf. Bde.

(I). Attention is drawn to S.S. 724 "March Discipline and Traffic Control".
(II). Representatives of all above serials will be on the main DOUAI-ORCHIES Road from 09.40 hrs onwards, and will not allow any portion of the serials move or form up along this road, until the President of the French Republic has passed. He is timed to leave DOUAI at 0930 hours and reach ORCHIES at 10.10 hrs. Advance parties will be E. of ORCHIES
(III). 37 Inf. Bde. Group (less 1 Bn. from CATTELET) may make a long halt for dinner E. of ORCHIES, provided they move via BEUVRY, and halt between ORCHIES and BEUVRY. No restrictions as regards Bn. from CATTELET.
(IV). 36th Inf. Bde. Group may make a long halt for dinner wherever convenient. by 1000 hrs.

app No 3

Copy No. 34

12th DIVISION ORDER No. 295.

Ref. Sheets 44 and 44.a.,　　　　　　　　10th November, 1918.
1/40,000.

1. (a) 12th Divisional Artillery will march to ROSULT area on the 11th November, under orders of C.R.A.

   (b) No restrictions as to time or route.

2. Billets will be arranged for by 12th Division "Q".

3. A C K N O W L E D G E.

J.H.Jackson Capt.
for Lieut.Colonel,
General Staff,
12th Division.

Issued at 13·45

Copies to :-

1. G.O.C.
2. G.S.O.1.
3. C.R.A.
4. C.R.E.
5. 35th Inf. Bde.
6. 36th Inf. Bde.
7. 37th Inf. Bde.
8. 5th Northamptonshire Regt. (Pioneers).
9. 12th Bn., M.G.C.
10. 12th Div. Signal Coy. R.E.
11. A.D.M.S.
12. D.A.D.V.S.
13. 12th Div. Train.
14. S.S.O.
15. D.A.P.M.
16. D.A.D.O.S.
17. 214th Div. Employment Coy.
18. Div. Reception Camp.
19. Camp Commandant.
20. Div. Gas Officer.
21. "Q".
22 & 23. VIII Corps.
24. 8th Division.
25. 49th Division.
26. 52nd Division.
27 & 28. War Diary.
29 - 34. G.S. and Records.

app no 4

PRIORITY.

G.R.A. C.R.E. 35th Bde. 36th Bde. 37th Bde.
12th Bn. M.G.C. Signals. Pioneers. "Q" A.D.M.S.
D.A.D.V.S. Train. E.S.O. D.A.Q.M. D.A.D.O.S.
214 Emp. Coy. Div. Reception Camp. Camp.Comdt.

G 194.   11

Corps wire begins AAA Hostilities will
cease at 11.00 on November 11th AAA
Troops will stand fast on line reached at
that hour which will be reported to Corps
Headquarters AAA Defensive precautions
will be maintained AAA There will be no
intercourse of any description with the
enemy AAA Ends /AAA Added. List Y.
AAA Acknowledge

12th Division.
0750

Off No 5

PRIORITY.

C.R.A. C.R.E. 35th Inf. Bde. 36th Inf. Bde.
37th Inf. Bde. 5th Northamptons. 12th Bn. M.G.C.
Signals. A.D.M.S. D.A.D.V.S. Train. S.S.O.
D.A.P.M. D.A.D.O.S. 214 Imp. Coy. Div. Reception
Camp. Camp Commandant. Div. Gas Officer. "Q"
8th Corps. 8th Divn. ~~58th Divn.~~ 49 Div. 52 Div.

G 201   11   AAA

35th Inf. Bde. with 37th Field Amboo. attached

will move to BONSECOURS area tomorrow AAA

No restrictions but Bns. working under C.R.E.

will carry out work as usual AAA 35th Bde.

to issue orders to C. Coy. 12th Bn. M.G.C.

to move to SAMEON tomorrow and rejoin Battn.

advance party to report to Billet 252 SAMEON

for Billets AAA No restrictions AAA

ACKNOWLEDGE AAA Addsd. List Y.

12th Divn.

1730

                                    Major, G.S.

By wire to 35th Bde. 12th Bn. M.G.C. "Q"
           A.D.M.S. C.R.E.   By D.R.L.S.
      to remainder.

APP No 6

Copy No. 29

12th DIVISION ORDER NO. 296.

Ref. Sheet VALENCIENNES.   23rd November, 1918.
    1/100,000.

1.   The Division will concentrate in the AUBERCHICOURT area on the 25th, 26th and 27th inst., in accordance with March Table herewith.

2. (a).   Units not mentioned in the March Table will move under orders being issued by 12th Division "Q".

   (b).   Administrative instructions are being issued by 12th Division "Q".

3.   Divisional Headquarters will close at SAMEON at 11.00 hrs. on 25th inst., and open at LASNY at the same hour.

4.   Acknowledge.

                               C. Ryan.
                                 Major,
                               General Staff,
                               12th Division.

Issued at 19.35 hrs.

Copies to :-

       1. G.O.C.
       2. G.S.O.1.
       3. C.R.A.
       4. C.R.E.
       5. 35th Inf. Bde.
       6. 36th Inf. Bde.
       7. 37th Inf. Bde.
       8. 5th Northamptonshire Regt. (Pioneers).
       9. 12th Bn. M.G.C.
     10. 12th Div. Signal Coy. R.E.
     11. A.D.M.S.
     12. D.A.D.V.S.
     13. 12th Div. Train.
     14. S.S.O.
     15. D.A.P.M.
     16. D.A.D.O.S.
     17. 214th Employment Coy.
     18. Div. Reception Camp.
     19. Camp Commandant.
     20. Div. Gas Officer.
     21. "Q".
     22 & 23. VIII Corps.
     24. 11th Division.
     25. 49th Division.
     26. 63rd Division.
     27. 24th Division.
     28 & 29. War Diary.
     30 - 35. G.S. and Records.
     36. Town Major ST. AMAND
     37.   "   "   AUBERCHICOURT.
     38.   "   "   SOMAIN.

March Table issued with 12th Division Order No.296.

Date	Serial	Unit or Formation	From	To	Route	Remarks
Nov. 25th	A	36th Inf.Bde.Group 36th Inf. Brigade 36th Field Amb.	LANDAS area	ECAILLON - BRUILLE area.	MARCHIENNES - SOMAIN	Not to enter MARCHIENNES before 12.00 hrs. March and billet under orders of B.G.C. 36th Inf. Bde.
	B	37th Inf.Bde.Group 37th Inf. Brigade 12th Bn. M.G.C. 38th Field Amb.	RUMEGIES area	AUBERCHICOURT area	To be notified later.	No restrictions. March and billet under orders of B.G.C.37th Inf.Bde except 12th Bn.M.G.C. who will billet at ANICHE under orders of 12th Division "Q".
	C	35th Inf.Bde.Group 69th) 70th)Field Coys. 87th) R.E. 35th Inf. Brigade. 5th Bn. Northamp- tonshire Rgt. (Pioneers) 57th Field Amb.	BONSECOURS area.	ST.AMAND	No restric- tions.	March and billet under orders of B.G.C. 35th Inf. Bde.
Nov. 26th	D	35th Inf.Bde.Group As in Serial C	ST.AMAND	SOMAIN and ANICHE	To be notified later.	No restrictions. March under orders of B.G.C. 35th Inf.Bde. 35th Inf.Bde. and 37th Fd.Amb. to billet at SOMAIN under orders of B.G.C. 35th Inf.Bde. 5th Northamp- tonshire Regt.(Pioneers) and Field Coys.R.E.at ANICHE under orders of 12th Division "Q".

P. T. O.

Date	Serial	Unit or Formation	From	To	Route	Remarks
Nov. 26th	E	12th Div. M.G.Bn.	SAMEON	MASNY	Via MARCHIENNES - MARCHIENNES - CAMPAGNE - VILLERS CAMPEAU.	Not to enter MARCHIENNES before 12.00 hrs. Lorries-MCT to move via MARCHIENNES or SOMAIN.
27th	F	12th Div. Arty.	ROEULT area	LEWARDE - ERCHIN.	As in serial B. (To be notified later).	No Restrictions.

(i) Attention is directed to S.S.724 "March Discipline and Traffic Control" as amended by G.R.O. 5536 of Nov.16th 1918.

(ii) Formations may make long halts for dinners if desired.

12th Division No.G.O. 884

ADDENDUM and CORRIGENDUM
No. 1.   to
12th DIVISION ORDER No. 296

24th November, 1918.

Reference March Table accompanying 12th Division Order No. 296.

1. Route for Serial "B".

    BRILLON - ELFRUT - MARCHIENNES.
    Not to enter MARCHIENNES before 13.30 hrs.

2. Route for Serial "D".

    RUE DUMONTEL - GRAND BRAY - WALLERS - HELESMES - H.R.

3. Route for Serial "F".

    Not to enter MARCHIENNES before 12.00 hrs, otherwise no restrictions.

4. Destination of 36th Brigade Group will be FENAIN - ERRE - HORNAING area and NOT ECAILLON - BRUILLE area.

5. Serial "B".

    Delete 12th Bn. M. G. Corps from 37th Bde Group. 12th Bn. M. G. Corps will move on the 26th inst. via MARCHIENNES - MARCHIENNES CAMPAGNE - VILLERS CAMPEAU to ECAILLON (NOT ANICHE), and will NOT enter MARCHIENNES before 12.00 hrs.

6. Acknowledge.

                                        G. Rapan
                                        Major,
                                        General Staff,
                                        12th Division.

Copies to all recipients of 12th Div.Order No.296.

App. No. 4

SECRET.
Copy No. 30.

12th DIVISION ORDER No. 297.

27th November, 1918.

1. 293rd Army Brigade, R.F.A. will move from ECUVIGNIES to the 12th Divisional Area on the 29th instant under orders to be issued by the 12th Divisional Artillery.

2. On arrival in 12th Division area, the 293rd Army Brigade R.F.A. will be under the orders of the C.R.A., 12th Division, and will be administered by and will form an integral part of the 12th Divisional Artillery.

3. 12th Divisional Artillery to acknowledge.

C. Ryan
Major,
General Staff,
12th Division.

Issued at

Copies to :-

1. G.O.C.
2. G.S.O.1.
3. C.R.A.
4. C.R.E.
5. 35th Inf. Bde.
6. 36th Inf. Bde.
7. 37th Inf. Bde.
8. 5th Northamptonshire Regt. (Pioneers).
9. 12th Bn. M.G.C.
10. 12th Div. Signal Coy. R.E.
11. A.D.M.S.
12. D.A.D.V.S.
13. 12th Div. Train.
14. S.S.O.
15. D.A.P.M.
16. D.A.D.O.S.
17. 214th Div. Employment Coy.
18. Div. Reception Camp.
19. Camp Commandant.
20. Div. Gas Officer.
21. "Q".
22.& 23. VIII Corps.
24. 11th Division.
25. 49th Division.
26. 63rd Division.
27. 24th Division.
28 & 29. War Diary.
30. - 35. G.S. and Records.

12th Division No. G.O. 483

7th November, 1918.

35th Inf. Bde.
36th Inf. Bde.
37th Inf. Bde.
C.R.A.
C.R.E.
12th Dn. M.G.C.
"Q".
A.D.M.S.

    Please forward any lessons learnt during the operations of the Division in October, illustrating them briefly by the instances that occurred during the advance.

for

Lieut.Colonel,
General Staff,
12th Division.

G.O.C.	
G.S.O. 1	
G.S.O. 2	
G.S.O. 3	

12 D.A. No. R.A. 1077.

12th Division (G),

Reference your No. G.O. 783.

The recent advance, owing to not meeting with much resistance, did not add much to experiences already gained during operations of a more active nature since August 8th. on the SOMME.

2. The plan of having four Artillery Brigades - two in action and two in support - worked admirably. Brigades got to know the Infantry and each other; smooth working resulted.

3. The Heavy Artillery acted throughout with energy and vigour. Until placed under Divisional control, they were inclined perhaps to push forward unnecessarily fast. In this enclosed country this leads to unnecessary congestion on roads at times.

4. The system of ammunition supply appears to admit of improvement. Omitting the first part of the advance, when conditions owing to bad roads were hardly normal, there has always been a feeling of anxiety with regard to ammunition supply behind the D.A.C.
This was fortunately never tested by any sudden demand, but I feel that the present system which works satisfactorily while stationary, is not suited to moving warfare, and I urge the importance of having the M.T. Ammunition Echelon in direct touch with the D.A. Column.

Br. General,
Commanding 12th Divl. Artillery.

8th Novr., 1918.

12th Div.

1. In answer to your No. 60783 of 7.11.18, the instructions contained in S.S. 143 were proved to be sound and met nearly every situation.

2. The operations during October showed more clearly than ever the value of the Brigade Group as a fighting unit. For this reason the more permanently units of other arms are affiliated to the infantry brigade the better. Only by mutual acquaintance and practice in working together, can thorough cooperation on the battlefield be attained. During the operations in question T.M. Cos, Artillery Brigades, and Fd. Cos R.E. were frequently changed. So far as possible this should be avoided.

3. The necessity for tactical training of all ranks was emphasised, especially the principles laid down in F.S.R. Part I in Protection on the move and when halted. One result of the long period of trench warfare is that Officers & O.R. are not sufficiently on the look out for guarding their flanks or for threatening the enemy's flanks. The advance afforded valuable experience and great improvement was made in this respect.

During the successful advance of this brigade on O.R. 12/10/18

~~At Dormand~~

Quant-line to the Haute-Deule Canal, the leading battalion (9th Essex) pushed on rapidly in spite of opposition & captured Courcelles. The support battalion (1/1 Cambs) had to be used to guard the flanks at Fosse VIII and Fosse IV and the reserve Bn (7th Norfolk) had ~~to form a defensive~~ formed a defensive flank on the left as the 36th Inf Bde ~~[illegible]~~ had not advanced from Henin-Lietard.

Liaison Posts

4. The importance of liaison posts with units on flanks, [illegible] of divisions, [illegible] patrols [illegible] for [illegible].

Liaison generally

5. The [illegible] to brigades by Divisional Staffs in keeping them informed of what the situation & action of brigades & divisions on either flank [illegible]. [illegible] the staff [illegible] are [illegible] extent. [illegible] Comdrs ~~[illegible]~~ flank brigades [illegible] them [illegible]. The better informed brigadiers are what the general situation the easier it is for them to ~~[illegible]~~ deal with ~~[illegible]~~ the complicated situation that constantly arise.

6.
Trench
Mortars

Undoubtedly superior the
German type of Light Trench mortar
is more valuable in attack than our
own T.M. Mortars, chiefly owing to their longer
range [illegible]. Head of Battalion
Commanders lacked four of these
M.G. attached to them, opposition
from enemy M.Gs could be overcome
much more easily by their use.

7.
L.G.
Platoons

A Lewis gun section of less than
1 N.C.O. + 6 men is of little value,
as sufficient drums cannot be
carried. A minimum of 12
drums is necessary, but 16 is
better.

There is a tendency to push
forward the L.G.s for too fast.
The loss men + the gun upset
of firing M.Gs cannot be overcome
under cover.

8.
Keeping
Direction

Definite instruction in the
art of keeping direction to
[struck through]

All N.C.O.s at least 3 men
per platoon should be taught
with the compass. All N.C.O.
should be map men.

History [illegible] invariable
to [illegible] and in [illegible] there is
there is a tendency to converge
towards points of resistance [illegible]
of [illegible] is often necessary to check

R.O.

9.

Rifle
Lectures

The Rifle is the most
valuable weapon we have, & the
it is still made apparent the
use of Rifle lectures must have
its full expression & so show
that they are in fact working
together.

I have found the men are
unwilling to attend self, & to
[illegible] them they do not attend
[illegible] to be at to have do not
great steady the idea of Lecturing
to be kept steadily in view &
[illegible]

10.

Strength
of Section

The [illegible] [illegible]
[illegible] should show by the
manoeuvre in line of the Sub-
alt section proved it [illegible]
but it is often the [illegible]
number think it of [illegible]
and it therefore be quicker
after similar [illegible] life
[illegible] section the battalion
reserve, or closing into close
[illegible] to [illegible] the End day
up [illegible] section [illegible] [illegible]
If a & XII section falls below
this strength it cannot form
a double so by habit, and
in the case of a L.g. section,
L g [illegible] & could cannot be
carried.

Headquarters,
12th Division "G"

Reference 12th Division No. G.O. 783 Lessons learnt during the Operations in October 1918.

The chief lesson learnt during August was that the trades and equipment in a Field Coy. R.E. must allow of better and more permanent work being done than in pre war days, though this referred mainly to water supply on that occasion.

In October exactly the same lesson was learnt but with reference to bridging and communications generally.

In short the lessons amounted to:-

(1). A Field Coy. R.E. should be fitted out to deal with iron work. The cases in which Stocks and Dies, Acetylene cutting plant etc. were wanted were so obvious that no detailed instances are required and it is useless for a Field Coy. to be dependent on formations or Units in back areas for these stores.

(2). A machine driven saw is essential for heavy bridge work and nearly all bridging has been of the heavy type. In particular this is required for cutting equal road bearers and decking.

(3). The Pontoon equipment was extremely useful but it should be altered to allow of easy and safe conversion to carry lorry traffic. The varnish on chesses should not be allowed or should be removed from time to time as it appears to be responsible for an excess of dry rot. The Shore Bays of the Pontoon Bridge should be longer and splayed as approaches are usually difficult.

(4). Unless there is a good moon or a very light night it is usually a bad policy to carry heavy bridging through the 24 hours. The men get overtired, both better and quicker work is got from working in daylight only.

(5). The transport of a Field Coy. is in many respects unsuitable and more attention is required to replacing some of the H.T. by M.T. vehicles.

(6). When considering the question of Field Coy. equipment it should be remembered that Field Coys. require things immediately and cannot delay to borrow equipment from other Units; nor would they usually find large dumps of sawn timber, Dogs nails etc. ready for use as occurred in the recent advance. They will have to improvise these things and require the means and material to do so.

Lieut. Colonel. R.E.
C.R.E., 12th Division.

18/11/18.

36th Inf. Bde. No. 136/S24.

12th Division.

URGENT

With reference to 12th Division No. G.O.783, dated 7th instant, no lessons were learned which had not already been brought out by the fighting in September. The following points, however, confirm previous experience:-

1. The value of the Battery Commander being at Battalion Headquarters was proved at the capture of ROUVROY on 10th October. Isolated Machine Guns were dealt with and artillery support was readily obtained for repelling a German counter-attack.

2. A section of Machine Guns should be placed at the disposal of Officers Commanding leading Battalions in open and semi-open warfare. O.C. Machine Gun Battalion or Company should not move these guns without consulting and informing Battalion Commander. This was exemplified during the operations which culminated in the capture of MONT DE LA JUSTICE and the western bank of the JARD CANAL. Battalion Commanders were able to indicate tasks to the O.C. Machine Gun Section who was able to keep in touch with the situation and place his guns so that they could be used for possible contingencies. On one occasion, however, they were ordered to be moved without the knowledge of the Battalion Commander. This resulted in the latter losing control of the section for a time. While it is realised that the Machine Gun Commander should decide how the allotted task is to be carried out, yet it is necessary for the Battalion Commander to know at all times where the section is so that he can send orders to the Commander and know what tasks it is practicable for the section to carry out.

3. The insufficient training of young Officers in map reading and use of compass was again noticeable throughout the operations

Brigadier-General,
Commanding 36th Infantry Brigade.

20th November 1918.

37th Inf.Bde.No. GO.1439

12th Division "G".

Herewith report in accordance with 12th Division No. G.O.783 dated 7th instant.

1. ARTILLERY SUPPORT

Close support of Forward Battalions by a Section or more of Field Artillery to engage fleeting targets and M.G's holding up the advance, has again proved of great value.

It is better that the Battery Commander, rather than the O.C. of any one Section, keeps in close touch with the Battn. Commander concerned. This does not imply that the whole Battery necessarily moves at the same time.

The Battery Commander has resources at his disposal whereby he can establish a forward O.P. with telephonic communication to a selected position, into which, say, one Section is moved and a satisfactory shoot conducted.

A Section Commander is practically limited to open sights (not always practicable) or transmitting his observations by flag or orderly.

The Battery remains throughout the day under the control of the Battery Commander and the Infantry are never without Artillery support owing to getting out of range or movement of guns.

EXAMPLE.- At Zero (the hour at which the Infantry advance), the Battery is in position of observation about 2000 yds. or 3000 yds. in rear of the Battalion it is detailed to support.

No.1 Section has teams up and is prepared to move forward directly the Infantry have made good a specified tactical feature or have gained a certain distance in the advance.

Battery Commander in Company with Battalion Commander moves forward, selects position for one or more Sections and establishes O.P. and communication, probably extending line from existing O.P. Selected position occupied by No.1 Section and targets engaged by this Section or Nos.2 and 3, or all as desired. Advance continues satisfactorily.

No.2 Section ordered to come into action near No.1. No.3 Section ordered to move past Nos.1 and 2 and take up a more advanced position as did No.1 at say Zero plus 20 minutes.

Repeat as often as necessary.

2. FILTRATION OF INFANTRY

Forward movement by filtration to within close proximity of the enemy by taking advantage of cover again proved of value at BRUILLE where the element of surprise was of great importance.

3. MACHINE GUNS.

Machine Guns, placed on tops of houses for close covering fire, proved useful at BRUILLE and BURIDON.

4. COMMUNICATION.

Visual Signalling was used with success, especially in the earlier stages of the advance; full advantage was taken of the numerous Fosses.

x "Light must be given from Receiving Station to Forward Station, and "R.D." Signalled. The risk of drawing enemy shell-fire must be taken, and from experience has not proved prohibitive.

x to establish Comm"

5.TRENCH MORTARS....

5. TRENCH MORTARS

The Trench Mortars attached to forward Battalions were of service in dealing with enemy Machine Guns.

Guns and ammunition were carried on limbers as far forward as possible and subsequently on pack animals.

The Mark I Base plate should be replaced by Mark II which can be fired from any position, either in a road or against the wall of a house, and the necessity for digging in is obviated.

x off mules to carry pack saddles.

8/11/1918.

Brigadier General,
Commanding 37th Infantry Brigade.

12th. Battalion, M.G.C. No. G.S./14.

Headquarters,
    12th. Division. "G"

   Reference 12th. Division No. G.S.783 dated 7-11-18.
   No new lessons have been learned during the operations in October, but various points gained during the Summer fighting have been emphasised.

8-11-1918.

W.G.A. Coldwell

Commanding 12th. Battalion, Machine Gun Corps.

8.11.18. Lieut. Colonel

H.Q., 12TH DIVISION (GENERAL STAFF). No. G.790 Date 8.11.18

G/ The chief lesson learnt during the operations of the Div. in Oct is :—
That it is essential that a responsible Officer should be appointed for duty at every Pontoon bridge to supervise & direct operations during the crossing of all transport. An Officer should be on duty the whole time. The work to be done in relays.

W.R.L. Marr
Q

16/11/18

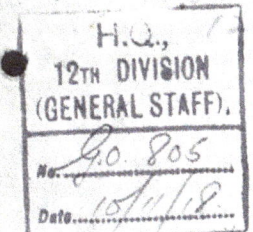

LESSONS LEARNT DURING THE OPERATIONS OF 12TH DIVISION DURING OCTOBER, 1918.

MEDICAL.

The Medical lessons learnt may be referred to under two heads :-

1. Clearing of Wounded.
2. Treatment of Sick.

(1). CLEARING OF WOUNDED.

There is little to be added to the report sent in on the September operations. The same scheme was adopted and found very suitable for a rapid advance. One or more squads of R.A.M.C. Bearers, together with a runner were attached to each Battalion, and the Bearer Divisions of Field Ambulances were affiliated to Brigades. The Bearers of any Brigade not in the line or in support were at the disposal of the A.D.M.S. as Reserves. The system enabled the Officers of the Bearer Divisions to keep in constant touch with the Infantry Brigades.

A feature of the advance was the destruction of roads and bridges by the retiring enemy. This destruction at times, rendered the clearing of casualties very difficult, but served to bring out the very great value of the small Ford Ambulances, which, owing to their speed and handiness were used to explore all possible routes between Advanced Dressings Stations and Regimental Aid Posts. On several occassions they were taken, with the aid of Infantry, across mine craters or pushed across bad bits of road that would have been quite impassable to heavy Cars. Having been got as far forward as possible, they would work back to the crater, or other obstacle across which casualties were carried on stretchers to a large car in waiting on the other side.

I should like to mention the close co-operation and the cordial relations that existed between the Infantry and Battalions and the Bearer Divisions.

(2). TREATMENT OF SICK.

During the rapid advance of the Division, the Field Ambulances could do little for the treatment of sick as it was essential they should remain mobile. A Tent Sub-division from each Division of the Corps has been taken to form a Corps Rest Station, but as it was not near C.C.S. a different system of cars would have been required to take patients to it. This was not carried out, owing probably to the rapidly increasing long distances to C.C.S. All sick, slight cases and severe, went to the latter place.

I have made a suggestion with regard to the saving of man power, that Corps Rest Station should be in the neighbourhood of C.C.S. I believe that one is now being formed in DOUAI, where the C.C.Ss. also have been placed, and it will be interesting to see if the association of the two will prove a success.

COLONEL
A.D.M.S. XII DIVISION.

12th DIVISION NO. G.O.

27th November, 1918.

C.R.A.	A.D.M.S.
C.R.E.	D.A.D.V.S.
35th Inf. Bde.	12th Div. Train.
36th Inf. Bde.	S.S.O.
37th Inf. Bde.	D.A.P.M.
12th Bn.M.G.C.	D.A.D.O.S.
12th Div. Signal Coy.R.E.	214th Emp. Coy.
5th Northamptonshire	Div. Recpn. Camp.
Regt. (Pioneers).	Camp Commandant.
12th M.T. Coy.	Div. Gas Officer.
"Q".	

----

1. It is probable that the Division will spend the winter in the present area. Plans of units and formations should therefore be made accordingly, and labour expended now in improving billets, recreation rooms, lecture-halls, messes and in construction of baths, football fields etc.etc., should be amply repaid in the coming months. As far as possible salvaged material should be used for all repair work.

2. (a). The attached map (To Bdes, R.A. and "Q" only. Traces showing Div. area on 1/100,000 scale have been forwarded to Div. units and also for the Bde. areas for salvage purposes referred to in para.10. 12th Div., S.Q.99 (Preliminary Administrative Instructions) shows the Divisional areas, and also inter-Brigade boundaries for the purposes of training, ranges, football fields etc.
    (b). 37th Inf. Bde. will allot an area to the Divisional R.E. and Pioneers.

3. Whilst the Division is in this area it will have to clear the salvage in the whole Divisional area. Detailed instructions regarding this salvage works are being issued by 12th Division "Q", but before any general salvage work is started Bdes. will be given a generous allowance of time for cleaning up thoroughly the area in the immediate vicinity of their billets.

4. During the next few months the task before all those responsible for training is :-
    (a). To maintain the present high standard of discipline and prepare the Division for the resumption of hostilities, should this take place.
    (b). To prepare men for their return to civil life, after demobilization.

5. As regards para.4 (b), instructions have been issued from time to time regarding educational work, and details of a Scheme for training tradesmen in ~~provisional~~ workshops will be issued separately.

6. As regards para.4 (a) and military training generally
    (a). This should consist for the most part of close order drill, ceremonial and Physical Training. All Commanders should ensure that their units are up to full strength in "specialists" and have a sufficient reserve of men trained. Musketry should be carried out and shooting competitions organized, but men should not be kept out on the range except when the weather is favourable. Every parade should begin with an inspection and finish with a march past the O.C. Parade, special attention being paid to saluting and smartness of carriage.
    (b). Route marches by Groups will be carried out once a week on the following days, provided the weather is suitable :-

/P.T.O.

Mondays.	Divisional Headquarters & 12th Bn.M.G.C.
Tuesdays.	35th Inf. Bde; 36th Field Ambulance.
Wednesdays.	36th Inf. Bde; 37th Field Ambulance.
Thursdays.	37th Inf. Bde; 5th Northamptonshire Regt and 38th Field Ambulance.
Fridays.	12th Division Artillery.

These marches can be short but the strictest attention must be paid to turn out and march discipline.

7. Brigadiers and other Commanders will be left a free hand in the organization of their salvage, but on "Salvage Parades" men will carry rifles and do at least 15 minutes "handling of arms" [rifle exercises + sword drill] before beginning work.

8. The Corps have intimated that a limited number of busses may occasionally be available for units to make trips to historical battlefields in the neighbourhood or to other places of interest in the Corps area, on the understanding that the party is accompanied by an officer qualified to describe the action or place.

9. Arrangements are also being made for the attachment of Officers for short periods to the 16th Squadron R.A.F. and 1st Balloon Wing. Further details will be issued later.

10. The Divisional A.R.A. Competition for the best platoon in a combined musketry and bayonet fighting test will be carried out in the course of the next two months, and a further notification will be made in due course.

Major,
General Staff,
12th Division.

✳ To Bgdes & RA only. Traces showing Div area on 1/40,000 scale have been forwarded to their units.

(Routine orders)

The probable that

(1) The Division will spend the winter in the present area. Plans of units and formations should therefore be made accordingly, and labour expended now in improving billets, recreation rooms, lecture halls, messes and in construction of baths, football fields etc should be amply repaid in the coming months. As far as possible salvaged material should be used for all repair work.

✳ (2)(a) The attached map shows the Divisional areas, and also areas Inter Bgde Boundaries for the purposes of training, ranges, football fields etc.
(b) 37 Infy Bgde will allot an area to the Divisional RE and Pioneers. Whilst the Division is in this area it will have to clear the salvage in the whole Divisional area. Detailed instructions regarding this salvage work are being issued by DADQ, but before any general salvage work is started Bgdes will be given allowed a generous allowance of time period for cleaning up thoroughly the area in the immediate vicinity of their billets.

(3) During the next few months the task before all those responsible for training is

(a) To maintain the present high standard of discipline and prepare the Division to the resumption of hostilities should this take place

(b) To prepare men for their return to civil life after demobilisation

and also for the Bgde areas for salvage purposes referred to in Para 10.12 Div SQ 99 (Preliminary Administrative Instructions Demobilisation)

5) As regards para 4 (b) instructions have been issued from time to time regarding educational work and details of a scheme for training tradesmen in Divisional workshops will be issued separately.

6) As regards (para 4 (a) and military training generally:-

(a) This should consist for the most part of close order drill, ceremonial and Physical Training. All commanders should ensure that their units are up to full strength in "specialists" and have a sufficient reserve of men trained. Musketry should be carried out and shooting competitions organised, but men should not be kept out on the range except when the weather is favourable.

(b) Route marches by Groups will be carried out on the following days, once a week provided the weather is suitable.

Monday   Div Hdqrs   and 12 Bn M.G. Corps.
Tuesday   35th Infantry Bgd.   2½ F. Amb
Wednesday 36th Infantry Bgde   37 F Amb
Thursday   8) 37th Infantry Bgde 5 Northants Regt
                                  . 33 F. Amb
Friday   12 Div Arty
           (and turn out)

These marches can be quite short but the strictest attention must be paid to march discipline.

(Every brigade should begin with a march past the G.O.C. in C of a brigade function, the tools and harness to exercise finish to take tops and harness of a parade.)

and other commanders.

7. Brigadiers will be left a free hand in the organisation of their salvage, but on "salvage parades" men should carry rifles and do at least 15 minutes "handling of arms" before beginning work.

8. The Corps have intimated that a limited number of busses may occasionally be available to make trips to historical battle fields in the neighbourhood or to other places of interest in the Corps area on the understanding that the party is accompanied by an officer qualified to describe the action or place.

9. Arrangements are also being made for the attachment of officers for short periods to the 16 Squadron R.A.F. and 1st Balloon Wing. Further details will be issued later.

10. The Divl. A.R.A. competition for the best platoon in a combined musketry and bayonet fighting test will be carried out in the course of the next two months and further notification will be sent made in due course.

GENERAL STAFF,

12th DIVISION,

DECEMBER 1918.

1918 DEC — 1919 JUNE

Ref. VALENCIENNES Sheet 1/100,000.

Army Form C. 2118.

Instructions regarding War Diaries and Intelligence Summaries are contained in F. S. Regs., Part II. and the Staff Manual respectively. Title pages will be prepared in manuscript.

WAR DIARY
12th DIVISION 1st DECEMBER 1918
INTELLIGENCE SUMMARY.
(Erase heading not required.)

Place	Date	Hour	Summary of Events and Information	Remarks and references to Appendices
MASNY	1st 2nd 3rd 4th 5th 6th 7th 8th		Brigades engaged in training.	
	9th		G.O.C. inspected and presented medal ribbons to 35th Infantry Brigade.	
	10th		G.O.C. inspected and presented medal ribbons to 37th Infantry Brigade.	
	11th	(Wet)	G.S.O.3 left to take up appointment at G.H.Q.	
	12th	(Wet)		
	13th	(Fine)	Brigades engaged in training. Lecture at 35th Infantry Brigade Headquarters by Professor ADKINS.	
	14th	(Fine)	G.O.C. inspected and presented medal ribbons to Divisional Signal Company, T.M. and 12th Bn. M.G.C.	
	15th	(Fine)		
	16th	(Fine)	Brigades engaged in training. G.O.C., G.S.O.1 and Brig.General Vincent went by invitation of G.O.C. 49th Division to see ceremonial parade of 49th Division. General Remy arrived. *Artwork of flies in ink*	
	17th	(Fine)	G.O.C. inspected Divisional Artillery. Brigades engaged in training.	
	18th	(Wet)		
	19th	(Stormy)	G.O.C. inspected and presented medal ribbons to 36th Infantry Brigade.	
	20th	(Stormy)	G.O.C. inspected and presented medal ribbons to 5th Bn. Northamptonshire Regiment (Pioneers).	

Page 2.
Army Form C. 2118.

WAR DIARY
12th DIVISION for DECEMBER 1918
INTELLIGENCE SUMMARY

Instructions regarding War Diaries and Intelligence Summaries are contained in F. S. Regs., Part II. and the Staff Manual respectively. Title pages will be prepared in manuscript.

(Erase heading not required.)

Place	Date	Hour	Summary of Events and Information	Remarks and references to Appendices
MASNY	21st		G.O.C. Inspected Mobile Vety. Section. Brigades engaged in salvage work.	
	22nd			
	23rd	(Stormy)	G.O.C. Inspected and presented medals to Royal Engineers	
	24th	(Fine)	G.O.C. went to lecture at VIII Corps, ORCHIES, by Dr. VAUGHAN CORNISH on the new Geographical Conditions resulting from the victory which affects the military Policy of the Nation.	
	25th	(Fine)		
	26th	(Fine)	Semi final Divisional Football Competition - 9th ESSEX 1, 62nd Bde R.F.A. nil. Semi final Tug-of-War 293rd Bde R.F.A. beat 5th Northamptonshire Regt. (Pioneers)	
	27th	(Wet)		
	28th	(Wet)		
	29th	(Wet)	Football semi final 5th Royal Berks 3, 6th R.W.Kents 1.	
	30th		G.O.C. held conference at AUBERCHICOURT.	
	31st	(Wet)	G.O.C. inspected roads with C.R.E. and Roads Officer.	

Major-General,
Commanding 12th Division.

Page 1.
Army Form C. 2118.

Ref. VALENCIENNES Sheet 1/100,000.

WAR DIARY

12th DIVISION for DECEMBER 1918
INTELLIGENCE SUMMARY

(Erase heading not required.)

Instructions regarding War Diaries and Intelligence Summaries are contained in F. S. Regs., Part II. and the Staff Manual respectively. Title pages will be prepared in manuscript.

Place	Date	Hour	Summary of Events and Information	Remarks and references to Appendices
MASNY	1st) 2nd) 3rd) 4th) 5th) 6th) 7th) 8th)		Brigades engaged in training.	
	9th		G.O.C. inspected and presented medal ribbons to 35th Infantry Brigade.	
	10th		G.O.C. inspected and presented medal ribbons to 37th Infantry Brigade.	
	11th		(Wet) G.S.O.3 left to take up appointment at G.H.Q.	
	12th		(Wet)	
	13th		(Fine) Brigades engaged in training. Lecture at 35th Infantry Brigade Headquarters by Professor ADKINS.	
	14th		(Fine) G.O.C. inspected and presented medal ribbons to Divisional Signal Company, R.E. and 12th Bn. M.G.C.	
	15th		(Fine)	
	16th		(Fine) Brigades engaged in training. G.O.C., G.S.O.1 and Brig.General Vincent went by invitation of G.O.C. 49th Division to see ceremonial parade of 49th Division. Inspection of Muscles gun lumb General Renny arrived.	
	17th		(Fine) G.O.C. inspected Divisional Artillery. Brigades engaged in training.	
	18th		(Wet)	
	19th		(Stormy) G.O.C. inspected and presented medal ribbons to 36th Infantry Brigade.	
	20th		(Stormy) G.O.C. inspected and presented medal ribbons to 5th Bn. Northamptonshire Regiment (Pioneers).	

Page 2
Army Form C. 2118.

WAR DIARY

12th DIVISION for DECEMBER 1918

INTELLIGENCE SUMMARY.

(Erase heading not required.)

Instructions regarding War Diaries and Intelligence
Summaries are contained in F.S. Regs., Part II.
and the Staff Manual respectively. Title pages
will be prepared in manuscript.

Place	Date	Hour	Summary of Events and Information	Remarks and references to Appendices
MASNY	21st		G.O.C. inspected Mobile Vety. Section. Brigades engaged in salvage work.	
	22nd			
	23rd	(Stormy)	G.O.C. Inspected and presented medals to Royal Engineers	
	24th	(Fine)	G.O.C. went to lecture at VIII Corps, ORCHIES, by Dr. VAUGHAN CORNISH on the new Geographical Conditions resulting from the victory which affects the military policy of the Nation.	
	25th	(Fine)		
	26th	(Fine)	Semi final Divisional Football Competition - 9th ESSEX 1, 62nd Bde R.F.A. nil. Semi final Tug-of-war 293rd Bde R.F.A beat 5th Northamptonshire Regt (Pioneers)	
	27th	(Wet)		
	28th	(Wet)		
	29th	(Wet)		
	30th		G.O.C. held conference at AUBERCHICOURT. Football semi final 5th Royal Berks 3, 6th R.W.Kents 1.	
	31st	(Wet)	G.O.C. inspected roads with C.R.E. and Roads Officer.	

[signature]
for Major-General,
Commanding 12th Division.

CONFIDENTIAL & URGENT.   VIII Corps No. G.b.127/1.

                                O.B./2307 of 9.12.18.

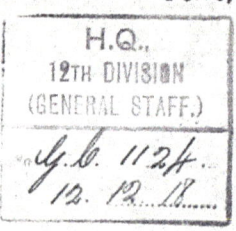

11th Division.
12th Division.
49th Division.
63rd Division.

1.   Notification has been received that it is proposed to reopen the Staff College at CAMBERLEY on the 1st February, 1919. The duration of the first course will probably be one year.

2.   Sixty vacancies are allotted to the British Armies in France.

3.   The following qualifications have been laid down :-

"Candidates should be officers of the Regular Army who have held Staff appointments and distinguished themselves in the field, and officers who have attended a Senior or Junior Staff Course.
        Age limit - 35 years, unless for exceptional reasons.
        Medical category - 'fit for general service'."

4.   The first selection will be made from those officers who, not having been to the Staff College, are at present holding first grade Staff appointments.

5.   Divisions will submit any names recommended to Corps Headquarters by the 16th instant, especial regard being had to the following claims

   (a) of officers who have served on the Staff during the war, but who now hold commands.

   (b) of second grade Staff officers and brigade majors of very outstanding merit who were likely to have been shortly selected for advancement if operations had continued.

   (c) of specially picked young Brigadier-Generals and unit commanders of very outstanding merit, in the case of whom, though they have not served on the Staff, it may be considered for the good of the service that they should go to the Staff College.

6.   It is very necessary that the utmost care should be exercised in the selection of candidates. It is notified that there is no guarantee that officers whose names are submitted will be accepted, but those who are not accepted for the 1919 course may be considered for future courses.

                                        for B.G., G.S.,
                                        VIII Corps.

Copy to :-   GSO1

G.O.C., R.A.
C.E.
"A".

12th Bn.M.G.C.No.A/829

12th Division G.

Reference 12th Division G.C.1140 dated 15th instant the following name is submitted in accordance therewith.

Lieut. Colonel W.G.A.Coldwell, 2nd Northamptonshire Regt. seconded 12th Bn.M.G.Corps.

W.G. Coldwell
Lieut. Colonel,
Commanding 12th Bn Machine Gun Corps.

18th Decr.1918.

12th Division.

36th Inf.Bde.No.170/104/1.

CONFIDENTIAL

With reference to 12th Division No.G.C.1140 dated 15/12/18 and K.R. para.721,

I wish to submit the name of Captain (Temp. Lieut.Col.) E.H.J.Nicolls, D.S.O., M.C., East Surrey Regt., cdg. 5th Royal Berkshire Regt.

This officer is qualified in every way as laid down in K.R. para.721. He was recommended as a suitable candidate for the Staff College before the war and was working for the entrance examination.

I recommend him very strongly.

Age 32½

22nd December 1918.

Brigadier-General,
Commanding 36th Infantry Brigade.

12th Divisional Artillery.

> H.Q.,
> R.A.,
> 12TH DIVISION.
> No. RA 1138
> Date...........

List of Officers who are recommended for admission to the Staff College - para. 721, King's Regulations.

31st December, 1918.

Rank and Name	Unit	Remarks
Major H.W.L. WALLER, D.S.O., M.C.	Brigade Major R.A.	Has already done about 4 years service on the Staff on active service and also in peace conditions, & has proved himself a Staff Officer of very high calibre.

J. F. Craig
Colonel,
Commanding 12th Divl. Artillery.

Headquarters,
   12th Division (G)

1st Jan. 1919.

List of Officers recommended for the Staff College
in accordance with para. 721 K.R.

Name	Unit	Age	Remarks
Captain (Temp. Lt. Col) E.H.T. NICOLLS DSO MC	East Surrey Regt. (Comdg 8th Royal Berkshire Regt.)	① 32½	Qualified in every way. Strongly recommended by Bde Commdr.
Captain (Temp. Lt. Col.) W.G.A. COLDWELL	Northamptonshire Regt. (Comdg 12 Bn. M.G.C.)	② 27½	
Major H.W.L. Waller DSO MC	Bde. Major 12th Divl. Artillery	33	recommendation forwarded Dec. 1918
Capt (Temp. Major) C.F.M.N. RYAN DSO MC	R.E. (Special Reserve) GSO2 12th Div.	③ 27	
Capt. (Temp. Major) G. MACDONALD MC	Gordon Highlanders DAAG 12th Div.	④	
Capt. (Temp. Lt. Col.) A.T. SHAKESPEAR DSO MC	R.E. CRE 12th Div.	34	recommendation forwarded Dec. 1918

First Army No. G034 (G).

T/32 of 4th January.

VIII Corps.

      It is notified for information that the School of Tactics, CAMBERLEY, will close on the 15th of January 1919.

                           (sgd) C.M. HIGSON, Capt.,
                                for Major-General,

6th January 1919.   General Staff, First Army.

-2-

VIII Corps No. G.b. 119/11.

7th January 1919.

11th Division.
12th Division.
49th Division.
63rd Division.

For information.

                         B.G., G.S.,
                         VIII Corps.

VIII Corps No. G.b. 127/5.

4th January 1919.

11th Division.
12th Division.
49th Division.
63rd Division.

[Stamp: H.Q. 12TH DIVISION (GENERAL STAFF.) No G.b.1255 Date 5.1.19]

It is notified for information that the opening of the Staff College, CAMBERLEY, is postponed till April 1st.

(Is that very appropriate) **ALL FOOLS DAY**

B.G., G.S.,
VIII Corps.

G.O.C.	
G.S.O. 1	
G.S.O. 2	
G.S.O. 3	

Copy to :-
    G.O.C., R.A.,
    C.E.
    "A" & "Q".

June 1919

WAR DIARY

12th Divn G S

DECEMBER 1916

WAR DIARY

12th Div GS

JANUARY 1914

Army Form C. 2118.

WAR DIARY
or
INTELLIGENCE SUMMARY.
12th Division. ~~Army Form~~ January 1919.

Ref.: VALENCIENNES Sheet 1/100,000.

Instructions regarding War Diaries and Intelligence Summaries are contained in F. S. Regs., Part II. and the Staff Manual respectively. Title pages will be prepared in manuscript.

Place	Date	Hour	Summary of Events and Information	Remarks and references to Appendices
MASNY	1st		(Fine)	
January	2nd		(Stormy) Brigades engaged in training	
	3rd		(Fine) Brigades engaged in training	
	4th		(Fine) Finals in Divl Tug-of-War and Football. Tug-of-War - 293rd Bde R.F.A. beat 9th Royal Fusiliers. Football - 9th Essex (3) - 5th R. Berks (0). G.O.C. presented prizes.	
	5th		(Wet) G.O.C. attended services at MASNY and AUBERCHICOURT. Then proceeded to Educational Conference VIII Corps	
	6th		(Fine) G.O.C. went to Corps point to point meeting	
	7th		(Fine) Brigades engaged in training and salvage work	
	8th		(Fine) G.O.C. inspected billets of the 'Queens' Regt	
	9th		(Wet) G.O.C. Inspected billets of R.E. afterwards attended Chaplains Conference	
	10th		(Fine) Brigades engaged in usual training	
	11th		(Fine) Do. Do. Finals of Divl Boxing Competition. Prizes presented by G.O.C.	
	12th		(Dull)	
	13th		(Fine) Classification of Animal demobilization for the 12th Div commenced	
	14th		(Fine) G.O.C. attended conference at VIII Corps	
	15th		(Wet)	
	16th		(Fine) G.O.C. attended Divl Education Conference - Lecture on the League of Nations by Lieut.Colonel Belgrave, D.S.O.	

Army Form C. 2118.

WAR DIARY
OF
INTELLIGENCE SUMMARY.
12th Division. Week ending January 1919

Instructions regarding War Diaries and Intelligence Summaries are contained in F. S. Regs., Part II. and the Staff Manual respectively. Title pages will be prepared in manuscript.

Place	Date	Hour	Summary of Events and Information	Remarks and references to Appendices
MASNY	17th		(Fine) GOC. inspected 35th Inf. Bde. Billets	
	18th		(Fine) G.O.C. inspected billets 36th Inf. Bde. - in the afternoon attended conference held by Archbishop of CANTERBURY at VALENCIENNES	
	19th		(Fine)	
	20th		(Fine) GOC. inspected billets and stables of Royal Artillery	
	21st		(Fine) 12th Divl Races. Final Leight-weight tug-of-war - won by 293rd Bde R.F.A	
	22nd		(Fine Frost) Brigades engaged on training	
	23rd		(Fine. Frost) GOC inspected billets of 37th Inf Bde.	
	24th		(Fine) GOC. inspected billets of 7th Royal Sussex Regt (36th Bde)	
	25th		(Hard Frost) Brigades engaged in training	
	26th		(SNow)	
	27th		(Thawing) G.O.C. inspected billets of 12th Div Signal Coy and 12th Div Train	
	28th		(Frost) G.O.C. inspected billets of 35th T.M.B. later had conference of Battn & Coy. Commanders at 35th Bde H.Q.	
	29th		(Hard frost) G.O.C. inspected billets of 293rd Bde R.F.A.	
	30th		(Hard frost) G.O.C. inspected billets of 6th Bn R.W.Kent Regt and 5th Northants (Pioneers)	
	31st		(Hard Frost) G.O.C. attended rehearsals of consecration and presentation of Colours to Battns 35th, 36th, and 37th Inf. Bdes.	
February	1st		(Snow) G.O.C. attended rehersal of presentation of Colours to Battns 35th, 36th and 37th Bdes.	

Major-General,
Commanding 12th Division.

Von Baeyer
Vorschal... HO
G
_____
February 1919

Army Form C. 2118.

WAR DIARY

12th Division for FEBRUARY 1919.
INTELLIGENCE/SUMMARY.

(Erase heading not required.)

Instructions regarding War Diaries and Intelligence Summaries are contained in F. S. Regs., Part II. and the Staff Manual respectively. Title pages will be prepared in manuscript.

Place	Date	Hour	Summary of Events and Information	Remarks and references to Appendices
MASNY	1st		G.O.C. attended rehearsal of Presentation of Colours to battalions of 35th, 36th and 37th Infantry Brigades.	
	2nd		(Frost) Address and discussion on reconstruction of the Church at Divisional Headquarters by Doctor TEMPLE.	
	3rd		(Frost) Prince of Wales arrived at Divisional Headquarters.	
ERRE	4th	1000	Colours presented by H.R.H. The Prince of Wales to 9th Battalion Royal Fusiliers, 7th Battalion Royal Sussex Regiment and 5th Battalion Royal Berkshire Regiment (36th Infantry Brigade.).	
SOMAIN	"	11.45	Colours presented by H.R.H. The Prince of Wales to 7th Battalion Norfolk Regiment, 9th Battalion The Essex Regiment and 5th Battalion Northamptonshire Regiment (Pioneers). (35th Infantry Brigade).	
AUBERCHICOURT	"	14.30	Colours presented by H.R.H. The Prince of Wales to 6th Battalion The Queen's (Royal West Surrey Regiment), 6th Battalion The Buffs (East Kent Regiment) and 6th Battalion The Queen's Own (Royal West Kent Regiment), (37th Infantry Brigade).	
MASNY	5th		(Frost) H.R.H. The Prince of Wales left Divisional Headquarters. Heavy fall of snow during the afternoon.	
	6th		(Slight Thaw) G.O.C. visited 12th Divisional Ammunition Column at ERCHIN.	
	7th		(Hard Frost) G.O.C. held a Conference at 35th Infantry Brigade Headquarters.	
	8th		(Hard Frost) Brigades engaged in training.	
	9th		(Hard Frost) "	
	10th		(Frost)	
	11th		(Frost)	
	12th		(Frost)	
	13th		(Frost)	

Army Form C. 2118.

WAR DIARY
12th Division   for   FEBRUARY 1919
INTELLIGENCE/SUMMARY.
(Erase heading not required.)

Instructions regarding War Diaries and Intelligence Summaries are contained in F. S. Regs., Part II. and the Staff Manual respectively. Title pages will be prepared in manuscript.

Place	Date	Hour	Summary of Events and Information	Remarks and references to Appendices
MASNY	14th		(Wet) Brigades engaged in training, and salvage work.	
	15th		(Wet) G.O.C. visited C.R.E. with reference to the revision of Mobilization Store Tables.	
	16th		(Fine) Brigades engaged in training, + salvage work.	
	17th		(Showery) G.O.C. visited 12th Bn. M.G. Corps and 35th Infantry Brigade with reference to the revision of Mobilization Store Tables.	
	18th		(Fine) G.O.C. visited 5th Bn. Northamptonshire Regiment (Pioneers) with reference to the revision of Mobilization Store Tables.	
	19th		(Fine) Final of Divisional Rugby Football Championship. 12th Division Signal Co. R.E. 9 Pts. v 62nd Brigade R.F.A. 5 Pts. Prizes presented by Major-General H.W.HIGGINSON, C.B., D.S.O.	
	20th		(Fine) G.O.C. proceeded to VALENCIENNES as President of Commission to enquire into the revision of Mobilization Store Tables. Brigadier-General B.VINCENT, C.M.G. assumed command of the Division.	
	21st		(Fine)	
	22nd		(Wet)	
	23rd		(Fine)	
	24th		(Fine) 12th Divisional Race Meeting at NOMAIN(?) - prizes presented by Brigadier-General B.VINCENT, C.M.G.	
	25th		(Fine)	
	26th		(Fine)	
	27th		(Wet) Draw of Divisional War Savings Certificate Lottery held at SOMAIN.	
	28th		(Fine)	

H.W. Higginson
Major-General,
Commanding 12th Division.

(6414) Wt. W3906/P1607 2,500,000 7/18 McA & W Ltd (E 3591) Forms W3091/4.   Army Form W.3091.

Cover for Documents.

Nature of Enclosures.

WAR DIARY
General Staff
12th Division.
MARCH 1919
(VOL   )

Notes, or Letters written.

Army Form C. 2118.

WAR DIARY
MARCH 1919
GENERAL STAFF 12th DIVISION.
(Erase heading not required.)

Instructions regarding War Diaries and Intelligence Summaries are contained in F. S. Regs., Part II. and the Staff Manual respectively. Title pages will be prepared in manuscript.

Place	Date	Hour	Summary of Events and Information	Remarks and references to Appendices
MASNY	1st	(Fine)	Major-General H.W. HIGGINSON, C.B., D.S.O. returned from VALENCIENNES and resumed command of the Division.	
	2nd	(Fine)		
	3rd	(Wet)	6th Bn. Royal West Kent Regt. and draft from 12th Divisional Artillery, 7th Bn. Royal Sussex Regt., 6th Bn. The Queen's, 12th Bn. Machine Gun Corps and 12th Divisional Signal Coy. proceeded by train from ANICHE to the Second Army. The Divisional Commander saw them off at ANICHE.	
	4th	(Wet)	Major-General H.R. DAVIES, C.B., Commanding VIII Corps arrived at SOMAIN and was met by Major-General H.W. HIGGINSON, C.B., D.S.O. A Silver Bugle was presented by the Corps Commander to the Drum and Fife Band of the 1/1st Bn. Cambridgeshire Regt., 35th Infantry Brigade, the winners of the Corps Drum and Fife Competition.	
	5th	(Fine)	The Divisional Commander visited the 62nd Brigade R.F.A. at DECHY.	
	6th	(Wet)	The Divisional Commander visited the 36th Infantry Brigade at HORNAING.	
	7th	(Stormy)	The last Race Meeting of the Division held at ANICHE. Prizes presented by Major-General H.W. HIGGINSON, C.B., D.S.O. -in-Chief	
	8th	(Wet)	Wire No. G.865 from VIII Corps stating that the First Commander would visit Divisional Headquarters at 11.45 hours on the 12th and wished to see Brigadiers.	
	9th	(Wet)	G.O.C. attended service at Divisional R.A.. A.C.G. First Army officiated.	
	10th	(Fine)	Wire No. G.885 sent ordering 36th Infantry Brigade to move to SOMAIN and VILLERS CAMPEAU on the 12th inst. Wire No. G.881 received from VIII Corps postponing the visit of the Commander-in-Chief by 24 hours (to Thursday 13th).	
	11th	(Fine).		
	12th	(Fine)	The Divisional Commander proceeded to VALENCIENNES as President of Committee to consider the readjustment of Mobilization Store Tables. 36th Infantry Brigade moved to SOMAIN and VILLERS CAMPEAU.	
	13th	(Fine)	The Commander-in-Chief paid a farewell visit to the Division. The Divisional Commander visited VIII Corps in the afternoon. VIII Corps wire No. A.863 received ordering Major-General H.W. HIGGINSON, C.B., D.S.O., to assume command of a Brigade of the 34th Division on the 18th instant.	
	14th	(Fine)	-	

Army Form C. 2118.

Page 2.

WAR DIARY

MARCH 1919

GENERAL STAFF 12th DIVISION.
(Erase heading not required.)

Place	Date	Hour	Summary of Events and Information	Remarks and references to Appendices
MASNY	15th	(Fine)		
	16th	(Showery)		
	17th	(Showery)	Major-General H.W.HIGGINSON, C.B., D.S.O. relinquished command of the 12th Division and proceeded to take over command of the 103rd Infantry Brigade, 34th Division. Brigadier-General B. VINCENT, C.M.G. assumed command of the Division.	
	18th	(Stormy)		
	19th	(Fine)	Orders received for Major G.MacDONALD, M.C. (D.A.A.G. 12th Div.) to proceed to G.H.Q. for temporary duty.	
	20th	(Snow)		
	21st	(Fine)	Major G. MacDONALD left to take up duties at G.H.Q.	
	22nd	(Snow)	Orders received for G.S.O.1 (Lieut.Col.J.D.BELGRAVE, D.S.O.) to proceed as G.S.O.2 II Corps on the Rhine.	
	23rd	(Fine)		
	24th	(Wet)		
	25th	(Fine)		
	26th	(Wet)		
	27th	(Wet)		
	28th	(Fine)	Divisional Headquarters moved to SOMAIN. Orders received for Major R.D.JOHNSTON/to (D.A.Q.M.G.) proceed to First Army as D.A.Q.M.G.	
SOMAIN	29th	(Fine)	Major R.D.JOHNSTON left to take up duty at First Army H.Q.	
	30th	(Snow)		
	31st	(Snow)		

G.A.Trent Colonel
for

Brigadier-General,
Commanding 12th Division.

Duplicate

War Diary
of

[stamp: H.Q., 12TH DIVISION, A.Q.'s BRANCH. No......... Date.........]

April 1919

Army Form C. 2118.

WAR DIARY
H.Q. 12th DIVISION for April 1919.
INTELLIGENCE SUMMARY.

(Erase heading not required.)

Instructions regarding War Diaries and Intelligence Summaries are contained in F. S. Regs., Part II. and the Staff Manual respectively. Title pages will be prepared in manuscript.

Place	Date	Hour	Summary of Events and Information	Remarks and references to Appendices
SOMAIN	Apl.1		Nothing to report.	
	2		2 officers 60 other ranks 5th Northamptonshire Regt. proceeded to 358 P.O.W. Coy.	
			2 " 61 " " " " " " 351 "	
			3 " 77 " 7th Bn. Norfolk Regt. " " 3 54 "	
			3 " 79 " " " " " " 352 "	
	3		3 " 80 " 7th Bn. Norfolk Regt. " " 320 "	
	4		Lieut.Colonel H.M.B.de Sales la TERRIERE M.C., 9th Essex, proceeded to England to report to the War Office.	
			Lieut.Colonel A.T.SHAKESPEAR D.S.O., M.C., C.R.E., proceeded to Disposals Branch for duty.	
			5 officers 24 O.R. 9th Bn. Royal Fusiliers proceeded to 17th Royal Sussex.	
			1 " 7 " 7th Bn. Royal Sussex " " 6th Bn.M.G.Corps.	
			1 " 33 " 12th Bn.M.G.Corps " " 6th Divisional Train.	
			1 " 7 " 12th Divisional Train " " 1st Divisional Train.	
			1 " 3 " " " " " 2 30 Divl.Employment Coy.	
			1 " 21 " 214 Divl.Employment Coy. " " 15th Bn.Essex Regt., 59th Division.	
	5		5 officers 17 O.R. 9th Bn. Essex Regt. " "	
	6		Nothing to report.	
	7		" "	
	8		" "	
	9		Revd. P.M.BRUNWELL,M.C. S.C.F.,P.Cs.Dept., proceeded to 34th Division.	
	10		Nothing to report.	
	11		Lieut.Colonel A.L.THOMSON D.S.O.,M.C., 36/M 7th Bn Royal Sussex Regt. proceeded to command 53rd Bn.Royal Sussex Regt., 34th Division.	
			Lieut.Colonel J.H.FLETCHER D.S.O.,M.C., 36th Field Ambulance, proceeded to England (for INDIA).	
	12		18 O.R. 214 Divl.Employment Coy. proceeded to 229 Divl.Employment Co., 32nd Division.	

Army Form C. 2118.

Page 2.

WAR DIARY
H.Q. 12th DIVISION for APRIL 1919.
INTELLIGENCE/SUMMARY.
(Erase heading not required.)

Place	Date	Hour	Summary of Events and Information	Remarks and references to Appendices
SOMAIN	April 13		Nothing to report.	
	14		1 officer 5 O.R. 9th Bn. Royal Fusiliers proceeded to 17th Bn. R. Sussex Regt., 59th Division.	
			" 14 " 5th Bn. Royal Berks Rgt. " 2/4th Bn. R. Berks Regt., 61st Division.	
	15		Brigadier General C.S.OWEN C.M.G.,D.S.O. proceeded to command 51st Welsh Regt., 1st Division.	
			Brigadier General A.B.INGLETON-WEBBER C.M.G.,D.S.O. proceeded to command 52nd Devon Regt.29th Div.	
			5 O.R. 1/1st Cambs.Regt. proceeded to 11th Suffolk Regt., 61st Division.	
	16		9 O.R. 9th Bn.Essex Regt. proceeded to 15th Bn.Essex Regt., 59th Division.	
			28 " 7th Bn.R.Sussex Regt. " 17th Bn.R.Sussex Regt., 59th Division.	
	17		Nothing to report.	
	18		Brigadier General B.VINCENT,C.M.G., proceeded to England.	
			Colonel G.A.TRENT C.M.G. assumed command of 12th Division Brigade Group.	
	19		Nothing to report.	
	20		"	
	21		"	
	22		6 O.R. 6th Bn.The Buffs proceeded to 6th Bn.R.W.Kent Regt., 34th Division	
			89 " 12th Bn.M.G.Corps. " 37th Bn.M.G.Corps.	
			6 " 214 Divl.Employment Co. " 229 Divl.Employment Co., 32nd Division.	
	23		Nothing to report.	
	24			
	25			
	26			
	27			
	28			
	29			
	30			

G. Aisworth,
Colonel.
Commanding 12th Division Brigade Group.

Duplicate.

War Diary
of.

[Stamp: H.Q., 12TH DIVISION, A.G.'s BRANCH. No...... Date......]

March 1919

(Vol.   )

Army Form C. 2118.

WAR DIARY
12th D. H. Q. for MAY 1919.
INTELLIGENCE SUMMARY.
(Erase heading not required.)

Instructions regarding War Diaries and Intelligence Summaries are contained in F. S. Regs., Part II. and the Staff Manual respectively. Title pages will be prepared in manuscript.

Place	Date	Hour	Summary of Events and Information	Remarks and references to Appendices
SOMAIN	MAY 1/2		Nothing to report.	
	3		Instructions received and issued to units for entrainment of cadres (see Appendix "A")	App."A"
	4		Preparation for entrainment proceeding.	
	5		Cadres detailed for first train in Appendix "A" left SOMAIN STATION at 19.10 hours for DUNKIRK.	App."A"
	6		Cadres detailed for second train in Appendix "A" left SOMAIN STN. at 19.20 hours for DUNKIRK.	App."A"
	7/10		Nothing to report.	
	11		Cadre of 12th Bn.M.G.Corps proceeded from ANICHE Station at 19.10 hours for DUNKIRK (see Appendix "B".)	App."B"
	12		Captain W.H.STIFF,D.S.O.,M.C.(Staff Capt. 49th Inf.Bde.) arrived and took up duties as Staff Captain 12th Divisional Headquarters.	
	13/18		Nothing to report.	
	19		Captain J.H.JACKSON, General List, proceeded for duty with Military Attache, BRUSSELS.	
	20/21		Nothing to report.	
	22		Captain H.P.McCABE, Staff Captain, 36th Infantry Brigade, proceeded to take up duties as Staff Captain, BOULOGNE BASE. Rev. H.P.BERKELEY proceeded to England to report to Chaplain General, War Office, for Home duty.	
	23/26		Nothing to report.	
	27		Notification received that trains for the conveyance of cadres would be available as follows:— one train on 30th, one on 31st May, and one on 1st June.	
	28		Administrative Instructions No.3 issued giving orders for entrainment of cadres (see Appendix "C".)	App."C"
	29		Preparation for entrainment proceeding.	
	30		Units detailed for train "A" (Appendix "C") left ANICHE Station at 13.30 hours.	App."C"
	31		Train B (see Appendix "C") did not arrive. Orders for units concerned were consequently postponed for 24 hours.	

[signature]
for Colonel,
Commanding 12th Division Brigade Group.

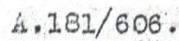

A.181/606.

**ADMINISTRATIVE INSTRUCTIONS IN CONJUNCTION
WITH FORECAST No. 7.**

Reference .... No. A.441 of 3rd inst.

1. Forecast No.7, will proceed by train from SOMAIN GUN PARK Siding to DUNKIRK on 5th and 6th May 1919.

2. Two trains are available and are made up as follows :-

   Each Train consists of   34 Flats (each Flat takes 3 axles).
                                 13 covered trucks (holds 40 men each).

3. 1st Train, Monday 5th May 1919.

   37th Infantry Brigade Headquarters.
   37th Light Trench Mortar Battery.
   7th Bn. Norfolk Regt.
   9th Bn. Essex Regt.
   37th Field Ambulance.

   2nd Train, Tuesday 6th May 1919.

   1/1st Bn. Cambridgeshire Regt.
   6th Bn. E. Kent Regt.
   70th Field Co. R.E.
   No.2 Coy. 12th Divl. Train.

4. Loading Parties.

   Loading Parties will report to R.T.O. SOMAIN (Gun Park Siding) at 08.00 hours on 5th and 6th inst. respectively.

Each Infantry Battn.)	1 officer.	30 Other ranks.
Brigade Headquarters)		3 " "
37th Field Ambulance.	1 N.C.O.	25 " "
70th Field Coy.	1 "	25 " "
No.2 Coy. Train.	1 "	10 " "

5. Extra horses are being detailed to assist units. (see appendix "A" attached).

6. For units leaving by 1st Train, rations will be issued on Sunday for consumption up till Wednesday inclusive.
   For units leaving by 2nd Train rations will be issued on Monday for consumption up till Thursday inclusive.

7. There will be two 1 hour HALTE REPAS, one at MONTIGNY, and one at TINCQUES; this will enable troops to procure hot drinks and food. Estimated duration of journey 12 hours.

8. Os.C. Units enumerated in Forecast No. 7 will render to this office by 12.00 hours 4th instant)
   Return A. A nominal roll of all (1) retainable officers, N.C.Os and men, (2) releasable officers, N.C.Os. and men surplus to Cadre.
   Return B. A nominal roll of all officers, N.C.Os. and men extra-regimentally employed absent with or without leave etc.

P.T.O.

9. All surplus stationery etc. will be properly packed, labelled "O.C. Reception Depot, Army Printing and Stationery Services, HAVRE" and sent to these Headquarters.

10. Winter Clothing will be handed ~~~~~ D.A.D.O.S. vide G.R.O. 6749.

11. Units will ensure that all claims and billeting certificates are settled before leaving.

(signed)
Captain,
A/D.A.Q.M.G.
12th Division Brigade Group.

3rd May, 1919.

Distribution:-

35th Inf. Bde.
7th Norfolks.
9th Essex.
1/1st Cambs.
36th Inf. Bde.
9th R.Fusiliers.
7th R.Sussex.
5th R.Berks.
37th Inf. Bde.
6th E.Kents.
12th Divl. Train.
C.R.E.
A.D.M.S.
D.A.D.O.S.
5th Northamptonshire Regt.
12th Div. Artillery.

12th Bn. M.G. Corps.
E.T.O. SOMAIN.
Camp Comdt.

Appendix "B"

A.181/637.

ADMINISTRATIVE INSTRUCTIONS No. 2.

1. 12th Bn. M. G. Corps will proceed by train from ANICHE STATION leaving at 18.00 hours 11th instant for DUNKIRK. Destination DEBGATE CAMP, SHORNCLIFFE.

2. 12th Divisional Artillery will detail 16 horses complete with drivers and harness to report to 12th Bn. M.G.C. H.Q. at 09.30 hours 10th inst. and 09.00 hours 11th inst.

3. 12th Bn. M. G.Corps will hand over on the 11th inst. all horses and mules on their charge and all surplus forage to 12th Divl.Arty., obtaining a receipt in duplicate, one copy of which will be forwarded to these H.Q.

4. Loading parties will report to R.T.O. ANICHE Station at 08.30 hours 11th inst.

5. Rations will be issued on the 10th for consumption up to 13th inst. inclusive.

6. All surplus stationery etc. will be properly packed and labelled O.C. Reception Depot, Army Printing and Stationery Services HAVRE, and sent to these H.Q.

7. Winter clothing will be handed in to D.A.D.O.S. vide G.R.O. 6749.

8. 12th Bn. M.G.Corps will ensure that all claims and billeting certificates are settled before leaving. A certificate that this has been done, and that all funds have been properly audited and found correct will be rendered to these H.Q. By 09.00 hours 11th inst.

9. 12th Bn. M.G.Corps will render to these H.Q. by 09.00 hours 11th instant :-

   Return "A". A nominal roll of all retainable officers, N.C.Os and men showing how posted.

   Return "B". A nominal roll of all releasable officers N.C.Os and men surplus to Cadre, together with demobilization papers for same.

   Return "C". A nominal roll of all officers, N.C.Os and men extra regimentally employed, absent with or without leave, giving particulars.

10. 12 th Bn. M.G.Corps will put up the following notice at ANICHE Station and Bn. H.Q. prior to moving off :-

    " All personnel of 12th Bn. M.G.Corps returning off leave etc. will report to 12th Div. H.Q. SOMAIN."

11. Reliefs of guards etc. will be carried out in accordance with Appendix "A".

12. C.R.E. will arrange for the removal of all fittings at the Baths, ECAILLON. 12th Bn.M.G.C. will provide the necessary transport at 12.00 Hours 12th inst.

(Signed) T. GILIAM, Captain,
A/D.A.A.G.
12th Division Brigade Group.

9.5.19.

To all units.

Appendix "A" issued in conjunction with Administrative Instructions No.2.

The following reliefs will take effect at 11.00 hours 10th instant :-

Guard	Situation	Strength N.C.O.	Strength O.R.	Found by	To be relieved by	Remarks
Dump	ANICHE H.7.b.7.7.	1	7	12th Bn. M. G. Corps.	R.E.	includes 1 cook. Mounts 19.00 hrs daily.
XY Dump and Intermediate Ordnance Collecting Station.	SOMAIN B.13.d.8.2.	2	18		12 D.A.	
German Amm.	Nr SOMAIN B.14.c.4.8.	1	3		12 D.A.	
Div. Baths.	SOMAIN		2		9th R.F.	
Div. Guard Detention Room.	SOMAIN	(1 (1	2) 3)		5th Berks 7 Sussex	1 Sgt. 1 Cpl.

Appendix 'C'

A.181/695.

12th DIVISION BRIGADE GROUP.

ADMINISTRATIVE INSTRUCTIONS No. 3.

Reference VALENCIENNES Sheet 1/100,000.   28th May 1919.

1. **Move of Cadres.**
One train will leave ANICHE on each of the following days to take Cadres as per Appendix 'A' to DUNKIRK :-

    30th May.
    31st May.
    1st June.

    Each train will be shunted into position during the early hours of the day of departure.
    Each train will depart at 13.00 hours.

2. **Composition of train.**
Each train consists of :-

    1 covered coach.
    12 covered trucks.
    35 flats (approx. 146 axles closely packed).

3. **Entrainment.**
Loading will commence daily at 06.00 hours. Units will be loaded in the order enumerated in the attached Appendix 'A'.
    All available space on trains A and B must be filled, the vehicles of units being pooled if necessary.
    All wagons must be at the wagon Park beside ANICHE Station or in position near the ramp by 18.00 hours on date prior to entrainment.
    Units will supply their own loading parties.
    H.Q. 12th Divisional Artillery will detail one officer for each train to superintend the loading of the whole train, under the R.T.O., in order to ensure continuity etc.

4. **Horses.**
O.C. 12th Divisional Train will place 2 pair horses with drivers and harness at the disposal of 87th Field Company R.E. on 29th instant to move wagons to ANICHE Station.
    On the evening of the 29th instant the O.C. 87th Fd.Co. will transfer the pair of horses on his charge to O.C. 69th Field Coy.R.E.
    O.C. 12th Divisional Artillery will arrange for all horses on charge of 62nd and 63rd Brigades R.F.A. to be taken over by 12th D.A.C. prior to departure.
    O.C. 39th Divisional Artillery will retain the horses with A/ 174 Brigade R.F.A.

5. **Guards.**
The following guards being found by the 12th Divisional Artillery will be withdrawn at 12.00 hours on 29th instant whether relieved or not :-

German R.E.Dump	MONCHECOURT	1 N.C.O.	3 men.
German Fuel Dump	BOUCHAIN	1 "	3 "
German Fuel Dump	SIN-LE-NOBLE	1 "	3 "

    The following guards /
    P.T.O.

5. Guards.
(Contd.)

The following guards will continue to be found by the 12th Divisional Artillery:-

XY Dump. near SOMAIN.	3 N.C.Os.	18 men
Salvage Dump. " LEWARDE.	1 N.C.O.	3 men.
Amn.Dump. " LEWARDE.	1 N.C.O.	6 men.
Div.Fuel Dump. AUBERCHICOURT.	1 N.C.O.) 3 men.)	at night only.

The guard of 1 N.C.O. and 7 men on R.E. Dump near ANICHE, H.7.b.7.7., at present being found by 69th and 87th Field Coys. R.E. will be found by 69th Field Co.R.E. after the 29th instant.

The guards being found by 39th Divisional Artillery will remain as at present.

6. Rations.

Unconsumed portion of rations for day of entrainment plus two days rations will be taken.

7. Returns.

The following returns will be rendered by Os.C. 62nd and 63rd Brigades R.F.A. and O.C. 87th Field Coy.R.E. to reach this office by 16.00 hours 29th:-

1. A certificate to the effect that no retainable men are proceeding with the cadre.

To reach this office prior to departure of unit :-

2. A nominal roll of all retainable officers, N.C.Os. and men showing how posted.

3. A nominal roll of all releasable officers N.C.Os and men surplus to cadre, together with demobilization papers for same.

4. A nominal roll of officers, N.C.Os and men extra-regimentally employed, absent with or without leave, giving particulars, together with all demobilization papers for personnel on leave etc.

5. A certificate to the effect that all billets occupied have been included in billetting certificates and that all claims have been settled, together with a clearance certificate countersigned by the Maire.

It is absolutely essential that the demobilization papers asked for are completed as far as possible.

8. Billets.

O.C. 12th Divisional Artillery will arrange for 12th D.A.C. to move to ANICHE on departure of 62nd Brigade R.F.A. Completion of move to be reported to this office.

[signature], Captain,
A/D.A.A.G.,
12th Division Brigade Group.

Distribution :-

12th Div. Arty.	12th Div.Signal Co.RE.
62nd Bde. R.F.A.	7th Bn.R.Sussex Regt.
63rd Bde. R.F.A.	9th Bn.R.Fusiliers.
12th D.A.C.	5th Bn.R.Berks. Regt.
293rd Bde. R.F.A.	5th Bn.Northamptonshire
39th Div. Arty.	Regt. (Pioneers).
174th Bde. R.F.A.	12th Div. Train.
C.R.E.	A.D.M.S.
69th Field Co.RE.	D.A.D.O.S.
87th Field Co.RE.	R.T.O. SOMAIN.

To accompany 12th Div.Admin.Inst.No.3.

APPENDIX 'A'.

Date of Entrainment	Serial number.	Unit.	Destination	O.C. Train.
30th May Train A.	A.393. A.185. A.186. A.187. A.188(portion)	87th Fd.Co.R.E. H.Q.62nd Bde.RFA) A/62nd " ") B/62nd " ") C/62nd " ")	BORDEN. CARTON - Sutton VENEY.	O.C. 62nd Bde. RFA.
31st May. Train B.	A.188(balance) A.189. A.190. A.191. A.192(portion)	C/62nd " ") D/62nd " ") H.Q.63rd Bde. RFA.) A/63rd " ") B/63rd " ")	-do-	O.C. 63rd Bde. RFA.
1st June. Train C.	A.192(balance) A.193. A.194. A.229.	B/63rd " ") C/63rd " ") D/63rd " ") A/174th " "	-do- BETTISFIELD CAMP.	Field officer to be selected by O.C. 63 Bde.RFA.

Fd Coy 28
62ⁿᵈ RFA 178
63ʳᵈ RFA 178
A/174 RFA 44
2 Coy Train 30

3) 458
152 *mules per train*.

3½ pm

Army Form C. 2118.

WAR DIARY

H.Q. 12th Division for June 1919.
INTELLIGENCE SUMMARY.

(Erase heading not required.)

Instructions regarding War Diaries and Intelligence Summaries are contained in F.S. Regs., Part II. and the Staff Manual respectively. Title pages will be prepared in manuscript.

Place	Date	Hour	Summary of Events and Information	Remarks and references to Appendices
SOMAIN	1st June		Owing to the non-arrival of a train for conveyance of cadres on 31st May, two trains were allotted for to-day to complete the programme in hand. For details of units see Appendix "A" to Administrative Instructions No.3 (Trains B and C) attached. Train B left at ANICHE at 13.20 hours and Train C at 21.10 hours.	Appendix I
	2nd	"	Colonel G.A.TRENT C.M.G. D.S.O. proceeded on leave to U.K. Lieut. Colonel A.K.MAIN D.S.O. assumed temporary command of the Divl. Brigade Group.	
	3rd/7th	"	Nothing special to report.	
	8th	"	Four trains available for conveyance of cadres, one each day from 8th to 11th inclusive.	Appendix II.
	9th	"	Units entrained in accordance with Appendix "A" to Administrative Instructions No.4 attached.	
	10th	"		
	11th	"		
	10th	"	Colonel G.A.TRENT C.M.G., D.S.O. returned from U.K. and resumed command of the Divl. Brigade Group.	
	12th/15th	"	Nothing to report.	
	16th	"	4 offrs. 149 O.R. proceeded to No.5 Concentration Camp for demobilization on reduction of cadres to equipment guards.	
	17th	"	Nothing to report.	
	18th	"	Equipment Guards of 186 Bde. R.F.A. and No.1 Signal Construction Coy. entrained for DUNKIRK in accordance with Administrative Instructions No.5 attached.	
	19th	"	295 Army Bde. R.F.A., 39th Divl. Artillery H.Q., 39th D.A.C. (less S.A.A. Sect.) 284 Coy.R.A.S.C. were transferred to VIII Corps H.A. for administration (vide Admin. Instr. No.6 attached).	
	22nd	"	Entrainment of Equipment Guards incordance with Administrative Instructions No.5. H.Q. 12th	
	24th	"	Division Brigade Group closed at 09.00 hours.	
DUNKIRK	23rd 24th -27th	"	Accommodated at No.1 Camp Dunkirk awaiting loading of equipment on ferry. Lieut-Col. G.A. TRENT. C.M.G. D.S.O. proceeded to U.K. independently on 21.6.19 when equipment is loaded on ferry personnel of equipment guard will proceed to BOULOGNE for demobilization. A/L1. Scott Capt. c/D.A.A.G. 12 Div. Bde. Group. 27.6.19	

APPENDIX "A"

to
ADMINISTRATIVE INSTRUCTIONS No.3.

Date of Entrainment.	Serial Number.	Unit.	Destination	O.C. Train.
30th May Train A.	A.393.	87th Fd.Co.R.E.	BORDEN.	O.C. 62nd Bde. RFA.
	A.185.	H.Q.62nd Bde.RFA)		
	A.186.	A/62nd " ")	CARTON -	
	A.187.	B/62nd " ")	SUTTON VENEY.	
	A.188(portion)	C/62nd " ")		
1st June	A.188(balance)	C/62nd " ")		O.C. 63rd Bde. RFA.
	A.189.	D/62nd " ")		
	A.190.	H.Q.63rd Bde.RFA)	-do-	
	A.191.	A/63rd " ")		
	A.192(portion)	B/63rd " ")		
1st June.	A.192(balance)	B/63rd " ")		Field Officer to be selected by O.C. 63rd Bde. RFA.
	A.193.	C/63rd " ")	-do-	
	A.194.	D/63rd " ")		
	A.229.	A/174th " "	BETTISFIELD CAMP.	
	ZA.476.	ZA.1 Coy. 12th Divl. Train.)	AINTREE.	
	ZA.477.	1 Coy. -do-)		

ADMINISTRATIVE INSTRUCTIONS NO.4.

1. Move of Cadres. Cadres will move by train in accordance with Appendix "A" attached.
Forecast issued with Divl. Orders No. 1090 dated 31-5-19 is cancelled.

2. Loading. All wagons must be at the station of entrainment or in the wagon park adjoining by 18.00 hours on the day prior to entrainment. Loading will commence at 08.00 hours daily. Units will load in the order enumerated in attached Appendix "A". Units will supply their own loading parties. Each train must be loaded to its greatest possible capacity. Vehicles must be carefully selected for each flat so that the maximum number of axles are got on each flat, vehicles of units being pooled where necessary. The entraining officer will pay particular attention to the above. He will report to the R.T.O. at 17.45 hours on the day of entrainment.

3. Guards. The guard of 1 N.C.O. and 3 men at ANICHE dump found by 69th Field Coy. R.E. will be withdrawn at 18.00 hours 7th inst. whether relieved or not. The guard at ANICHE Station of 2 N.C.Os. and 9 men found by 5th Northamptonshire Regt. will be withdrawn at 18.00 hours 11th inst. 12th Divl. Arty. will make the necessary arrangements to guard these wagons from 18.00 hours 18th inst.
The night watchman at Div. Fuel Dump AUBERCHICOURT found by 5th Northamptonshire Regt. will be relieved by 12th Divl. Arty. on night of 9th/10th June.

4. Rations. Unconsumed portion of rations for day of entrainment plus two days rations will be taken.

5. Returns. The following returns will be rendered by Os.C. units entraining
to reach this office by 18.00 hours 7th:-
1. A certificate to the effect that no retainable men are proceeding with the cadre.
To reach this office prior to departure of unit:-
2. A nominal roll of all retainable officers, N.C.Os. and men showing how posted.
3. A nominal roll of all releasable officers, N.C.Os. and men surplus to cadre, together with demobilization papers for same.
4. A nominal roll of officers, N.C.Os. and men extra-regimentally employed, absent with or without leave, giving particulars, together with all demobilization papers for personnel on leave &c.
5. A certificate to the effect that all billets occupied have been included in billeting certificates and that all claims have been settled, together with a clearance certificate countersigned by the Maire.

It is absolutely essential that the demobilization papers asked for are completed as far as possible.

6. Horses. Horses to convey wagons to the station and for running wagons up the ramp will be furnished in accordance with Appendix B attached, complete with drivers and harness.
Units handing their horses over will obtain a receipt in duplicate, one copy of which will be forwarded to this office.

THGillam Capt.
A/D.A.G.
12th Div.Bde.Group.

APPENDIX "A" TO ADMINISTRATIVE INSTRUCTIONS No. @.

Date of entrainment.	Train.	Entraining Station.	Unit	Serial No.	Destination	Entraining Officer	O.C. Train.
JUNE 8	A	SOMAIN	5th R.Berks.Regt.	ZA.495.	GEORGETOWN (Scottish Command).	To be detailed by O.C.5th R. Berks. Regt.	O.C.9th R.Fus.
			9th R.Fusiliers.	ZA.496.	–do–		
			7th R.Sussex Regt.	ZA.474.	AINTREE (Northern Command).		
			36th Field Ambce.	ZA.478.	–do–		
			As much as possible of 69th Field Coy.R.E.	ZA.480.	–do–		
" 9	B	ANICHE.	Remainder of 69th Field Coy. R.E.	ZA.480.	–do–	To be detailed by 12th D.A.C.	O.C.12th D.A.C. party.
			As much as possible of 12th D.A.C.	ZA.483.	–do–		
" 10	C	SOMAIN.	H.Q.174 Bde. R.F.A.	A.228.	BETTISFIELD CAMP (Western Command)	To be detailed by 174 Bde.R.F.A.	O.C. 174 Bde R.F.A.
			B/174 Bde.	A.230.	–do–		
			C/174 "	A.231.	–do–		
			D/174 "	A.232.	–do–		
			H.Q.35th Inf.Bde.	ZA.472.	AINTREE.		
			35 L.T.M.B.	A.390.	PREES HEATH.		
			H.Q.36th Inf.Bde.	A.473.	BORDEN.		
			36 L.T.M.B.	A.503.	CATTERICK.		
" 11	D	ANICHE.	Balance of 12 D.A.C.	ZA.483.	AINTREE.	To be detailed by 12th D.A.C.	O.C. D.A.C. party.
			X/12 T.M.B.	ZA.484.	–do–		
			Y/12 T.M.B.	ZA.485.	–do–		
			23rd M.V.S.	ZA.481.	GEORGETOWN.		
			5th Northamptonshire R.	ZA.486.	AINTREE. (If train accommodation is available).		

APPENDIX "B".

No of horses.	By whom found.	to report to	Time	Date	To be handed over to	Place	Time	Date
2	5th Royal Berks	5th Royal Berks.	-	"	12th Div. Train.	Somain Station.	18.00	7th
6	12th Div. Train.	5th Royal Berks.	14.00	7th	"	"	"	"
2	9th Royal Fusiliers	9th Royal Fusiliers.	-	"	12th Div Artillery	Station Somain	18.00	7th
6	12th Div. Artillery	9th Royal Fusiliers	14.00	7th	"	"	"	"
4	7th Royal Sussex.	7th Royal Sussex.	-	"	12th Div. Artillery.	Somain Station.	18.00	7th
6	12th Div. Artillery	7th Royal Sx.	14.00	7th	"	"	"	"
2	36th Field Ambulance.	36th Field Ambulance	-	"	12th Div. Train.	Somain Station	18.00	7th
2	12th Div. Train.	36th Field Ambulance	14.00	7th	"	"	"	"
2	69th Field Coy. R.E.	69th Field Ambulance	-	"	"	"	"	"
2	12th Div. Artillery	69th Field Coy. R.E.	14.00	7th	"	"	"	"

No of horses	By whom found	to report to	Time	Date	Date to be handed over to	Place	Time	Date
8	12th Div Train	Entraining Officer SOMAIN.	07.45	8th	"	"	"	"
4	12th Div. Train.	69th Field Coy. R.E.	14.00	8th	"	"	"	"
2	69th Field Coy. R.E.	69th Field Coy. R.E.	"	"	12th Div Train	ANICHE STATION.	18.00	8th
10	12th Div. Artillery	Entraining Officer ANICHE Stn.	07.45	9th	"	"	"	"
2	35th Inf. Bde. H.Q.	35th Inf. Bde. H.Q.	"	"	12th Div Train,	SEMAIN STATION	18.00	9th
4	12th Div. Train.	35th Inf. Bde. H.Q.	14.00	9th	"	"	"	"
6	12th Div. Train.	36th Inf. Bde. H.Q.	14.00	9th	"	"	"	"
10	/39th Div. Artillery.	Entraining Officer SOMAIN Stn.	07.45.	10th	"	"	"	"
2	5th Northants	5th Northants.	"	"	12th Div. Train,	ANICHE STATION.	18.00	10th.
10	12th Div. Train.	5th Northants	14,00	10th	"	"	"	"
10	12th Div. Artillery	Entraining Officer ANICHE	07.45.	11th	"	"	"	"

Transport arrangements for 174th Bde. R.F.A. will be made by 39th Div. Artillery.

APPENDIX TO WAR DIARY

of

GENERAL STAFF

12th DIVISION

AUGUST and SEPTEMBER, 1918.

NARRATIVE OF OPERATIONS

and

MAP SHOWING ADVANCE OF DIVISION

from 8th AUG. to 30th SEPT. 1918

0-0-0-0-0-0-0-0-0-0

12th Division No. G.O /278

18th March, 1919.

Historical Section of War Cabinet,
2 Whitehall Gardens,
London, S.W.

With reference to First Army letter No. 3166 (G) dated 9th March 1919 I forward herewith

(a) Report on operations by 12th Division 2nd August to 30th September 1918,

(b) Report on operations by 12th Division 6th to 29th October 1918.

B. Belgrave Lt Col.

for Brigadier-General,
Commanding 12th Division.

REPORT ON OPERATIONS BY 12th Division.

PHASE I.

August 2nd to August 21st 1918.

AUGUST

2nd to 4th

Between August 2nd and 4th the Division took over the centre sector III Corps front, astride the River ANCRE. At this time the enemy was in process of evacuating DERNANCOURT and of giving up all the ground West of the River.

On the 4th the G.O.C. was informed at a conference that an attack would take place on the 8th in which the Division on our right would take part, but which would not affect the front held by the 12th Division.

5th.

On the 5th the B.G.,G.S., III Corps arrived at Divisional Headquarters at 10.00 hours and gave verbal orders for the 12th Division to take part in the attack on a one Brigade front, South of the River ANCRE. The portion of our front North of the ANCRE was to be taken over by the 47th Division.

A conference was held at Divisional Headquarters at 21.30 hours attended by Brigade Commanders and the C.R.A., at which the proposed plan was explained. The objective is shown on Map 'A'. The idea was to secure a suitable jumping off place for an attack on the Spur N. and N.E. of MORLANCOURT. The 35th Infantry Brigade (Brig.General B.VINCENT, C.M.G.) was ordered to carry out this attack.

6th.

Orders were received on the evening of the 6th that the 36th Infantry Brigade (Brig.General C.S.OWEN, C.M.G., D.S.O.) would come under orders of the G.O.C. 18th Division (Major-General R.P.LEE, C.B.) for the operations on the 8th. This was owing to an attack which the Germans had made on the morning of the 6th, in which they had captured some trenches held by the 18th Division on our right, and also owing to the fatigue and depletion of the 18th Division units consequent upon this attack, and the subsequent counter-attack delivered by them.
In order that the German trenches on our front could be bombarded and the wire cut, it was decided that the attack by the 12th Division should not take place until two hours after the attack had been launched on our right.

7th.

Zero hour for the 58th and 18th Divisions on our right was fixed at 04.20 hours; for the 12th Division at 06.20 hours.

8th.

From 22.00 hours 7th until 22.30 hours 8th the enemy shelled the area North and East of BARETT WOOD, and the area K.12. very heavily with Mustard Gas. This made the march to assembly positions difficult, and caused casualties, especially to units moving into areas which had been shelled, after the shelling had ceased. The necessity was again emphasised for the strictest gas discipline and also for Commanders to post sentries round areas which have been shelled with gas in order to warn troops entering those areas.

Troops were in their assembly positions by 05.30 hours, and at 06.20 hours the attack was launched on a three battalion front in a thick mist, which prevented the troops seeing more than 30 yards. The 6th Queen's Regt., 37th Infantry Brigade, had been placed under orders of the G.O.C. 35th Infantry Brigade, and was in support. The 5th Northamptonshire Regt, (Pioneers) was also placed under orders of the G.O.C. 36th Infantry Brigade in reserve for defensive purposes. The 37th Infantry Brigade (Brig. General A.B.INCLEDON-WEBBER, D.S.O.), less 1 battalion, was in Divisional reserve at FRANVILLERS.

AUGUST.

8th (Contd)
The attack of the centre and left Battalions (7th Bn. Norfolk Regt. and 9th Bn. Essex Regt. respectively) was entirely successful, and consolidation was begun at once on their objective line from about the T of MORLANCOURT to the River ANCRE, from which line patrols were sent forward with the object of gaining the crest of the spur.

The left Company of the right Battalion (1/1st Bn. Cambridgeshire Regt.) reached its objective, but the right Company met with strong opposition owing to the troops on its right having been unable to go forward - strong machine gun and rifle fire came from the trench K.14.a.4.6. to K.8.c.7.7. and from the road K.14.b.2.6. to K.8.d.7.5. Eventually both leading Companies of this Battalion were driven back to our front line. Lt.Col. E.T.SAINT, D.S.O., the Battalion Commander, went to Brigade Headquarters and requested that his Battalion should be allowed to make another attack, the objective to include the trench K.14.a.4.6. to K.8.c.7.7. Artillery support was arranged by Brigadier-General B.VINCENT, C.M.G., the Brigade Commander, with his affiliated Artillery Brigade Commander. The Division arranged for Heavy Artillery fire, and with the 18th Division that their left should advance at the same time. A Tank which happened to be in the neighbourhood was ordered to assist.

At 12.15 hours the 1/1st Bn. Cambridgeshire Regt. attacked again with great gallantry and was completely successful. The attack was carried out by two Companies totalling less than 200 Officers and men. 316 wounded and unwounded prisoners were captured, and upwards of 30 were killed. In addition 14 M.Gs., 6 light T.Ms. and 2 medium T.Ms. were taken. This success afforded immediate relief to the Brigade on our right and to our own troops on the left who had been much harassed by snipers and M.G. fire from their right flank and rear. It was a good example of a well arranged attack carried out at short notice under a resolute Commander.

The line held and consolidated during the night, together with advanced posts, is shown on the map, touch being obtained with flank Divisions at the points indicated.

At 16.00 hours orders were received that the 37th Infantry Brigade (less 1 Battalion with 55th Infantry Brigade) was to be placed under the orders of the 18th Division. This Brigade moved accordingly to the ROMA - BALLARAT Line (J.23., 17 and 10.) arriving about 21.00 hrs.

Night 8/9th
At 20.45 hours orders were received by telephone that the attack would be continued by the 12th Division on the left, and the 58th Division, (with the 131st American Regt. attached.) on the right; with the 1st and 2nd objectives as shown on the map. Eight tanks were allotted to the 12th Division.

Zero would probably be at 04-30 hours.

The G.O.C. summoned a conference of Brigadiers at the Brigade Headquarters of the rear Brigade. Orders were sent to the 37th Infantry Brigade for two Battalions to assemble in the K.2.a. and one Battalion about CLONCURRY TRENCH (K.13.d.), ready to pass through the 55th Infantry Brigade, and attack at dawn. C.O's. were ordered to assemble at Brigade Headquarters, and Company commanders at Battalion Command posts, close to their assembly positions.

The G.O.C. went by car to Rear Brigade Headquarters of the 55th Infantry Brigade and issued orders for the attack, together with maps marked with boundary lines and objectives. At 00.10 hours 9th August., III Corps telephoned that it was proposed to postpone the hour of attack to 05.30 hours. The G.O.C. replied that in his

-1-

AUGUST.
Night 8/9th (Contd)

opinion the hour of Zero should remain unaltered or the operation be postponed until much later, as troops waiting in assembly positions would be seen by the enemy. At 01.40 the G.O.C. returned to Divisional Headquarters, and at 01.45 the attack was postponed till the evening by telephone order from III Corps.

The 37th Infantry Brigade Headquarters were on the move, but were informed as soon as possible. They were, however, unable to stop the attack of their right battalion, the 6th Buffs, whose leading Companies had commenced the assault and had already penetrated the enemy's positions in K.14.b. and d., without the assistance of a barrage, when the order reached them that the operation was postponed. They captured some prisoners and a machine gun. The time from receipt of orders by telephone at Divisional Headquarters to the commencement of the attack by this Battalion was roughly 9 hours. The Brigade was under another Division when the first order was issued, and the final order from Divisional Headquarters cancelling the attack caught Brigade Headquarters on the move; but 7 hours may be taken as a minimum in which an attack can be arranged, and 3 hours must be added for every change in orders to reach Company Commanders.

9th.

The attack was finally ordered to take place at 17.30 hours under a creeping barrage and with the assistance of tanks. At that hour one battalion (6th Buffs) 37th Infantry Brigade, advanced from K.14.a. and c., South of MORLANCOURT, and two battalions, 6th Queen's and 8th R.W.Kent Regt., having formed up in K.9.a. and c., moved North of the village.

The 6th Bn. R.W.Kent Regt. made a fine attack and reached the second objective. Their advance was much assisted by the tanks and by the machine guns specially placed in the railway embankment North of DERNANCOURT, in K.20. and K.15., to enfilade the valley in K.28. These were very successful and obtained many direct targets at the enemy running away from the advance of our tanks and infantry on the spur and in the valley in K.27. and K.28. The troops on the right met with considerable opposition, and a large number of the enemy were taken prisoner or killed. The 18th Division on our right also met with stubborn resistance, and at 20.00 the line ran as shown on the map.

About 350 prisoners were taken, with machine guns, trench mortars, and two 77 mm. guns.

10th

The 9th Bn. Essex Regt., 35th Infantry Brigade, was placed under orders of the G.O.C. 37th Infantry Brigade and orders were issued for the attack to be renewed at 18.00 hours on the 10th. This attack, supported by tanks, was successful, and the main line of the old AMIENS defences was captured. The trench running through the 150 contour in K.29. was cleared by the tanks and some of our men entered it, but we were unable to retain it.

The 58th Division on our right attacked simultaneously, and as soon as they had passed through the 36th Infantry Brigade, the latter reverted to the orders of the 12th Division.

The 7th Bn. Royal Sussex Regt. was attached to the 37th Infantry Brigade and moved in close support to its right during the advance on the evening of the 10th. After the attack this battalion was ordered to relieve the 9th Bn. Essex Regt. (35th Infantry Brigade, attached 37th Infantry Brigade) in the right sub-sector, and to push out strong patrols to make good the trench running through contour 150 in K.29. This they were unable to do owing to the severity of the hostile M.G. fire, but posts were established as shown on the map.

AUGUST.

Night 10/11th

During the night the front line was consolidated by the battalions in the line. Strong points were dug by the 69th and 70th Field Coys., R.E. at about K.10.b.0.0. and K.3.b.5.7. The Pioneers wired the front line. A battalion of the 108th Regiment United States Engineers was attached to the Division and did some wiring along the Reserve line, which was taped from K.10.b.0.5. through SOLITARY TREE to K.3.b.5.7., and thence to E.27.a.1.4. and to the River about E.21.c.4.2. This American battalion also dug a strong point close to SOLITARY TREE.

The front line held by the Division on August 10th is shown in red on the map.

12th.

On the evening of the 12th the 36th Infantry Brigade took over the right and centre sub-sectors from the 37th Infantry Brigade. There were two Brigades in the line.

    36th Infantry Brigade - on the right on a two battalion front.
    37th Infantry Brigade - on the left on a one battalion front.

At 04.55 hours on the 13th an attack was made on the trench running through the 150 contour in E.29.in accordance with orders issued by the Division. The attack was carried out by two Companies of the right battalion 36th Infantry Brigade (7th Bn. Royal Sussex Regt.) and two Platoons left battalion (9th Bn. Royal Fusiliers) under a heavy concentration of guns. Part of the trench was occupied and some prisoners, machine guns and trench mortars captured; but a counter-attack made at 06.30 hours from the valley in K.6.a. and E.29.a. drove our men back to their former positions with the loss of 1 officer and 66 other ranks.

This ended the First Phase in the operations as far as the 12th Division was concerned.

PHASE II

13th to 21st.

During this pause in the operations, the line held was consolidated and wired, while a good trench was dug and wired as shown on Map 'A'.

Our patrols were very active and the enemy's line was accurately located.

Divisional Headquarters were at RIENCOURT.

The Division was ordered to prepare a scheme for an advance to the high ground about F.20. on the right with its left refused along the spur South of MEAULTE to the bend of the River ANCRE in E.22.a., thus forming a flank to the further advance of the Fourth Army.

Plan of attack for Aug.22nd.

The scope of the operations was afterwards extended and an attack was ordered for the 22nd August.

The first essential was a rapid movement into the Eastern end of MEAULTE to allow troops of the 18th Division, which was now on the left of the 12th Division, to pass between the village and the River and to gain a footing on the spur between MEAULTE and ALBERT in order to cover the crossing of the river between those places. These troops were to be brought across the River ANCRE for this purpose and formed up immediately behind the left Battalion of the Division.

The attack was to be carried out by the 35th Infantry Brigade on the right, with the 1/1st Cambridgeshire Regt. and 7th Bn. Norfolk Regt. in front, and the 9th Bn. Essex Regt. and 6th Bn. The Buffs (placed under their orders for this operation) in close support.

of the G.O.C. 35th Inf. Bde.

- 4 -

The 36th Infantry Brigade was to attack on the left. Its right battalion, the 9th Bn. Royal Fusiliers, was to be followed by the 7th Bn. Royal Sussex Regt. in close support. The left battalion, the 5th Bn. Royal Berkshire Regt., was given the task of clearing the village of MEAULTE and was to be covered by a special barrage which was to advance at the rate of 100 yards in 2 minutes.

As this barrage was timed to move quicker than the barrage on the remainder of the front it was necessary to make special arrangements to keep down rifle and machine gun fire from the trench running from E.29.a. to the E of MEAULTE. For this purpose 'D' Special Company R.E. were to fire 50 drums of burning oil into the head of the valley in E.29.a. at Zero; Heavy Artillery fire was to be directed on the trench; and a 4.5" Howitzer battery was to fire on the trench till the creeping barrage on the rest of the front came up.

On the remainder of the front the barrage was arranged in co-ordination with the 58th Division on our right and was to move at the rate of 100 yards in 4 minutes, halting for 20 minutes on a line protecting the first objective, subsequently creeping forward at the same rate to a line protecting the final objective. During the pause on the first objective the three supporting battalions were to leap-frog and capture the second objective. In the meantime the special barrage for the 5th Bn. Royal Berkshire Regt. was to halt on the approximate line of the road E.17.c.6.0. to E.17.c.2.7. where it was to wait till Zero plus 68 minutes, at which time it was caught up by the barrages on either flank. It was then to creep forward with them at the rate of 100 yards in 4 minutes.

Eight tanks were to co-operate in the attack, of which three were allotted to the front of the right Brigade and five to that of the left Brigade.

August 22nd.

At 03.00 hours the 18th Division reported by telephone that their troops had overcome the resistance of the enemy on the line of the River ANCRE and had already reached the line of the VIVIER MILL - ALBERT Road. It would therefore be unnecessary for any troops of the 18th Division to form up with the 5th Bn. Royal Berkshire Regt.

The barrage opened at 04.45 hours, at which hour the attack began. The morning was very misty till about 09.00 hours. The section of tanks detailed to work with the right Brigade got into a concentration of gas which delayed their advance so that they were not available to deal with the trench as in E.29. and K.5. Severe casualties were sustained here, but the resistance was overcome and the first objective, the BROWN LINE, was reached without much further difficulty about 06.40 hours. There were a few machine gun nests in MEAULTE, but these were dealt with by the tanks, one of which moved up and down the main street of the village while two others moved on either side of it. The "leap-frogging" battalions moved through, and, on the left Brigade front, they reached their final objectives capturing 14 prisoners. On the right Brigade front, however, the enemy had taken up a position on the high ground about F.20. between the MEAULTE - BRAY and the FRICOURT - BRAY Roads, which was chosen with great tactical skill and defended with resolution. As men of the 35th Infantry Brigade moved up the hill they were met and stopped by machine gun fire sweeping the crest, and were then subjected to heavy trench mortar fire directed on the Western slopes.

AUGUST.

22nd
(Contd.)

The Division on our right (47th) reached its objective on the Southern slope of the high ground, but the Germans on the Eastern side of the hilltop were under cover from them and from our men who now held the Northern and Western slopes. The enemy was able to bring an intense machine gun fire on to any troops who came into view over the crest of the hill and had covered lines of approach and retreat down the valleys leading to the FRICOURT - BRAY Road. Continued advance to the North and South would have enveloped this position, but the troops there had reached the furthest objectives assigned to them. The tanks, seeing our men in position on the crest to the right and left, and, being by now in danger of running short of petrol, returned to their rendezvous.

The Germans were quick to take advantage of the situation. About 14.00 hours they attacked the Division on our right and drove them back. The situation appeared to be unsatisfactory and the 37th Infantry Brigade was ordered to safeguard the flank, but a line was formed by the 35th Infantry Brigade, *as shown on the map "Z"*, with one battalion 37th Infantry Brigade in support about K.5.b and K.6.a.

9 officers and 470 other ranks of the enemy passed through the Divisional Cage. A considerable number of others were captured by the Division but went through other cages.

The night was quiet and the front was wired and consolidated.

23rd.

In the morning the G.O.C. held a conference at the 36th Brigade Headquarters at 11.30 hours and orders were issued verbally for the 37th Infantry Brigade to take over the whole Divisional front during the night of the 23rd/24th, but subsequently, in view of an order received from the IIIrd Corps, at a second conference held in the afternoon Lieut.Colonel J.D.BELGRAVE, D.S.O. (G.S.O.1) conveyed orders from the G.O.C. to the effect that an attack would be made (taking advantage of the moonlight) at 01.00 hours on the 24th instant by two battalions of the 37th Infantry Brigade on the right and one battalion of the 36th Infantry Brigade on the left, with the object of gaining the line F.20.central - F.14.central - F.7.b.8.8. where contact was to be obtained with the 18th Division. Any success was to be vigorously exploited and for this purpose 1 squadron of (NEW ZEALAND) XXII Corps Cavalry and 1 Company XXII Corps Cyclists were placed under the orders of the Division.

The day passed quietly except for persistent shelling of MEAULTE and without any infantry action other than a weak attack by the enemy on the 7th Bn. Royal Sussex Regt. at 05.30 hours which was easily repulsed and prisoners taken.

Previous to this the 18th Division had advanced their line at 04.45 hours and the 36th Infantry Brigade had obtained touch with them about E.12.d.6.6.

24th.

On the evening of the 23rd, orders were received from the Corps that a further attack was to be made at 16.00 hours on the 24th instant, and Major C.N.RYAN,D.S.O.,M.C., (G.S.O.2) was sent at once to warn both the 36th and 37th Infantry Brigades, who were attacking at 01.00 hours, that they would have to be prepared to continue the advance in the afternoon and that, after the completion of the earlier operation, as many men as possible should be kept back under cover of the high ground in F.13. in order to form up for the later attack.

In the meantime the attack was delivered as ordered at 01.00 hours, but was not successful. The attack was delivered in the same direction as that on the 22nd instant

AUGUST.

24th (Cont'd) and was held up in a similar manner. The 6th Bn. Royal West Kent Regt. made some progress but by 08.00 hours they had been driven back by heavy machine gun fire to the road in F.10.c. on both sides of the SEATHER. The 6th Bn. Queen's Regt, attacking on the left of the 6th Bn. Royal West Kent Regt., made a slight advance and succeeded in gaining touch on their left with the 7th Bn. Royal Sussex Regt. who reached their objective, and were holding the line F.14.c.5.5. - F.7.b.8.7.

The 47th Division on our right gained their objective, but, though we had now made an advance on both flanks of this strong point in F.20.a., the enemy still maintained his position throughout the morning of the 24th instant and at 15.30 hours defeated a further attack (delivered this time from the direction of F.15.central) by the 6th Bn. Royal West Kent Regt. assisted by three whippet tanks which had been placed under the orders of the 37th Infantry Brigade and had rendezvous in the valley in F.13.c. In this attack two of the tanks were knocked out and the third came back with its guns jammed. During the whole of the fighting for the possession of this knoll the enemy put up a most determined resistance and much assistance was given by a considerable artillery barrage to his machine guns whose fire was also very heavy.

During the morning the intention of advancing at 16.00 hours was abandoned by the Corps, the operation being postponed to 02.30 hours on the 25th instant.

At 18.00 hours the 47th Division reported that the enemy had vacated his position in F.20.a. and patrols at once followed up and occupied his posts. In view of the operation already planned for early the next morning no attempt was made to carry out a general advance before that time

25th. 25" The attack was delivered as ordered at 02.30 hours and met with practically no opposition. A very thick fog, however, hindered operations considerably and it was 07.00 hours before definite news was received that either of the attacking Brigades were on their objectives. At 06.30. hours the 18th Division reported that their right Brigade had reached FRICOURT craters in F.3.a. and c. and was in touch with the 36th Infantry Brigade, and at 07.15 hours the 38th Division reported that they had reached their objective throughout and had taken prisoners who stated that the enemy had withdrawn to SUSAINE. In the meantime orders had been issued at 07.15 hours for the 35th Brigade group under Brigadier General A.T. BECKWITH C.M.G., D.S.O., to form the advanced guard to the Division, to concentrate in the valley of the BRAY - FRICOURT road in F.9. and F.15. and move forward as soon as the XXII Corps Mounted Troops had made good their first bound, viz., the high ground CARNOY - MONTAUBAN.

Between 07.00 hours and 09.00 hours several reports were received from the 36th Infantry Brigade and 37th Infantry Bde. that their patrols had not been able to gain touch with the enemy West of the CAFTET WOOD - FRICOURT road, that the fog was still very thick and it was impossible to see more than 50 yards.

Between 09.00 hours and 11.00 hours, however, it began to clear and subsequently the day was very fine. At 11.45 hours a report was received from the 36th Infantry Brigade locating the enemy about 100 strong on the high ground West of MONTAUBAN, and later the Cavalry reported a few enemy still in MAMETZ at 12.15 hours. Orders were therefore issued by the advanced guard Commander instructing the 1/1st Bn. Cambridgeshire Regt. on the right and the 7th Bn. Norfolk Regt. on the left to advance through the 36th and 37th Infantry Brigades and gain the high ground CARNOY - MONTAUBAN. The leading troops of these battalions crossed the line F.16.central - F.10.central about 15.00 hours.

AUGUST

25th (Contd)   The enemy was found to be holding the ground West of
CARNOY and East of MAMETZ in some strength with machine guns,
and, in spite of the great heat and of a long preliminary
march, these battalions forced their attack home with
great skill and determination.   From 15.00 hours onwards
they were continually in touch with the enemy but took every
advantage of the broken state of the ground and of the
many old trenches that existed in this area to work their
way steadily forward in the face of heavy artillery and
machine gun fire.   By 16.45 hours they had reached the
general line F.18.a.central - F.11.central and by dusk they
had reached the line shown on map 'Z' with posts pushed
well forward and E. of CARNOY.   The enemy was holding
the vicinity of the APPLETREES in A.1.b. strongly and
repulsed all our attempts to advance in this direction.
During the day the 18th Division and the 58th Division
(who had relieved the 47th Division) made equally
successful advances, the latter after severe fighting in
BILLON WOOD where the artillery fire was particularly heavy.
By night touch was obtained with these Divisions by the
36th Infantry Brigade.

In the meantime orders were issued during the morning
for the 37th Infantry Brigade to take over the whole of the
old front line from the 36th Infantry Brigade, who were to
concentrate in F.8.b. and d. preparatory to moving through
the 35th Infantry Brigade as advanced guard on August 26th.

Divisional Headquarters moved during the day from
RIBEMONT to MORLANCOURT, K.9.b.8.7., opening at the latter
place at 12.00 hours.

26th.   In view of the fact that the enemy was still offering
organised resistance it was considered necessary that the
36th Infantry Brigade should carry out a definite attack,
after passing through the 35th Infantry Brigade, supported
by as much artillery fire as was possible.   Orders were
framed at Divisional Headquarters and the G.S.O.1 left
with them about 23.00 hours, 25th instant, for 36th Infantry
Brigade Headquarters which he reached at 00.10 hours 26th
instant.   Brigadier General C.S.Owen, C.M.G.,D.S.O.,
proceeded with the G.S.O.1 to the Battalion Headquarters
of the 5th Bn. Royal Berkshire Regt. where he then issued
his orders verbally to the commanders of the units of his
Brigade Group about 01.00 hours, giving them marked maps
previously prepared with objectives and boundaries and
start line of barrage.   In order to conform to the action
of the 58th Division the attack had to take place at 04.00
hours, which was one hour earlier than was originally
intended.   The attack was to be made by the 5th Bn.
Royal Berkshire Regt. on the right and 7th Bn. Royal Sussex
Regt. on the left, the first objective to be the spur
A.3.b. and d., A.2.b and d., and the second the MARICOURT
HIXQUEBUTIN road.   Considerable difficulty was found in
fixing the details of the artillery support as the position
of the most advanced troops of the 35th Infantry Brigade
was not accurately known and the barrage of the 58th
Division could not be made to conform to ours.
Eventually the artillery programme was as follows :-
4.5 hows. to bombard TALUS BOISE from 04.00 to 04.30 hours
and the 18 pdrs. to fire E. of the N. and S. grid line
through A.5.c.0.0. from 04.00 to 04.30 hours and E. of a
N. and S. grid line through A.4.c.0.0. from 04.30 to 04.50
hours, subsequently only firing on observed targets in
support of the Infantry.   In order not to interfere
with the operations of the 58th Division there was to be
no fire within 200 yards of the inter-Divisional boundary.
The results of not knowing the exact position of the 58th
Infantry Brigade were obvious during the day, for the areas
in which the enemy was to put up the most vigorous resistance,

- 8 -

AUGUST

26th (contd.) namely A.1.b. and A.7.b., were entirely unaffected by our preliminary artillery bombardment.

The attack was delivered as ordered though the greatest difficulty was experienced in getting the troops off in time. Owing to the nature of the fighting the artillery support was weaker ~~compared to~~ *than* the troops normally expected and, as explained above, it did not cover the area which the enemy was holding in strength. The attack met with a great deal of artillery and machine gun fire, and throughout the day the hostile artillery fire over the whole of the Divisional forward area was very heavy. The enemy was holding the high ground in A.2.a. and all craters in A.8.a. strongly and little progress beyond the *line held by* the 35th Infantry Brigade, was made by the 7th Bn. Royal Sussex Regt. During the morning there was heavy fighting including a great deal of bombing round the craters in A.8.a. in which the 1/1st Bn. Cambridgeshire Regt. was involved as well as the 7th Bn. Royal Sussex Regt. On the right, in ground which was dead to the enemy further north, the 5th Bn. Royal Berkshire Regt. made fair progress and their leading troops reached trenches on the forward slope facing the TALUS BOISE in A.8.d. and A.14.b. These however were cut off and the majority killed by a German counter-attack cleverly delivered about 09.00 hours from the N.W. so as to take every advantage of the spur in A.8.b. and the advanced position of this party of the 5th Bn. Royal Berkshire Regt. to the South of it. By 10.00 hours the 35th Infantry Brigade were holding the general line through A.14.a., A.8.c. and a. and A.14.central. By midday the salient South of the APPLE TREES ridge had been pushed further out and its point was about A.2.d.3.0. whence the line ran back in a W.N.W. direction with the enemy still holding out in the highest part of the ridge. About 16.00 hours the enemy commenced to withdraw from the vicinity of the APPLE TREES, and a little later the 18th Division captured POMMIERS REDOUBT with 40 prisoners, and their advanced troops reached the north western outskirts of MONTAUBAN.

Little further progress was made this day, however, and the main line of resistance during the night was approximately as shown on Map 'Z' with posts pushed out in front in squares A.9. and A.3.

During the day Divisional Headquarters moved to B.23.b.2.5. South of MEAULTE where they opened at 19.00 hours.

At 23.25 hours orders were issued for the action of the 57th Infantry Brigade group on the 27th instant - warning of which had been given to the Brigade early in the morning. The attack was to be carried out under a creeping barrage moving at the rate of 100 yards in 4 minutes with the MARICOURT-BRIQUETERIE road as the first objective, and the general line HARDECOURT - MALTZHORN FARM as the second objective. The 58th Division were co-operating on our right at the same hour, but after a certain time their barrage was to move forward at the rate of 100 yards in 6 minutes. Consequently, special arrangements had to be made to ensure that no interference was caused to our own infantry operating within our Divisional boundaries. On the left the 18th Division were attacking at the same hour but not from the eastern outskirts of MONTAUBAN. Their plan was to advance through S.22. and 23., then turn South and capture BERNAFAY and TRONES WOOD from the north, moving under a creeping barrage on an E. and W. line. Troops of the 18th Division were to emerge from the southern edges of these woods about two hours after Zero, and special arrangements were made for them to attack the BRIQUETERIE from the rear, in the event of the enemy still holding out there.

-9-

AUGUST
27th.

27th

The attack was carried out as ordered. Zero hour was 04-55 hours. The night had been fairly quiet except for intermittent "crashes" and the 37th Infantry Brigade was able to move up to its assembly positions without serious interference. The attack was carried out by the 6th Bn.Buffs Regt on the right, and 6th Bn Royal West Kent Regt on the left.

At 06.15 hours a report was received that the latter had reached A.4.c. and by 07.30 hours reports had been received from 37th Infantry Brigade that both their leading Battalions were on their final objectives. These reports, however, proved to be erroneous. At 11.15 hours the line was reported approximately as shown in map 2, and the enemy brought strong machine gun fire to bear on any movement East of this line from FAVIERE WOOD or from MAISY HORN FARM Ridge. During the morning FAVIERE WOOD and A.6.c. were shelled by our Field and Heavy Artillery, and in the afternoon the 6th Bn.Buffs Regt succeeded in infiltrating into FAVIERE WOOD and driving the enemy out of most of it. No touch with the 58th Division, however, was obtained east of A.10.b.7.8.

Meanwhile, the operations of the 18th Division were not carried out quite according to the original plan. The enemy was found to be holding HERBAPAY and TRONES WOOD very strongly, and after a great deal of severe fighting the 18th Division found themselves at midday holding the whole of HERBAPAY WOOD, and with a footing in the northern end of TRONES. This result was obtained after the defeat of a heavy counter attack between 09.00 hours and 11.00 hours by the enemy along the valley in A.6.a. in which 200 of the enemy were taken prisoners. To meet this counter attack the 35th Infantry Brigade was ordered at 09.30 hours to send a battalion at once to the HINDENBURG area, to come under the orders of the 37th Infantry Brigade. In addition one Company 30th Machine Gun Battalion was also sent forward. No definite news of this counter attack had however been received by 10.30 hours at which hour the 35th Infantry Brigade was ordered to move up, occupy and consolidate the line of the HARICOURT HINDENBURG Road and in the event of this line having already been lost, to make an immediate counter attack to retake it. The 36th Infantry Brigade was also warned to be ready to deliver a deliberate counter attack in the afternoon, should the 35th Infantry Brigade be unable to reach this line. As a matter of fact the enemy counter attack did not develop on the 18th Divisional Front, and after the 35th Infantry Brigade was established on the main line of resistance given above, the Bn sent forward to the 37th Infantry Brigade reported to ~~their command.~~ *its own brigade.*

In the afternoon the 18th Division shelled TRONES WOOD steadily, and at 19.00 hours they attacked with complete success and captured the whole of it. During the day, after very heavy fighting in which they inflicted severe losses on the enemy, the 18th Division captured about 236 prisoners from 10 regiments of 6 different Divisions.

The left Bn of the 37th Infantry Brigade pushed forwarded posts in the evening to conform the new line of the 18th Division.

At 20.45 hours orders were issued for the attack to be renewed the next morning at 04.55 by the 36th Infantry Brigade on the right and the 35th Infantry Brigade on the left. The latter, being fresher than the 36th Infantry Brigade, was given a wider front and was to attack with two Bns. - the former with one Bn.

-10-

AUGUST.

27th (Contd)

The objective was the HARDECOURT - HALTZHORN FARM Ridge, this line to be held as a line of observation, with a main line of resistance on the western slopes of the spur. The usual difficulties were experienced in fixing the start line for the barrage, and in the orders issued at 20.45 hours this line was put well to the East, giving a liberal margin of safety to what was thought to be the position of our most advanced troops. In view, however, of later information that it had been found possible to withdraw certain advanced posts, this line was amended in a further order issued at 22.40 hours bringing it 500 yards further West.

Arrangements were made for a platoon of the 36th Infantry Brigade to form up with the troops of the 58th Division and attack CLAPHAM FARM under their barrage.

28th.

The attack took place as ordered, with the 9th Bn. Royal Fusiliers (36th Infantry Brigade) on the right, 1/1st Cambridgeshire Regt. in the centre, and the 9th Bn. Essex Regt. on the left. The attacking troops had to go down one side and up the other of a deep, fairly steep valley, that ran across their line of advance. This enabled the 12th Bn. Machine Gun Corps to render very effective assistance by an overhead direct fire M.G. barrage, which materially assisted the success of the day's operations. On the right the 9th Bn. Royal Fusiliers had considerable fighting in HARDECOURT, where many Germans were killed, but by 11.00 hours they were firmly established East of the village in touch with the 58th Division at CLAPHAM FARM, but not then in touch with the 35th Infantry Brigade in the outpost line. Some difficulty was experienced by the 58th Division in clearing BOIS D'EN HAUT and, for a time, isolated enemy machine guns from there gave trouble to the 9th Bn. Royal Fusiliers. On the left the 9th Bn. Essex Regt. reported at about 07.00 hours that a prearranged success signal had been sent up from the hill of the objective, and that prisoners were coming back, and by 08.30 hours it was known that both bns. of the 35th Infantry Brigade were on their objective throughout their front. Their advance met with a good deal of opposition, over 100 prisoners were taken and many Germans, particularly machine gunners, who fought their guns to the end, were killed with the bayonet.

During the afternoon the enemy shelled the forward area very heavily, and movement on the forward slopes of the ridge was impossible owing to hostile machine gun fire. There was some sniping down the valley in A.5.d. from its head in S.30.c. and this valley was searched at frequent intervals with all calibres of shells. No infantry attack, however, was made though two enemy 77 mm. guns firing from the direction of ANGLEWOOD (B.1.d.) worried our advanced troops considerably.

After 20.00 hours, however, hostile artillery and M.G. fire decreased considerably and the night was quiet.

At 20.15 hours orders were issued for the Division to remain in its present position and consolidate. Patrols were to be particularly active and were to maintain touch with the enemy throughout the night. The XXII Corps Mounted Troops were ordered to be ready to move off from CARNOY at 07.00 hours next morning.

Later, at 21.00 hours, every indication (both from prisoners and the unusually quiet attitude of the enemy) pointing to the fact that he meant intended to continue his withdrawal, the 57th Infantry Brigade Group was detailed to form the advanced guard on the next day. It was not, however, the intention to attack the enemy if he was found in strength.

- 11 -

AUGUST.

29th.

At 02.00 hours a warning order was issued saying that the Division would be relieved by the 47th Division on the night 29th/30th and would be withdrawn to the area RIDGE LOOP STATION (F.27.) - BECORDEL (F.8.) and the old AMIENS Defences.

Patrols pushed out after daylight found that the enemy had withdrawn, and at 07.00 hours a cavalry patrol was sent forward to obtain touch with the enemy. This was followed up by infantry patrols; in the meantime the 18th Division reported their troops were making rapid progress. At 09.25 hours they reported their advanced guard through GUILLEMONT, with the enemy holding SAVERNAKE WOOD, and at 09.50 hours they reported their advanced guard had reached LEUZE WOOD at 08.50 hours. Orders were at once issued for a cavalry patrol to move through the 18th Division area and get touch with the enemy on the 12th Divisional front; at the same time the 37th Infantry Brigade were to move at once and attack the enemy, if encountered. By this time, however, infantry patrols from the 35th and 36th Infantry Brigades had moved forward and at 12.30 hours the 9th Bn. Royal Fusiliers were entering MAUREPAS, which was still held by a few enemy machine guns. These withdrew hurriedly on the arrival of our infantry. Patrols of the 9th Bn. Essex Regt. (35th Infantry Brigade) also moved to OAKHANGER WOOD and the spur South of FALFEMONT FARM, where they did not get in touch with the enemy.

About 13.30 hours the leading battalion of the 37th Infantry Brigade (6th Bn. The Queen's Regt.) passed through the patrols of the 35th and 36th Infantry Brigades with the 6th Bn. The Buffs in support on the right and the 6th Bn. Royal West Kent Regt. in support on the left. On leaving the Eastern outskirts of MAUREPAS they at once came under hostile artillery fire, and particularly when they advanced across the old WINDMILL Spur, B.9.d., B.15.b. By 17.00 hours it became clear that the enemy was holding a line from LE FOREST (inclusive) to SAVERNAKE WOOD (exclusive), and the 37th Infantry Brigade prepared to attack this position, the 6th Bn. The Buffs coming up into line on the right. This attack was delivered with great vigour, in spite of the very long preliminary advance, and over 60 prisoners were taken. Touch was obtained with the 18th Division on the left, but on the right the 58th Division were some way behind, and a patrol of the 6th Bn. The Buffs worked its way across their front and obtained touch with the Australians at HILL 110 in B.23.c. and d.

Owing to these operations the relief of the Division in the manner already ordered became impossible, and at 16.30 hours the original warning order was cancelled. The 142nd Infantry Brigade (leading Brigade of the 47th Division) passed through the 35th and 36th Infantry Brigades during the day and was in reserve to the 12th Division during the night Aug. 29th/30th West of MAUREPAS. The plan for this Brigade was to pass through the 37th Infantry Brigade on the morning of the 30th and continue the attack.

Divisional Headquarters moved from MEAULTE to HIDDEN WOOD, where they opened at 15.30 hours.

30th.

The attack was carried out successfully at 06.00 hours and the command of the sector passed to the G.O.C. 47th Division (Major-General Sir G.F.GORRINGE, K.C.B.,K.C.M.G., D.S.O.). The original area allotted to the Division in which to bivouac and reorganise was cancelled, and the Brigades were disposed as follows :-

35th Infantry Brigade - BRIQUETERIE Area.
36th Infantry Brigade - CARNOY and TALUS BOISE
37th Infantry Brigade - FAVIERE WOOD.

19th DIVISION.

NARRATIVE OF OPERATIONS 4th to 8th SEPTEMBER 1918.

PHASE III

Prior to the commencement of the operations carried out by the Division between the 4th and 8th of September the 55th and 57th Infantry Brigades had been in training and resting in the areas about the BRIQUETERIE, S.E. of MONTAUBAN and FAVIERE WOOD, W. of HARDECOURT respectively. The 56th Infantry Brigade was in reserved to the 47th Division and disposed in the area B.10. and 11.

Divisional Headquarters were at COMBLES.

3rd Sept.

Divisional orders were issued for an attack on NURLU and the trench system N. of it, as far as the left Divisional boundary, on the morning of the 5th.

When the NURLU trench system was captured the 56th Infantry Brigade Group, with two troops of Corps cavalry, were to become the advance guard of the Division.

4th/5th September.

During the night 4th/5th the 55th and 56th Infantry Brigades relieved the 53rd and 55th Infantry Brigades, 18th Division, in the front line, which at that time consisted of a line of posts running approximately from the CANAL DU NORD about C.12.b.8.5., thence along the southern and eastern edges of RIVERSIDE WOOD to about V.29.c.3.2. and thence to about U.18.d.8.0.

The relieving troops had a very difficult task owing to the extreme darkness, the uncertainty as to the exact position of the troops of the 18th Division, the heavy gas shelling by the enemy and the fact that small parties of the enemy were still holding parts of RIVERSIDE WOOD. The relief was, however, successfully carried out and the troops of the 55th and 56th Infantry Brigades formed up for attack along the eastern edge of RIVERSIDE WOOD.

5th Sept.

Zero hour was fixed for 06.45.
The attacking troops were formed up as follows:-

56th Infantry Brigade (on the right of the Divisional front)

7th Bn. Royal Sussex Regt. in front.

8th Bn. Royal Berkshire Regt. in support.) In the southern
) part of
9th Bn. Royal Fusiliers Regt. in Reserve.) VAUX WOODS.

55th Infantry Brigade (on the left of the Divisional front)

7th Bn. Norfolk Regt. on the right.
9th Bn. Essex Regt. on the left.
1/1st Bn. Cambridgeshire Regt. in Brigade Reserve, echeloned in rear of the 7th Bn. Norfolk Regt.

Advanced Divisional Headquarters were just N. of RANCOURT.

The attack duly commenced at Zero hour. Considerable opposition was met with from the high ground in the neighbourhood of NURLU. The strong wire in front of the enemy's trenches was also a source of great trouble but, in spite of this, the 9th Bn. Essex Regt. and a small party of the 7th Bn. Norfolk Regt. were able to force their way into FAUCON TRENCH, where they were held up by heavy machine gun fire, the bulk of which came from a hostile strong point in V.29.c.

On the right the 1/1st Bn. Cambridgeshire Regt. reached VESTA TRENCH and part of AJAX TRENCH, but were forced to evacuate the former owing to heavy enfilade artillery fire

-/3-

5th Sept.
(Contd)

from about V.29.b. A position in the open some 20 yards W. of the trench line was taken up and the troops dug themselves in.

After our attack had been temporarily held up, strong enemy parties infiltrated from the N. and E. of NURLU into the trench system immediately W. of the village.

The 7th Bn. Royal Sussex Regt. 36th Infantry Brigade, which had moved up on the right of the 35th Infantry Brigade also came under heavy M.G. fire, and owing to very thick wire in front of VESTA TRENCH, were at first unable to enter the trench. They dug themselves in W. of the wire and immediately commenced infiltrating through a gap which was found. About 100 prisoners of the 6th Cavalry Division were captured: these troops who had been railed down from YPRES had only come into the line the night before.

During the day orders were issued that the 7th Bn Royal Sussex Regt would attack NURLU at 7.30 p.m., the 1/1st Bn Cambridgeshire Regt to co-operate on the left by attacking the strong point V.29.a.

Orders did not reach 1/1st Bn Cambridgeshire Regt in time for them to co-operate, but at the hour stated the 7th Bn. Royal Sussex Regt. with the 47th Division on the right, attacked.

The attack was not successful, strong opposition being encountered from NURLU TRENCH.

In case this attack was not successful, orders had been issued to the 36th Infantry Brigade that they would be prepared to attack and capture NURLU and trench system S. of it to Divisional southern boundary on the morning of the 6th.

G.O.C. 36th Infantry Brigade thereupon ordered the 5th Bn. Royal Berkshire Regt. to move up, with a view to passing through and attacking the same objective, and to push out patrols at dawn to occupy any ground from which the enemy had withdrawn.

After dark the enemy made a strong bombing attack against the left of the 35th Infantry Brigade which at that time was holding a very extended line to connect with the Division on our left at the Eastern outskirts of MANANCOURT.

The main strength of this bombing attack was directed against the 9th Bn Essex Regt, which had suffered heavy casualties during the day. Our men were forced back out of FAUCON TRENCH.

A fresh attack by the 35th Infantry Brigade was ordered to take place at 08.00 hours on the 6th instant.

6th Sept.

At 08.00 hours the attack was renewed under an artillery barrage.

The 5th Bn. Royal Berkshire Regt. 36th Infantry Brigade attacked on the right of the Divisional front with the 1/1 Bn. Cambridgeshire Regt. (35th Infantry Brigade) in the centre and the 9th Bn. Essex Regt. (35th Infantry Brigade) on the left.

At 10.30 hours a report was received from the 5th Bn. Royal Berkshire Regt. that the objective had been taken, that touch had been obtained with the 47th Division on the right, but not with the 35th Infantry Brigade on the left, also that patrols were being sent out to establish touch.

Later reports showed that the attack had been a complete success, in spite of very formidable wire and strong opposition.

During the day the 35th and 36th Infantry Brigades took up the line of LIERAMONT CEMETERY - SOREL WOOD, with patrols in front of this line. The Division was in touch with the 47th Division on the right, N.E. of LIERAMONT, and with the 21st Division on the left between SOREL WOOD and SOREL LE GRAND. 1 Officer and 40 men of the 6th Cavalry Division were captured.

-14-

6th Sept.
(Contd.)

Orders were issued to the 37th Infantry Brigade that they would continue the advance on the 7th under an artillery barrage, with the object of capturing the eastern outskirts of GOUZEAUCOURT and the railway E. of TRESCAULT, Zero hour to be 08.00.

Divisional Headquarters moved to WELK WOOD, V.29.a.5.5.

7th Sept.

At Zero hour the attack was launched with the 6th Bn. The Buffs on the right, the 6th Bn. Royal West Kent Regt. on the left, and the 6th Bn. The Queens in support.

The reply of the enemy's artillery to our bombardment was not very heavy, but increased as the attack progressed. M.Gs. were very active from the start.

At 08.30 hours the 6th Bn. The Buffs was reported to be held up on the high ground E.1.a. by enemy M.G. fire from E.7.b., E.1.d., and SAULCOURT WOOD. The 6th Bn. Royal West Kent Regt. was reported to have gained the valley, V.29.a.

At 08.55 hours the Buffs reported that the enemy had been driven out of his posts in E.1.d. and E.7.b.

On approaching GUYENCOURT the Buffs found the trenches West of the village held by strong posts. A Battery Commander who was with the O.C. brought the fire of his battery to bear on the trench with such accuracy and success that the Infantry were able to advance and occupy GUYENCOURT at 10.10 hours. The enemy had evacuated a strong position.

At 13.50 hours a report was received from the O.C. 6th Bn. the Buffs that his battalion had reached the SUNKEN ROAD in E.4.a. and d. and the 6th Bn. Royal West Kent Regt. came up on the left of the Buffs in V.29.c. and d.

This line was eventually reached by the whole Brigade, but the attack could not be continued owing to heavy M.G. fire, consequently orders were issued that Battalions would dig in, and consolidate the line reached.

During the afternoon, an E.A. flying low over our lines was brought down by L.G. fire, just beyond our front line. The occupants, an Officer and N.C.O. endeavoured to escape, but were pursued and captured by an N.C.O. and some men of the Buffs who brought them back to our lines.

Orders were issued that the 58th Division would continue the advance, passing through the 12th Division at Zero hour on the 8th inst., but that endeavour was to be made during the night 7th/8th to gain possession of the objectives originally ordered. If these were found to be held in strength, the 37th Infantry Brigade was to establish itself on the line of the trench system running from E.5.d.8.0. through E.5.b., V.29.d. and b., and obtain touch with Flank Divisions.

The advance was therefore continued at 20.00 hours and during the night the line ordered was reached.

Orders were issued that the 58th Division would pass through at 07.30 hours on the 8th and that to enable a suitable barrage to be arranged for the advance of the 58th Division all troops E. of a N. and S. line through V.29. central were to be withdrawn immediately West of that line.

8th Sept.

At 07.30 hours the 58th Division passed through the 37th Infantry Brigade, command of the Sector passing at that hour to the G.O.C. 58th Division.

-15-

8th Sept. (Contd.)	The Division was then withdrawn in to Corps Reserve, and was disposed as follows:-

Divisional Headquarters.   VAUX WOOD.
35th Infantry Brigade.   In vicinity of RIVERSIDE WOOD.
36th Infantry Brigade.   Area West of NURLU.
37th Infantry Brigade.   VAUX WOOD.

NARRATIVE OF OPERATIONS FROM 10th to 30th SEPTEMBER, 1918

PHASE IV.

On the conclusion of the NURLU operations, the
Division commenced training and refitting. Unfortunately
the weather was very unsettled, and in consequence the
full benefits of the period out of the line were not
obtained.

The 58th Division which had relieved the 12th, had
found the villages of PEIZIERE and EPEHY to be strongly
held. It was therefore decided that the 12th Division
should carry out a prepared attack, which would form part
of an attack on a large scale.

On the 12th September a Conference of Divisional
Commanders and G.S.O.1. was held at III. Corps Headquarters.

This was followed later in the day by a conference of
Brigade Commanders at Divisional Headquarters. At these
Conferences the plans of a big attack, in which the Division
was to take part, were discussed.

In the meantime the Division had, in the event of an
enemy attack, been allotted the role of defending the
VIECOURT-NURLU Line. Defence orders were therefore issued
and the necessary reconnaissances made by Staff and
Regimental Officers.

On the 14th, Divisional Order No. 262, relative to
the attack mentioned above, was issued. This was
subsequently cancelled by Order 263. which was issued on
the 16th. This order gave the complete plans of the
attack so far as the 12th Division was concerned. Copies
of the maps issued with these orders marked "C" and "D"
respectively are attached.

The objectives of the Division were to capture the
village of EPEHY and to continue the advance, if possible, to
the BLUE LINE, or line exploitation, vide Map "D".

The plan of attack which is shown diagrammatically
on Map "D" was as follows:-

The 35th Infantry Brigade was to attack on the left
in a north-easterly direction from the approximate line
E.12.d.8.7. to E.12.a.6.7. This attack was to be carried out
by the 7th Bn. Norfolk Regt. and the 9th Bn.Essex Regt. on
right and left respectively, with 2 Companies of the
1/1st Bn. Cambridgeshire Regt., following in rear for mopping
up and finding garrisons for the Posts in the village,
while 1 Company 1/1st Bn. Cambridgeshire Regt. was to
form up on the right of the 58th Division and advance
with troops of this Division in a due easterly direction.
Two tanks were to accompany the 35th Infantry Brigade for
the purpose of mopping up EPEHY.

The main attack of the 36th Infantry Brigade on the
right was to be made from the Railway line in F.7.b,a. and
c. and F.1.d. To enable this to be done the 35th Infantry
Brigade was ordered to detail sufficient troops to move
forward on the right of the 35th Infantry Brigade at Zero
and clear up the area west of the Railway, so that by Zero
plus 90 minutes the two attacking battalions of the Brigade
(9th Royal Fusiliers and 7th Royal Sussex Regt. on right and
left respectively) could advance with 35th Infantry Brigade
on to the first objective.

The 37th Infantry Brigade was to move forward in rear
of the 35th and 36th Infantry Brigades and form up close
to the barrage ready to advance on the RED LINE at Zero
plus 190 minutes. The main objective of this Brigade was
the LITTLE PRIEL FARM Spur, including the Farm itself
and KILDARE POST Spur.

-17-

After the capture of the RED LINE, the 57th Infantry Brigade was to exploit the success as far as the BLUE LINE. The 5th Bn. Royal Berkshire Regt. (36th Infantry Brigade) was attached to the 57th Infantry Brigade to be employed as supports to the troops holding the RED LINE.

17th Sept.

Divisional Headquarters moved to EPINETTE WOOD, D.15.d.7.5.

Night. 17/18th.

During the evening of the 17th, Brigades moved up to Assembly positions between GUYENCOURT and the front line held by the 58th Division.

On the right of the 36th Infantry Brigade, the 18th Division was attacking, and on the left of the 35th Infantry Brigade the 58th Division was to attack PEZIERE and advance as far as the first objective, viz:- The GREEN LINE.

Zero hour was fixed for 05.20

There was a considerable amount of hostile Gas Shelling during the night, especially in the vicinity of GUYENCOURT. Orders had, however, been issued that there was a probability of Gas Shelling and all precautions were to be taken. The assembly positions themselves, were not badly gassed.

18th Sept.

The forming up of the attacking troops was successfully carried out, and at Zero hour the attack was duly launched. The heavy rain which had fallen consistently from midnight onwards, combined with a thick mist, accentuated the darkness and made it quite impossible to distinguish any landmarks.

On the right, the 36th Infantry Brigade was able to clear the area up to the railway, without difficulty. At 06.52 hours the 35th Infantry Brigade reported that the 7th Bn Norfolk Regt. had passed F.1.d.7.0. and F.1.d.7.5. and that by this time enemy M.G. fire had slackened down and the hostile artillery fire was now of only moderate intensity.

About 08.00 hours a report was received at Divisional Headquarters that the enemy was using tanks. This report proved to be incorrect. It was due to one of our own tanks which came into EPEHY from the north to assist our troops, but which then lost direction and ran about firing in the direction of our own men. It caused a considerable amount of confusion and delay amongst our attacking troops.

At 09.00 hours a message was received from the 35th Infantry Brigade to the effect that the 1/1st Bn Cambridgeshire Regt. was reported to be in the north end of EPEHY and that the 7th Bn. Norfolk Regt. was in PRINCE RESERVE TRENCH, East of the village, and that 50 prisoners were reported captured. The 9th Bn. Essex Regt. was held up on the Eastern edge of EPEHY by M.G. fire.

Owing to the darkness, a gap occurred between the left of the 35th Infantry Brigade and the 173rd Infantry Brigade of the 58th Division, (who were attacking PEZIERE) on their left. Owing to this gap the left of the 7th Bn Norfolk Regt. was held up by the enemy who were holding FISHER'S KEEP strongly with the result that the troops of the 35th Infantry Brigade had only cleared the southern end of EPEHY.

The G.O.C., 35th Infantry Brigade therefore ordered the 1/1st Bn. Cambridgeshire Regt. to make a fresh advance into EPEHY, from the S.W. and the 173rd Infantry Brigade 58th Division, was asked to co-operate by pushing down S.W. through PEZIERE and to get into touch with the 35th Infantry Brigade at the North end of FISHER'S KEEP and at WEEDON POST.

The result of this operation was that the 1/1st Bn. Cambridgeshire Regt. established itself in portions of the village with its left near the south face of FISHER's KEEP which was still in the enemy's hands.

18th Sept.
(Contd)

The 7th Bn. Norfolk Regt. and 9th Bn. Essex Regt. were established between a point 200 yards south of the Railway junction in F.1.b. thence along PRINCE RESERVE to the station F.1.b.

At 10.00 hours an officers' reconnaissance reported the line of the 36th Infantry Brigade to be as follows:- The 9th Bn. Royal Fusiliers - Post at North east end of MAY COPSE - RIDGE RESERVE to DEVLISH AVENUE, thence up latter towards OLD COPSE, which was held by enemy. The enemy was also found to be holding MALASSIGE FARM. The 9th Bn. Royal Fusiliers Regt. were in touch with the 7th Bn. Royal Sussex Regt. along the trench of RIDGE RESERVE. The 7th Bn. Royal Sussex Regt. were in touch with the 35th Infantry Brigade at F.2.c.0.9. The 36th Infantry Brigade was not in touch with the 18th Division on its right.

At 11.50 hours the G.O.C. 37th Infantry Brigade returned from PEZIERE, and reported that enemy Machine Guns were still firing from the village, that two Companies of the 6th Bn. Royal West Kent Regt. were in X.26.c. and the remaining two Companies, which were west of PEZIERE, were moving up. This battalion had been ordered to advance on KILDARE POST, keeping on the North side of the Spur in X.26. and 27. The 37th Infantry Brigade was, however, required later on to form a defensive flank to the 21st Division along LARK SPUR until the situation on the GREEN LINE was cleared up.

The 9th Bn. Essex Regt. had very heavy fighting in the southern portion of the village, as shown by the large number of British and German dead found lying face to face in the streets.

During the afternoon, CULLEN POST, WINDON POST and FISHER'S KEEP were still in the hands of the enemy, who from these places gave considerable trouble to our troops east of the village. Enemy snipers were also active from PEZIERE. In addition to this, there were still a good number of Germans hiding in the cellars in EPEHY. In accordance with orders issued by the 35th Infantry Brigade, the 9th Bn. Essex Regt. pushed up CHESTNUT AVENUE and established a bombing block about 250 yards east of PRINCE RESERVE. The 7th Bn. Royal Sussex Regt. and 7th Bn. Norfolk Regt. were by this time respectively only about 130 and 170 strong.

About 17.30 hours a party of 150 Germans, principally machine gunners, who had formed part of the garrison of EPEHY and PEZIERE succeeded in getting out of the village and retired in a N.E. direction.

At 17.30 hours the 5th Bn. Royal Berkshire Regt. (36th Infantry Brigade) less one Company was placed under orders of the G.O.C., 35th Infantry Brigade. Two Companies of this battalion were employed in co-operation with 1/1 Bn. Cambridgeshire Regt. in clearing up EPEHY from the S.W. Two Companies 5th Bn. Northamptonshire Regt. (Pioneers) were also placed under orders of the G.O.C., 35th Infantry Brigade.

The 1/1 Bn. Cambridgeshire Regt. made good FISHER'S KEEP, and at 19.15 hours the 5th Royal Berkshire Regt. reported the village clear and their casualties slight. Even after this, however, trouble was given by some of the enemy who had not been mopped up, and it was not until after midnight, 18th/19th that the village was definitely cleared. After passing through the village the two Companies of the 5th Bn. Royal Berkshire Regt. were assembled of the right of the 7th Bn. Norfolk Regt. in F.1.b.

At 20.15 hours the 5th Bn. Royal Berkshire Regt. attacked the trenches running south from CHESTNUT AVENUE and the trench running south from N.E. end of TETARD WOOD.

18th Sept. (Contd). The attack proved successful, the whole of CHESTNUT TRENCH being occupied and bombing blocks established in CHESTNUT AVENUE and in THIRD TRENCH as far South as F.2.central. The casualties in this minor operation were few.

During the night a further advance was made by the 5th Bn. Royal Berkshire Regt. and by 09.00 hours on the 19th the line shown on Map "Z" for that hour had been reached.

19th Sept. At 11.00 hours the 37th and 35th Infantry Brigades continued the attack, the 37th Infantry Brigade passing through the 36th. The enemy's counter barrage came down three minutes after Zero and was fairly heavy, especially in the vicinity of MALASSISE FARM and THIRD WOOD.

On the right the 37th Infantry Brigade succeeded in advancing the line about 1,000 yards, while on the left the 5th Bn. Northamptonshire Regt. and the 5th Bn. Royal Berkshire Regt. still under the orders of the G.O.C. 35th Infantry Brigade, made a gallant attack and established themselves in BOOM and CLARENDON TRENCHES. Before their capture considerable opposition had been met with from these trenches, which were strongly held by the enemy.

Orders were issued that Brigades were to consolidate during the night on the line gained.

During the night the 37th Infantry Brigade took over from the 18th Division as far South as PATRICK'S AVENUE, inclusive.

20th Sept. Little progress was made during the day owing to the hostile opposition; BRANTON and HEXTHORPE POSTS in F.5.c. and 4.b. in particular were strongly held.

21st Sept. An attack was ordered for 05.40 hours on the 21st, which was to be carried out by the 37th and 35th Infantry Brigades, the 18th Division co-operating on the right.

As a result of this attack our troops captured MULE TRENCH and its junction with DUBLIN AVENUE. There was heavy fighting in the vicinity of this trench junction, the enemy, apparently, attaching great importance to it.

On the right the enemy, by a counter attack, forced the 18th Division back along POMPEIOUS LANE and reoccupied *The 37th Inf. Bde.* TOMBOIS FARM, thereupon formed a defensive flank by manning DOSE TRENCH and placing machine guns with infantry escorts in and near YAK and ZEBRA POSTS.

22nd Sept. At 12.15 hours the attack was continued, the objectives being the same as for the 21st, viz., Trench system F.5.c.6.0.- HEXTHORPE POST - HEXTHORPE LANE - LITTLE PRIEL FARM and CRUCIFORM POST.

The 6th Bn. Royal West Kent Regt (37th Infantry Brigade) on the right were at first unsuccessful being held up by the wire in front of the trenches and by heavy machine gun fire, but a further determined attack was made under the personal leadership of Lieut.Colonel W.R.A.DAWSON, D.S.O.; the Germans were driven in disorder from the trenches, the whole of the objectives were gained and heavy casualties were inflicted on the enemy. On the left of the 6th Bn. Royal West Kent Regt. the 5th Bn. Royal Berkshire Regt. (36th Infantry Brigade) attacked and after heavy fighting in and around HEXTHORPE LANE captured HEXTHORPE POST and LITTLE PRIEL FARM.

During the night the 35th Infantry Brigade moved forward and took up a line through RELIEF COPSE and across CATELET VALLEY, the object being to join up with the 21st Division.

Thus the objectives of the attack were captured by an early hour, notwithstanding strong opposition along the BRANTON POST LINE and heavy enfilade fire from KILDARE POST, which was still held in strength by the enemy

3rd Sept.

There was a certain amount of scattered hostile shelling during the day, otherwise no change in the situation took place. On our left the 175 Infantry Brigade, 58th Division made some progress and captured KILDARE POST.

On the night 23/24th, the 36th Infantry Brigade relieved 175th Infantry Brigade extending the Divisional post to the new Northern Divisional Boundry, viz;-the East and West Grid line between X.20 and 26, and including DADOS LANE and STONE LANE, and carried the line forward to include DADOS LOOP and DADOS LANE.

24th Sept.

At 03.00 hours the 18th Division on our right, attacked and improved their position in FLEECEALL and POMPONIOUS LANES. The 37th Infantry Brigade maintained touch with them at F.11.b.0.4.

At 11.30 hours a heavy enemy barrage was put down along the Divisional Front, especially on the left Brigade Sub-sector. About half an hour later the S.O.S. signal was reported to have gone up north of LITTLE PRIEL FARM.

On the right Brigade Front, no infantry action took place, but on the left, an enemy force estimated at 6 Companies attacked from KILDARE AVE. Southwards. The attack was everywhere repulsed, except at DADOS LANE and DADOS LOOP, where the enemy succeeded in gaining a footing between X.22.d.8.0. and X.22.d.5.4. Observers reported that heavy casualties were inflicted on the enemy by our M.G. and rifle fire, especially by the machine guns posted in MULE TRENCH and firing across CATELET VALLEY.

By 15.00 hours the 9th Bn. Royal Fusiliers had succEEded in recapturing 300 yards of the trench occupied by the enemy. From this time onwards DADOS LANE and DADOS LOOP became the scene of many bombing encounters, as owing to the position of these trenches on the high ground, their retention was of great importance to both sides.

During the enemy's attack, his aircraft were active, flying low over our lines, one machine was brought down in the vicinity of RONSSOY by our Lewis Gunners.

During the night an unsuccessful attempt was made by the left Brigade to eject the enemy from DADOS LOOP and the Junction of that trench with STONE LANE.

25th Sept.

At 05.15 hours the S.O.S. signal was reported to have gone up on the left Brigade Front. This was occasioned by a silent attack by the enemy (estimated strength 4 Companies) against FRANTON POST. It was, however, completely repulsed by our rifle and Machine Gun Fire though some of the Germans reached our lines. One prisoner was left in our hands, thirteen enemy dead were left in the trench, and quite as many could be seen lying in front. The prisoner, who belonged to the 8th Division, stated that they had been ordered to capture and hold the trench at all costs. Their repulse was partly due to the gallant action of an N.C.O. of the 9th Bn. Essex Regt. who stood on the parapet of the trench firing a Lewis gun from his hip.

A Gas Projector Shoot was successfully carried out during the night on enemy positions in S.29.d. from emplacements in the sunken road west of HEYTHORP LANE.

26th Sept.

During the early morning the 36th Infantry Brigade carried out another minor operation, with artillery support, against the part of DADOS LOOP and DADOS LANE in the enemy's hands. Posts were established at X.22.d.8.3. and X.22.d.8.6. Almost immediately after, the enemy made a strong counter attack which forced our troops back to their original positions. Fighting went on here during the whole day, the ultimate result being that our troops held the blocks at X.22.d.8.3. and at the junction of DADOS LOOP and STONE LANE at X.22.d.9.3.

26th Sept. (Contd.)	The 33rd Division, on the left, owing to heavy opposition was unable to come up on the left of the Division.
Orders were issued relative to an attack which was to be carried out by the 27th American Division on the 27th inst. The objective of the attack was the old British Line from A.26. to A.1. The 12th Division's role was to push out patrols to secure points of tactical importance and to protect the left flank of the Americans. The advance of these patrols would be covered by an Artillery barrage.
27th Sept.	At the American Division attacked and captured the KNOLL and our patrols pushed forward. The QUARRIES in X.29.d. and LARK POST were found to be strongly held by the enemy and no progress could be made at these points. On the left, our post in DADOS LOOP was advanced but a strong counter attack, which the enemy made with Gas bombs, forced our troops back to their starting off positions. On the right of the Division the enemy forced the Americans back off the KNOLL in F.12.a.
28th Sept.	Preparations were begun and orders were issued for a big attack which was to be carried out by the Fifth and Fourth Armies on the 29th, and in which the Division was to take part. The objective of the 12th Division's Operation being (1)- To cover the left flank of 18th Division who were to attack on our right. (2)- To mop up the area between the present front and the CANAL. (3)- In the event of the 33rd Division on our left not being able to get on, to form a defensive flank along LARK SPUR facing North towards OSSUS. The co-ordination of the Divisional barrage with that of the 18th and 33rd Divisions was very difficult. The plan of the 18th Division had to be modified at the last moment owing to the enemy having recaptured the KNOLL.
29th Sept.	The attacked was successfully launched at 05.50 hours in spite of heavy hostile gas shelling in the early morning. On the Divisional front the enemy made a strong stand, but our troops kept up a continual pressure on him. The Attack of the 6th Bn. Buffs Regt. on the right was personally directed by the C.O. from his observation post at BRABTON POST. He had with him an Artillery F.O.O. and a machine gun section Commander. 18 pounders and M.G. fire were brought to bear on the enemy who could be seen in the trenches across the valley. Our men who had gained a footing in the southern end of LARK TRENCH were thus enabled to work northwards. By the evening the following line had been made good by this fine battalion of the 37th Infantry Brigade. - TINO TRENCH - LARK TRENCH - QUARRIES in X.29.d. CATELET TRENCH was also captured and Touch maintained with 18th Division on the right. 150 prisoners and many machine guns were captured at the QUARRIES. captured CATELET TRENCH but
The 6th Bn. Royal West Kent Regt. on the left, found the enemy still strongly holding DADOS LOOP. Fighting continued there most of the day, but practically no ground was gained. At 15.20 hours the enemy counter-attacked up CATELET VALLEY. Their attack was, however, a complete failure, being easily repulsed by our fire.
Orders were issued that the general attack would be continued on the 30th, the main effort of the attack being on the front South of that held by the 12th Division. The role of the Division was to press the enemy and feel for his weak spots by means of strong fighting patrols supported by other troops.
30th Sept.	During the night constant pressure was kept up on the enemy who still held part of DADOS LOOP. An organised attack in the early morning was repulsed, but the 6th Bn. Royal West Kent Regt. showed great determination and during the forenoon forced the enemy out of the trench, inflicting many casualties on him.

30th Sept. (Contd.)

The Germans were steadily pushed back and STONE LANE, STONE TRENCH, FALCON AVENUE, the BIRDCAGE and practically the whole of KILDARE AVENUE were occupied by the 37th Infantry Brigade. In the afternoon, the 6th Bn. Royal West Kent Regt. (37th Brigade) and 9th Bn. Essex Regt. (35th Brigade) pushed on and established themselves North and South of OSSUS WOOD at X.24.c.9.1. and 9.6. From there patrols moved forward, occupied BELOW TRENCH, and ultimately reached the CANAL. 4 prisoners, one 77 m.m. gun and numerous M.Gs. were captured in the day's fighting.

During the night 30th September/1st October, the Divisional front was taken over by the 55th Infantry Brigade, 18th Division.

1st Oct.

The Infantry Brigades of the Division moved by bus during the day to the PROYART area preparatory to entraining for the VIII Corps area (VIMY SECTION).

During the period from August 8th to August 27th the 25th Divisional Artillery (BRIG. GEN. K.J.KINCAID-SMITH, C.M.G., D.S.O.) was attached to the Division in place of its own Artillery, which was attached to the Canadian Corps. The 12th Divisional Artillery (BRIG. GEN. H.M.THO C.M.G., D.S.O.) returned and took over on August 27th. The able handling of the Divisional Artillery and the effective manner in which it co-operated with the Infantry were most marked throughout the operations and largely contributed to our successes. All ranks of the Infantry by their gallantry, untiring zeal and determination in spite of all difficulties of terrain, bad weather and continuous fighting during long periods without rest prove themselves equal to all occasions and the masters of their determined enemy of over 4 years. The work done by the R.Es. and Pioneers was of a high order throughout. Special mention must be made of the manner in which the water supply was maintained when crossing the waterless area between FRICOURT and the CANAL DU NORD, and of the fin and efficient work done by the R.Es. employed searching for "booby traps". The Medical Services were ably and efficiently carried out in spite of the many difficulties. The services of supply were most efficient in spite of the state of the roads, length of the lines of communication and other disadvantages. Throughout the operations all ranks of the Division displayed the greatest energy and cheerfulness, worthily upholding the splendid traditions of the British Army and adding fresh laurels to those already gained by the Division during the war.

12th Division.

Captures and Casualties.

August 8th, 1918 to September 30th, 1918.

Prisoners of War captured 29 Officers 1432 other ranks.

Material Captured.

4.2 Howitzers	8
5.9 "	1
77 mm. guns	13
M.Gs. Heavy	12
" Light	308
T.Ms. Heavy	4
" Medium	30
" Light	38
Anti-tank rifles	8
Granatenwerfer	2
Minenwerfer, Medium	3
" Light	8

Casualties.

	Killed		Wounded		Missing	
	Offrs.	O.R.	Offrs.	O.R.	Offrs.	O.R.
35th Infantry Brigade	34	281	61	1580	2	255
36th " "	27	230	46	1247	2	160
37th " "	16	184	60	1059	2	278
Royal Engineers	-	3	5	40	-	-
Divisional units	3	71	32	540	-	11
	80	769	204	4466	6	704

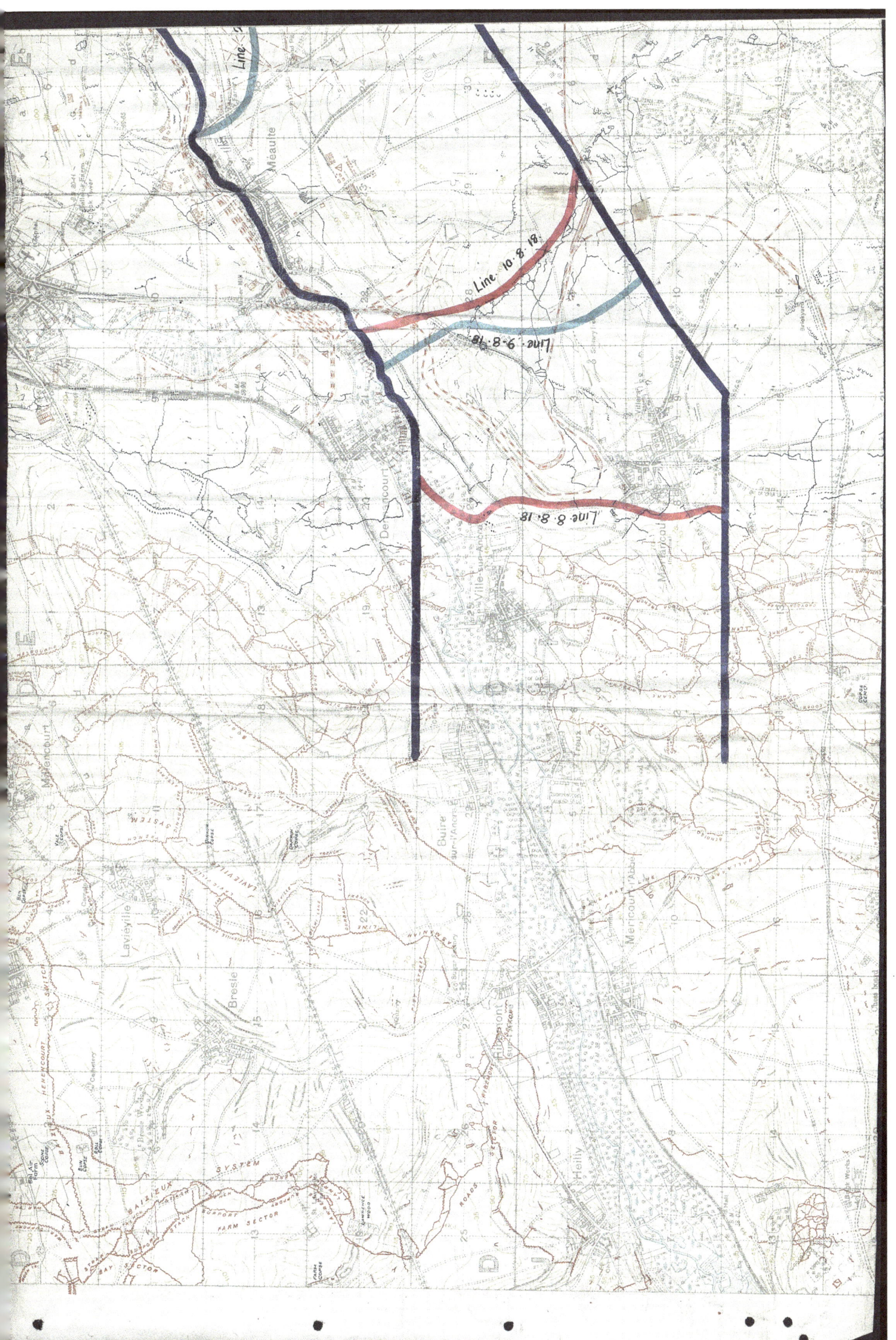

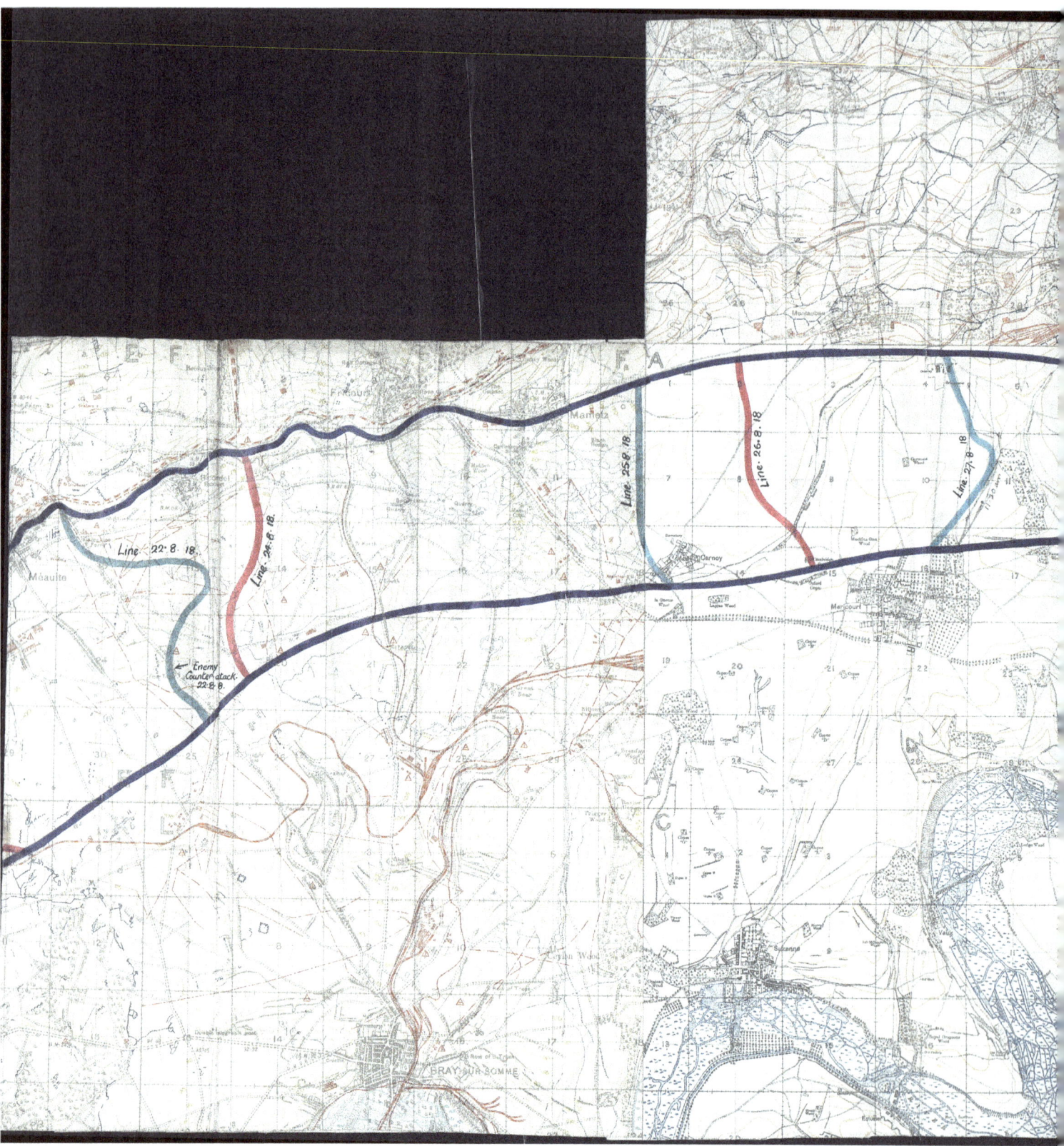

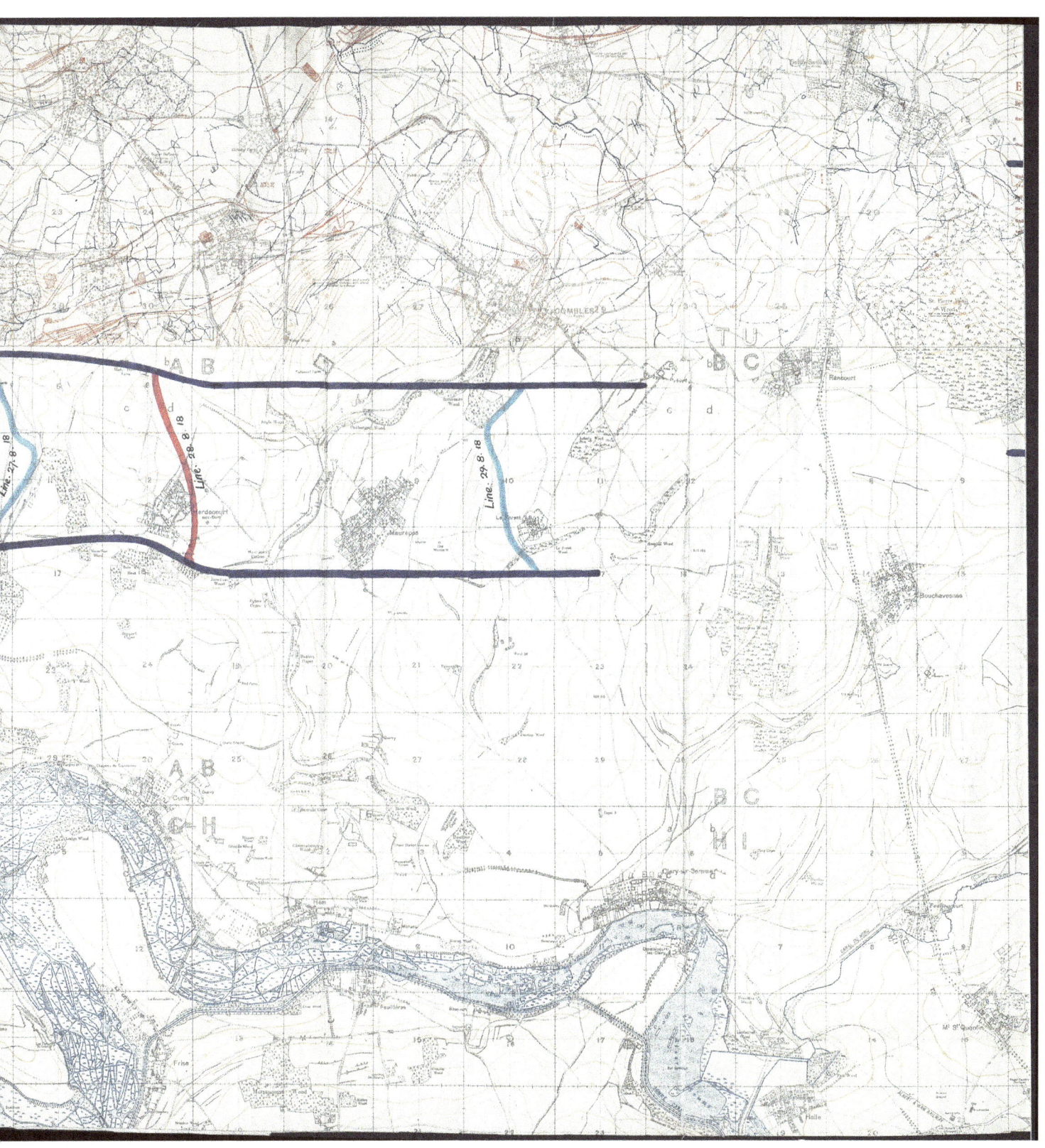

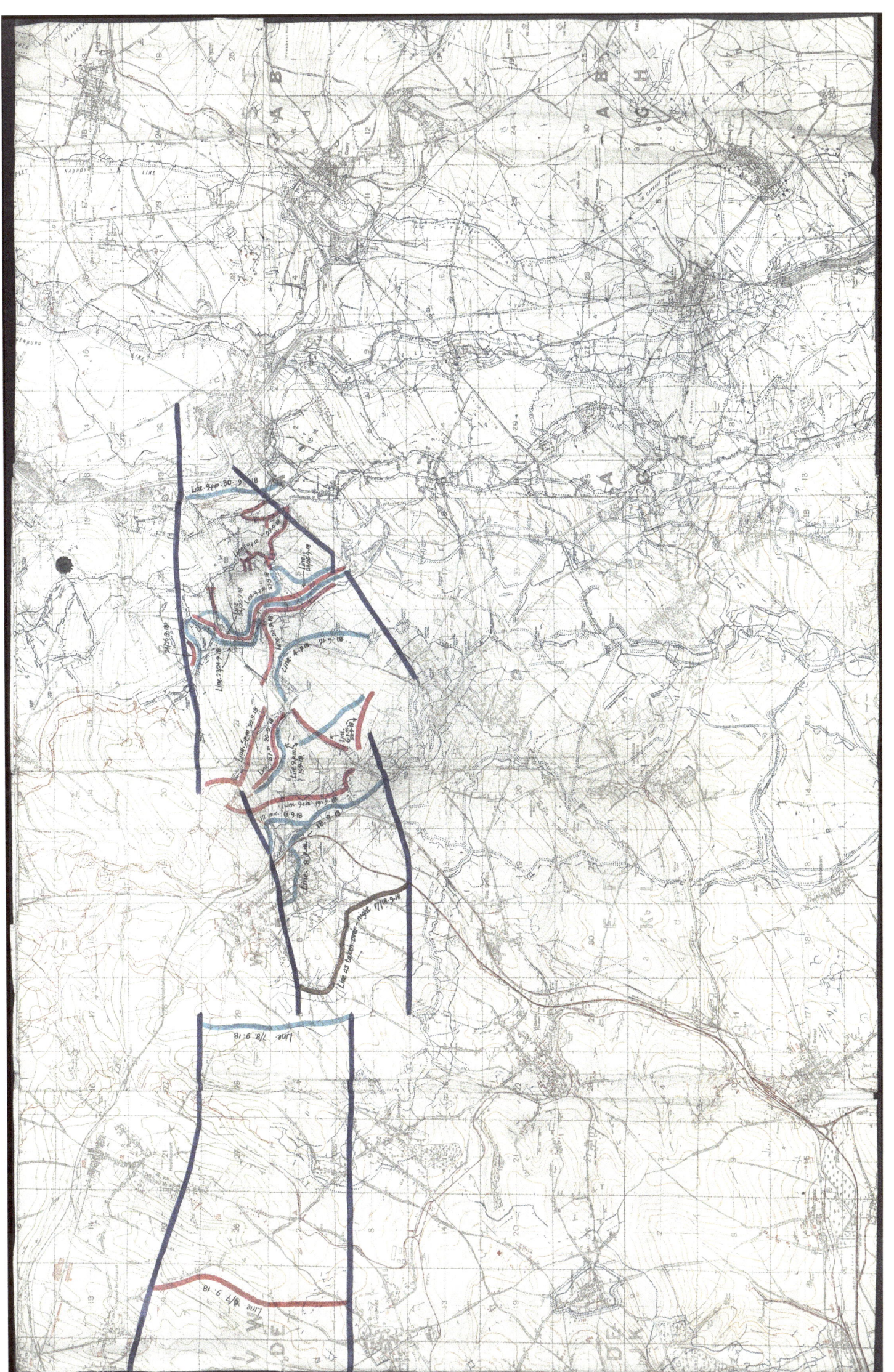

MAP Z

12ᵗʰ Division

Operations
8ᵗʰ Aug - 30ᵗʰ Sept
1918

www.ingramcontent.com/pod-product-compliance
Lightning Source LLC
Chambersburg PA
CBHW080836010526
44114CB00017B/2320